History

An Inquiry into the Development and Evolution of Historical Writing; the Historians' Methods and Themes; and the Assessment of Historians by Other Historians

Paul A. Hays
16 April 2008

By

Paul A. Hays

ISBN 0-7414-4672-3

Published by:

INFINITY
PUBLISHING.COM
1094 New DeHaven Street, Suite 100
West Conshohocken, PA 19428-2713
Info@buybooksontheweb.com
www.buybooksontheweb.com
Toll-free (877) BUY BOOK
Local Phone (610) 941-9999
Fax (610) 941-9959

Printed in the United States of America

Printed on Recycled Paper

Published April 2008

Preface

"History has a history."

Kelly Boyd, Introduction to *Encyclopedia of Historians and Historical Writing*, 1999. [1]

Paul Kennedy is a British born (1945-   ), Yale University historian who wrote *The Rise and Fall of the Great Powers, Economic Change and Military Conflict from 1500 to 2000,* in 1987. The last chapter speculates about the 21st century. During a television book review on C-SPAN, Kennedy was asked about predictions for the future. He replied that he could not predict the future "because I have difficulty predicting the past."

That profound statement astonished and intrigued me. Since then I have increased sensitivity to the language used on non-fiction book dust covers to describe the books' contents and the authors' thematic approaches. During the past several years I've been a member of the History Book Club and received the information sheets describing the new titles. Those descriptions and the blurbs on the back of the dust covers are marketing tools, but provide the grist to analyze the contents as written by that particular author compared to other authors on the same subject.

Those publishers' "come-ons" make one wonder about the veracity of previous books covering that same subject. I do admire the skill of the publishers' writers to generate wonderful phrases to entice you to buy the book:
"a groundbreaking new approach"
"a revisionist history"
"a provocative theory"
"best modern analysis"
"a unique book filled with novel approaches"
"bases his interpretation on already published sources"
"his quirky vision and candid views"
"challenges conventional wisdom"
"splendid new look"
"revisionist study refuting conventional wisdom"
"stimulating and controversial"
"challenges the official story"
"transcends the tunnel vision that characterizes much of the previous work published on the subject"
"One of the central theses of the book is that too many writers have followed the lead of 19th century scholars in unjustifiably narrowing the range of possible interpretations of this crucial battle."

The above phrases raise questions about the truthfulness of a given history and the historians' motivations. What facts should I believe? Which historian should I believe?

The blurbs above are a major part of the modern era's commercialized history books. They also raise questions about the historians of the past, not just of the past 200-300 years but the historians of the far distant past of 2,000 to 2,500 years ago. My naïve perceptions of history and historians became more fragile as my research unfolded.

This inquiry will explore the development of historical writing from before the time of Christ to the modern day. The historians will be introduced in a general chronological order, with his/her life span, nationality/locale and placed in the context of the era and other activities in order to gain an appreciation of the physical and philosophical environments in which they wrote. Their major writings will be identified, since those are the things that contributed to their lasting fame, and also became the target of other historians' critical analyses. The motivations to write history have evolved over time and provide a further basis to understand why and how they wrote. Another part of this effort will be to understand who is an historian, from full-time professionals to part-time autobiographical authors. General and specific lessons learned about historians and historical writing will be provided at the end of each chapter.

Historians properly maintain the foreign language titles of many works because those manuscripts are maintained in libraries under the original titles. To make my work more readable to the average non-historian, I've taken liberties to put some titles in English with less than a perfect translation. There is nothing more frustrating to the average reader of history than having to guess the meaning of foreign words sprinkled throughout the text. Definitions of academic historian-used words are provided to assist the reader.

Many of the characters were involved in other interesting fields, but I tried to maintain discipline not to tell about their non-historical efforts. For some historians I provide the number of citations if there is a significant number. Each citation represents a different author, not the number of times in a book. Two basic types of historians are discussed; those who actually wrote about past events and those who wrote about the meaning or philosophy of history (study of historical scholarship).

Warning to potential readers: I have tried to make this book reader friendly, but, I confess, I am both the writer and the target audience of this book. It was designed to satisfy my learning desires and to fill up my retirement years. "...for I write books to educate myself and my thirst for knowledge has been growing since my earliest consciousness."[2]

My research method was to look in the indexes of over forty bound-books about historians and develop an alphabetical card file of the historians cited. The cards of one name from different books were put together. I thought perhaps there would be some matter of importance of the historian based on the number of citations. Perhaps not. From time to time I will provide the number of citations. I soon discovered many citations were just name-dropping exercises, probably to show other historians the breadth of their research. Maybe I'm guilty of the same.

I made frequent use of Wikipedia, one of the Internet encyclopedias. It is high in the listing of resources when a name is Googled, and it provides much of the information I needed to quickly get started writing about the individual. Traditional historians will be unhappy and say it is not accurate. After you have read several chapters in this work, you will conclude that Wikipedia could not possibly be *more inaccurate* than many of our esteemed historians of the past. There will be further discussion about Wikipedia as a resource under Geoffrey of Monmouth in chapter 4.

The pictures of the historians, photos, prints and statues, were taken from Wikipedia and are all in the public domain. The pictures of places and buildings were taken by my wife, Margaret, and me during our travels. She also did a superb job of editing my work and assisting when I was stymied by the Adobe Photoshop 4 complexity.

Oxford and Princeton professor Lawrence Stone wrote, "…we should follow the advice of E.H. Carr and before we read history, examine the background of the historian."[3] Students studying for a master's degree in history should find this material helpful to learn about historians and their writings, before they read them.

"Writing a book is an adventure. To begin with, it is a toy and an amusement; then it becomes a mistress, and then it becomes a master, and then a tyrant."

Winston Churchill (1874-1965), quoted in William Safire, Gifts of Gab for '95." *New York Times Magazine* (December 18, 1994) [4]

Contents

Chapter

Chapter 1

Points to Ponder

"Everyone is entitled to his own opinion, but not his own facts."[1]

Daniel Patrick Moynihan, 1927-2003
Four-term U.S. Senator from New York

Senator Moynihan was an astute politician and academic, but he did not know historians very well, because he was wrong about the facts in the above quotation. My research led me to conclude that every historian chooses the facts according to his needs, adds his opinion about the facts, and then mixes them to produce his works. People who then read those books accept things as facts, unless they are historians themselves and undertake a critical analysis of those facts. The Wikiquote for Moynihan has three different quotations for the same idea, although they differ only in punctuation.

One should not begin a book by providing definitions of a word "history," for which we all know the meaning. But, I believe that it is appropriate now, for we will see many versions of "history." According to the Merriman-Webster Collegiate Dictionary, *history* has the following definitions:
1. TALE, STORY
2. a: a chronological record of significant events (as effecting a nation or institution) often including an explanation of their causes
   b: a treatise presenting systematically related natural phenomena
   c: an account of a patient's medical background
   d: an established record
3. a branch of knowledge that records and explains past events
4. a: events that form the subject matter of a history
   b: events of the past
   c: one that is finished or done for
   d: previous treatment, handling, or experience

Chronicle: a historical account of events arranged in order of time, usually without analysis or interpretation.

Historiography:
     a: the writing of history; especially the writing of history based on the critical examination of sources, the selection of particulars from authentic materials, and the synthesis of particulars into a narrative that will stand the test of critical methods.
     b: the product of historical writing; a body of historical literature

Hagiography:
     a. biography of saints or venerated persons
     b. idealizing or idolizing biography

1

These definitions may seem like overkill on such a simple subject as history. However, we will soon be swimming back and forth between chronicles, history, rewriting by translation and interpretation of the chronicles, historiography by authors, and then finally the onslaught in the last two centuries by academic historiographers who make their name, and money, by criticizing anybody and everybody. Thus Professor Kennedy's quote in the introduction, "…I have difficulty predicting the past."

We will end with the 20th century history writers who make their money by churning out books, pushed by their publishers, on the same old material with maybe up to one percent something new, which is really not new. They have just selected different facts to present this time around, Senator Moynihan notwithstanding. After all, it is about the money, the money, the money! The readership has changed dramatically over the two millennia, and so historians have adapted to the changing history-book market.

There are numerous ways and opinions to identify the difference between chronicles and history. Harry Elmer Barnes, 1889-1968, an American historian, whose *A History of Historical Writing* was most helpful to me, cited Reginald Lane Poole, 1857-1934, as differentiating between medieval chronicles and medieval histories on the basis of the excellence of composition. If the work is dry and plodding, it is a chronicle. If interesting and vigorous in style and independent in judgment it is history. Poole wrote:

> "The historian and the chronicler have the same intention and use the same materials, but their manner of treatment is different and their form unlike. For the historian proceeds in ample and elegant style, whereas the chronicler writes simply and with brevity. The historian aims at relating facts as they really happened, but he does so in a literary form; he pleases his readers by the gracefulness with which he describes men and manners. The chronicler, on the other hand, sets down the years of Grace, calculates the months and days, notes shortly the doings of kings and princes, and records events, portents or miracles."

Barnes admitted the idea was interesting but not to be accepted in full. He cites several different ways the issue might be looked at.[2] In chapter 4, Gervase of Canterbury will be discussed, as he is credited with an early medieval discourse on the differences between chroniclers and historians.

There are numerous labels applied to differentiate the kinds of history. One of the most obvious and useful labels is a chronological period, which is helpful to the reader to select her book. The other categories normally overlap considerably, so it is not always easy to use just one label. The following list (not inclusive) is offered to help, or confuse, you on what kind(s) of history you are reading: general, political, educational, religious, economic, social, family, local, architectural, biographical, intellectual, literary, regional, cultural, legal, or empirical.

I developed a simple list of the possible uses of history. They are generally in chronological order as the writing of history developed over nearly three thousand years. You can use this list to help you decide the motivations of the over 350 historians you will meet.
- Remember heritage
- Promote religion
- Promote culture
- Revise heritage
- Revise political background
- Record/embellish life story

- Career as a scholar
- Provide meaning for the educated classes
- Influence the future
- Earn more money
- I want to know

You will meet a variety of (mostly) men who have varied backgrounds, education and styles of writing. They each find their own writing style based on their skills and available material. Each has his own motivation. There is no one correct or best way. You will find that they love to criticize the style of earlier writers in sometimes much-earlier times. Lucian of Samosata, c. 117 AD-c. 180, was from Samosata (believe it or not), which is currently in modern Syria along the Euphrates River. He was a satirist and rhetorician, and not a historian. He wrote a tract, *How To Write History*, which was in the form of a letter about the Parthian War, 162-165 A.D. His ideas about writing history from that tract follow. They will provide a basis to make judgments about the historians and writing descriptions in this inquiry.

"-People think it is simple and easy to write history, just put down whatever comes to mind.

-Most neglect to record events and spend time lauding rulers and generals.

-Occasional praise is okay, but must be within reasonable limits to avoid displeasing future readers.

-Eulogies may be pleasing to one man, him who is praised, and annoying to others, especially if they contain monstrous overstatements.

-Most of our historians today are like that, courting private whim and the profit they expect from their history.

-His headings were too pompous for the place his books can hold.

-Because of the weakness in matters of importance or ignorance of what to say, they turn to this sort of description of scenery and caves.

-In the middle he stuffed a lot of words that were cheap, vulgar, and mean.

-Introductions are brilliant, dramatic, and excessively long—followed by bodies tiny and undistinguished.

-Others produce bodies without introduction.

-Should future be in a history?

-Power of expression requires practice, continual toil and imitation of the ancients.

-Let the historian's mind be free, let him fear no one and expect nothing, or else he will be a bad judge who sells his verdict to curry favor or gratify hatred.

-Only to truth must sacrifice be made. When a man is going to write history, everything else he must ignore. In short, the one standard is to keep in view not your audience but those who will meet your work hereafter. Whoever serves the present will rightly be counted a flatterer.

-That is the sort of man the historian should be: fearless, incorruptible, free, a friend of free expression and the truth.

-Tone should be pacific, his thought coherent and well-knit, his language exact, and statesmanlike, of a kind to set forth the subject with the utmost clarity and accuracy.

-His language should set forth the matter exactly and expound it as lucidly as possible, using neither unknown nor out-of-the-way words nor that vulgar language of the market-place, by such as ordinary folk may understand and the educated commend.

-Let his mind have a touch and share of poetry, since that too is lofty and sublime.

-Let his diction nevertheless keep its feet on the ground, rising with the beauty and greatness of his subjects.

-Facts should be assembled only after much laborious and painstaking investigation. When he has collected all or most of the facts let him first make them into a series of notes, a body of material as yet with no beauty or continuity. Then after arranging them in order, let him give it beauty and enhance it with the charms of expression, figure and rhythm.

-All should be in moderation, avoiding excess, bad taste, and impetuosity.

-Let him bring a mind like a mirror, clear, gleaming-bright, accurately centered, displaying the shape of things just as he receives them, free from distortion, false coloring, and misrepresentation.

-To give a fine arrangement to events and illuminate them as vividly as possible.

-Write a preface or use a virtual preface to clarify what he is going to say. What will instruct and interest his audience, will get attention if what he is going to say will be important, essential, personal, or useful.

-Let the transition to the narrative be gentle and easy.

-Finish the first topic, introduce the second, fastened to it and linked to it just like a chain. First and second should have common matter and overlap.

-Look at the subject matter to give adequate treatment to important matters. Avoid appearances of tasteless display of word-power or indulging my own interests.

-Eulogy and censure will be careful and considered, free from slander, supported by evidence, cursory, and not inopportune.

-Tell myths—not believe it and let the audience decide.

-Aim at eternity and write for posterity, not just for the present.

-This is the rule and standard for impartial history."[3]

Eighteen hundred years ago Lucian set an impossible group of standards. As you will soon discover, my cast of characters do not even come close to Lucian's advice. In fact, many of them fall far short of it. But their purposes dictate that they violate some (many?) of Lucian's points in order to achieve their goals. Many of them did not write impartial histories, and made no pretense about it.

Chapter 2

Classical

This chapter covers historians from the 8ᵗʰ century BC to the 6ᵗʰ century AD, or as it is now known Common Era (CE). They were primarily Greek and Roman pagans, that is, not believers in Christianity. They overlapped with the Christian historians of the next chapter, but are differentiated by belief or non-Christian beliefs, although they did have their own multiple gods.

As stated in the preface, the historians will be introduced with his/her life span, nationality/locale and placed in the context of the era and other activities in order to gain an appreciation of physical and cultural environment in which they wrote. Their major writings will be identified, since those are the works that contributed to their lasting fame, and also became the target of other historians' critical analyses. Let us try that format on our first character in this inquiry.

Homer, 8ᵗʰ or 7ᵗʰ century BC, was a Greek poet whose major works were the *Iliad* and the *Odyssey*. Homer's two works are universally praised as brilliant and influential. Now we run into a little bit of trouble. Tradition holds that Homer was blind, and various Ionian cities (western part of Greece) claim to be his birthplace, but otherwise there is very little known about Homer's life. There is no concrete evidence that shows Homer was a real person. It has been repeatedly questioned whether the same poet was responsible for both the *Iliad* and the *Odyssey*. Most scholars generally agree that the *Iliad* and the *Odyssey* underwent a process of standardization and refinement out of older material beginning in the 8ᵗʰ century BC. Most classicists would agree that the Homeric poems are the product of an oral tradition, a generations-old technique that was the collective inheritance of many singer-poets.[1]

There were six citations for Homer. Gilderhus points out the Homer's poems were not history but were legends, myths and fables in which gods, goddesses and heroes acted together, and supernatural events often accounted for the progression in human affairs.[2] "The work of Homer is not research, it is legend; and to a great extent it is theocratic legend. The gods appear in Homer as intervening in human affairs in a way not very different from the way they appear in the theocratic histories of the Near East."[3] The other four citations can be classified as name-dropping, throwing out a name without further explanation. This is the way the profession operates, always assuming that the readers are superior-intellect historians, as they think they are.

My readers are now prepared to describe Homer and his works to their relatives and friends, if they dare. As the old saying goes, do not try this at home.

Hesiod, 7ᵗʰ century BC, was a Greek poet frequently paired with Homer. Historians have debated which lived first, and some authors have even brought them together in an imagined poetic contest. Both lived before recorded history and Herodotus, below, admits his dates for the two are just his own opinion. Hesiod's writings serve as a major source for knowledge of Greek mythology, farming techniques, archaic Greek astronomy and ancient time-keeping. Hesiod's work, *Works and Days,* is a poem of 800 verses which revolves around two general truths: labor is the universal lot of Man, but he who is willing to work will get by. This work lays out the five Ages of Man (gold, silver, bronze, heroes and iron), as well as containing advice and wisdom, prescribing a life of honest labor and attacking idleness and unjust judges.[4] We should say with emphasis that Hesiod was an astute observer of mankind.

Croce makes the case that before Homer, Hesiod and Herodotus, there was history, because it is impossible to conceive of men who did not think and narrate their deeds in some way or other.[5]

Hellanicus of Lesbos, 490 BC-c. 405 BC, was a Greek logographer born on the island of Lesbos, which is just 6 miles off the western coast of modern Turkey. A logographer is one who uses a letter, sign or symbol to represent an entire word. His work includes the first mention of the legendary founding of Rome by the Trojans; he writes that the city was founded by Aeneas when accompanying Odysseus on travels through Latium. Some thirty works are attributed to Hellanicus; chronological, historical and episodical, which include the following:

- *The Priestesses of Hera at Argonm*: a chronological compilation, arranged according to the order of succession of the functionaries
- The *Carneonikae*: a list of the visitors in the Carnean games (the chief Spartan festival), including notices of literary events
- An *Atthis*, giving the history of Attica from 683 to the end of the Peloponnesian War (404), which is referred to by Thucydides, who says that he treated the events of the years 480-431 briefly and superficially, and with little regard to chronological sequence
- *Phoronis*: chiefly genealogical, with short notices of events from the times of Phoroneus the Argive first man to the return of the Heraclidae
- *Troica* and *Persica*: histories of Troy and Persia

Hellanicus authored works of chronology, geography and history, particularly Attica, the Greek province surrounding Athens, in which he made a distinction between what he saw as Greek mythology from history. He was not content to repeat the traditions of the poets and endeavored to lay the foundations of a scientific chronology. Because of this, his contemporaries called him untrustworthy. His style, like that of the older logographers, was dry and bald.[6] This last sentence strikes me as an unnecessary criticism. I am not sure how a writer using a letter, sign or symbol for a word can develop stylist prose to satisfy a modern historian.

Barnes writes that Hellanicus prepared the way for Herodotus by the breadth of his interests. "He not only dealt with the history of Persia and Greece from a broad social point of view, but was also the earliest of the Greek historians to recognize the necessity of a comprehensive system of chronology. The latter, with relative success, he attempted to supply."[7] "Neither Herodotus nor Thucydides made any serious attempt at solving the problem of chronology."[8] Chronology, according to Webster, "the science that deals with measuring time by regular divisions and that assigns to events their proper dates," was unknown about 500 BC. Chronology requires some baseline starting date from which to go forward, or backward, which we now take for granted.

Herodotus of Halicarnassus, 484 BC-c. 425 BC, was a Greek historian who is regarded as the "father of history." He is almost exclusively known for writing *The Histories*, a collection of 'inquiries', the Greek word which passed into Latin and took on the modern connotation of 'history.' His work looked into the origins of the Persian invasions of Greece which occurred in 490 and 480/479 BC. Herodotus included a narrative account of that period that was poorly documented and had many long digressions concerning the various places and peoples he encountered during wide-ranging travels around the Mediterranean. His work was written between 431 BC and 425 BC and was divided by later editors into nine books. Herodotus also earned the twin titles of *The Father of History* and *The Father of Lies,* as there has been a long debate concerning the truthfulness of his tales and the extent to which he knew himself to be creating fabrications. By his day's standards, he was reasonably accurate, respectful of evidence and a master of narrative.[9] Herodotus wrote, "Throughout the entire history it is my underlying principle that it is what people severally said to me, and what I have heard that I must write down."[10]

There were seventeen citations for Herodotus, many of which are in the category, "since Herodotus." Elton wrote, "...history had barely begun when Thucydides (to be discussed shortly) attacked the methods and purposes of Herodotus. Debates among historians are coeval (of the same or equal age) with the writing of history, and like the heresies of Christianity all the possible positions were worked out quite early, to be repeated in resounding counterpoint through ages of controversy."[11] "Herodotus celebrates the romance of the jealousies of the gods"[12]

Schorske writes, "Arnaldo Momigliano correctly observed the 'strange truth that Herodotus has really become the father of history only in modern times.' The reason for this is that Herodotus allowed culture (in the wide anthropological sense) to play a critical role in his *Histories*. While the narrative core of his work was the Persian Wars, he treated the conflict between Greeks and barbarians as a clash of cultural systems. Herodotus' integrated historiography was unseated by the sharper but narrowed political historiography of Thucydides."[13] Herodotus "was obsessed by an insatiable curiosity, and spent years traveling about the world, penetrating into places where no Greek has hitherto ventured, and prying into the secrets, past and present, of many nations and religious cults. He is as great a geographer as he is an historian; and his book is as valuable to the student of comparative religion as it is to the student of political institutions and social life."[14]

Now I will introduce a modern writer (partial historian), Ryszard Kupuscinski, 1932-2007, Polish, who had a strong affinity for Herodotus, because he saw himself as a modern-day Herodotus. Please review the salient points above about Herodotus, as they seem to be capsulated in Kapuscinski's quotes:

"Herodotus works hard on the road—he is a reporter, an anthropologist, an ethnographer, a historian. And at the same time a typical wanderer, or, as others like him will late be called in medieval Europe, a pilgrim."

"There is no anger in him, no animus. He tries to understand everything, find out why someone behaves in one way and not another. He does not blame the human being, but blames the system; it is not the individual who is by nature evil, depraved, villainous—it is the social arrangement in which he happens to live that is evil. That is why Herodotus is a passionate advocate of freedom and democracy and a foe of despotism, authoritarianism and tyranny—he believes that only under the former circumstances does man have a chance to act with dignity, to be himself, to be human. Look, Herodotus seems to be saying, a small handful of Greeks felt free and for that freedom were willing to sacrifice everything."[15]

Thucydides, c. 460 BC-c. 395 BC, was a Greek historian and author of the *History of the Peloponnesian War*, which recounts the 5th century BC war between Sparta and Athens. This is widely considered the first work of scientific history, describing the human world as produced by men acting from ordinary motives, without the intervention of the gods. I found 23 citations for Thucydides, which places him high in the eyes of later historians. Of course, many of the citations are name-dropping whenever an author wishes to cite an early historian in a general way. Almost everything we know about him comes from his own writing. Several quotations from Thucydides are worth remembering and having some reflective thoughts about them.

   -"The strong do what they can and the weak suffer what they must."
   -"It is the general rule of nature that people despise those who treat them well, and look up to those who make no concessions."
   -"War takes away the easy supply of daily wants, and so proves a rough master, that brings most men's characters to a level with their fortunes."
   -"The cause of all these evils was the lust for power arising from greed and ambition; and from these passions proceeded the violence of parties once engaged in contention."[16]

Thucydides tends to be paired up with a near contemporary, Herodotus, who was more "story-teller" versus Thucydides the "scientific."[17] Thus, Thucydides assumes the role of the ancient historian by which follow-on scientific historians might be compared. "No one can, as we mentioned, have a pretension to be greater historian than Thucydides." lectured Leopold von Ranke.[18] As we will see later, an opinion from such as von Ranke carries much weight. Under Herodotus above, I mentioned that Thucydides gained much long term fame for attacking Herodotus' methods. In the opening paragraph of the introduction, I quoted Paul Kennedy. Eric Foner, a 20th and 21st century historian, mentions in his preface that an eager young reporter from *Newsweek* asked him, "Professor, when did historians stop relating facts and start all this revising of interpretations of the past?" Foner answered her that it started about the time of Thucydides.[19] If I had put this item in my introduction, following Kennedy, I could have written a two-paragraph book.

Athens-Acropolis-Parthenon

Evans cites Raphael Samuel, since Thucydides historians have fought with the problem of "measuring words against deeds, and attempting to judge their representativity."[20] Historians accept Thucydides to be the founder of scientific and critical history. Barnes states that Thucydides was probably the first historian to state the alleged value of the writing and study of history. Thucydides wrote, "…the accurate knowledge of what has happened will be useful, because, according to human probability, similar things will happen again."[21] Gilderhus cites David Hume writing, "The first page of Thucydides is the beginning of all true history."[22] The first paragraph of Thucydides follows:

"Thucydides, an Athenian, recorded the war between the Peloponnesians and the Athenians, writing how they waged it against each other and beginning his work as soon as the war broke out in expectation that it would be a major one and notable beyond all previous wars, basing this assumption on the fact that both sides came into it flourishing in overall preparedness and on seeing that the rest of the Hellenes were aligning themselves with one or the other, some immediately and others at least intending to. This was certainly the greatest disturbance to effect (sic) the Hellenes and is considerable number of barbarians—one might say the majority of mankind."[23]

Xenophon, c. 431-355 BC, was a Greek soldier and historian born near Athens. He was a participant in a war in Persia, was on the losing side in the area of Mesopotamia (Iraq) and they had to fight their way back to Greece. Xenophon kept a record of the journey, which became known as *Anabasis* (The Expedition). It was late used by Alexander the Great as a field guide on his expedition into Persia. *Anabasis* is often read by beginning students of Greek.[24] "...the story of the romantic exploits of the Ten Thousand Greek warriors is told with moving simplicity and power. It is a tale of adventure so stirring that the schoolboy reading it forgets the difficulties of grammar in his eagerness to know the outcome."[25]

Priscus of Panium, 5th century BC, was a Greek sophist and historian. Since sophist is definitely not in my normal vocabulary, and I really had no idea what it meant. Let me quote from Webster and see if the definitions might color the credibility of Priscus:

1. Philosopher
2. any of a class of ancient Greek teachers of rhetoric, philosophy, and the art of successful living prominent about the middle of the fifth century B.C.
   for their adroit subtle and allegedly often specious reasoning
3. a captious or fallacious reasoner

Priscus is the bald fellow with the book and some grey hair, and his buddy is Attila the Hun.

Panium was in Thrace, which includes part of southern Bulgaria, eastern Greece and the European part of modern Turkey. Panium could not be located more exactly. Priscus was the author of a historical work in eight books (the *Byzantine History*), probably from the accession of Attila the Hun, 434, to that of Zeno (433-474). Priscus accompanied Maximin, the ambassador of Theodosius II, to the court of Attila in 448. His description of Attila and his court and the account of the reception of the Roman ambassadors is a valuable piece of contemporary history. His writings are usually impartial and objective, contrary to what I might have tried to lead you to by definition 2 above.[26]

Timaeus, c. 345-c. 250, was a Greek historian born at Tauromeniun (Taormina) on the northeast coast of Sicily about 20 miles north of the volcanic Mt. Etna. His great historical work was *The*

Histories, which consisted of some 40 books. This work was divided into unequal sections: containing the history of Greece from its earliest days until the first Punic war in 265 BC; the history of Italy and Sicily in early times; of Sicily alone; and of Sicily and Greece together. Timaeus is credited with the introduction of the system of reckoning time by the Olympiads, which was adapted by later Greek historians but not accepted in everyday life.[27]

This picture of the amphitheater at Taormina shows the beautiful view the audience enjoyed, and also features my wife, Margaret in the right foreground and our Princess cruise ship at top left.

Taormina Amphitheater

Manetho (Manethon of Sebennytos), c. 3rd century BC, was an Egyptian historian and priest. His principal work, *History of Egypt*, was an account of the pharaohs of Egypt, and is used often as evidence for the chronology of the reigns of the pharaohs. It was organized chronologically and divided into three volumes, and his division into dynasties was a new innovation. He is credited with coining the word dynasty (in Greek=governmental power) to represent groups of rulers with a common origin. He introduced new dynasties whenever he detected a discontinuity, whether geographical or genealogical. Some historians believe he was involved in a nationalistic competition with Herodotus over whether Greece or Egypt had the oldest civilization.[28]

Berossus (also Berossos or Berosus) was a Hellenistic Babylonian writer who was active at the beginning of the 3rd century BC. He published the *History of Babylon* sometime around 290-278 BC for the Macedonian/Seleucid king, Antiochus I. The complete text is now lost, and what remains comes from secondary sources of classical writers. It is suggested that it was commissioned by Antiochus I, perhaps desiring a history of one of his newly-acquired lands, or by the Great Temple priests, seeking justification for the worship of Marduk in Seleucid lands. Only Eusebius and Josephus preserve narrative material, and both had agendas. Eusebius was looking to construct a consistent chronology between the pagan and Christian worlds, while Josephus was attempting to refute the charges that there were people older than the Jews.[29] Please reread the previous three sentences, but now only think about the motivations of the three people, one original author and two later historians. We might criticize today's historians for crass commercial motivations, but the three above all had strong motivations to please a larger audience with selective facts (?) to prove their points. Which motivation is better, or worse?

Quintus Fabius Pictor, c. 254-? BC, was one of the earliest Roman historians and considered the first of the annalists. He wrote in Greek. He was used as a source by Polybius, Livy and Dionysius of Halicarnassus, and his work had been translated into Latin by the time of Cicero. Pictor dated the founding of Rome to be in the "first year of the eighth Olympiad," or 747 BC, according to Dionysius of Halicarnassus.[30]

Polybius, c. 203-120 BC, was a Greek historian born in Megalopolis, an Achaean city in the northern part of the Peloponnesse peninsula, which is the southern part of mainland Greece. I believe that the Cornith Canal now separates the two parts, but that does not qualify for making an island from a peninsula. Polybius is best known as the author of *The Histories* or *The Rise of the Roman Empire*, which covered the period 220-146 BC. Polybius was one of the first historians to attempt to present history as a sequence of causes and effects, based upon a careful examination of tradition and conducted with keen criticism. He narrated his History upon what he had himself seen and upon the communications of eye-witnesses and actors in the events. In a classic story of human behavior, Polybius captures it all: nationalism, xenophobia, duplicitous politics, horrible battles, brutality, etc.; along with loyalty, valor, bravery, intelligence, reason and resourcefulness. With his eye for detail and characteristic critically reasoned style, Polybius provided a unified view of history rather than a chronology. Some consider him to be the successor to Thucydides in terms of objectivity and critical reasoning, and the forefather of scholarly, painstakingly historical research in the modern scientific sense.[31] I found 12 citations about Polybius. Gilderhus credits Polybius with passing on to the Romans the best of the Greek traditions of historical writing. Polybius insisted that a historian must travel to the sites, participate in public events and utilize the documentary records.[32] Davies writes, "He is an analyst rather than an historian; and with all its wisdom and accuracy his work cannot escape the charge of being dull."[33] "Polybius sought out the causes of facts in order that he might apply them to analogous cases, and held those unexpected events to be of inferior importance whose irregularities place them outside rules;..."[34]

Thucydides was discussed earlier in this chapter, and now we are on Polybius. It is appropriate now to quote from Smith tying the two together.

> "Yet so ingrained is the picture of the Greeks as having produced the first "modern" historians that students required to write papers on Thucydides or Polybius almost invariably express astonishment at their modernity, hail them in conventional terms as the originators of our present-day notions of historical process, and doggedly read into them a view of history as progress that was in fact completely alien to their way of thought."[35]

> "Thucydides and Polybius stress the degree to which the blind workings of fate control humans and see the role of historians as that of forearming their leaders to endure the vicissitudes of fortune with equanimity."[36]

Julius Caesar, July 12 or July 13, 100 BC- March 15, 44 BC (the Ides of March), was a Roman military and political leader and one of the most influential men in classical antiquity. He was the author of two major works, *Commentaries on the Gallic War* and *Commentaries on the Civil War*. Other works are attributed to him, but the authorship is doubted. "The best-known of all Roman historical writers is Julius Caesar, his *Commentaries on the Gallic War* has been the first book to be put into the hands of learners of Latin. Generations of schoolboys have pondered over its pages, intent only upon the construction of its short, crisp sentences, yet probably quite inappreciative of its many excellent qualities, historical and literary."[37] Caesar's firsthand accounts of his military exploits against the Gauls, Germans, and Britons were unique and original works. Barnes writes about Caesar's writings, "Generally accurate and always clear, forceful and direct in his style, Caesar's apologies for his public career--The *Commentaries on the Gallic* Wars and the *Civil War*—were the best historical memoirs produced in the ancient world and rank well with those of any period.. Caesar's historical writing represents about the cleverest *ex parte* exposition in all historical literature. By maintaining a subtle self-restraint and an apparent personal modesty, he adroitly argued his case and portrayed his genius with the utmost effect."[38] Many later historians used Caesar's commentaries in their own works.

Diodorus Siculus, c. 90 BC-c. 30 BC, was a Greek historian born at Agyrium (Agira) in east central Sicily, about 30 miles west of Mt. Etna. His work was named *Bibliotheca historica* (Historical Library), because he acknowledged that he was assembling a composite work from many sources. The work consisted of forty books, which were divided into three sections. The first six books are geographical in theme, and describe the history and culture of Egypt, Mesopotamia, India, Scythia (a region that includes modern Kazakhstan), Arabia, North Africa, Greece, and Europe. The second part was from the Trojan War to the death of Alexander the Great. The third section concerns the historical events from the death of Alexander to 60-45 BC (the end was lost)

Mt Etna and me

Our English cousins have a distinct way of expressing their intellectual elitism. Perhaps it is an intellectual love/hate relationship. For example, the author of comments on Diodorus in the *1911 Encyclopedia Britannica* wrote:

> "The faults of Diodorus arise partly from the nature of the undertaking, and the awkward form of annals into which he has thrown the historical portion of his narrative. He shows none of the critical facilities of the historian, merely setting down a number of unconnected details. His narrative contains frequent repetitions and contradictions, is without colouring, and monotonous; and his simple diction, which stands intermediate between pure Attic and the colloquial Greek of his time, enables us to detect in the narrative the undigested fragments of the materials which he employed."[39]

For his critique of Diodorus, the author of the Encyclopedia Britannica quotation was obviously the typical English academic snob for whom nothing is satisfactory unless he wrote it. **He deserves my utmost contempt for unfairness in applying standards of 1900 years later to a writer!**

Voltaire, 1694-1778, in his Philosophical Dictionary, wrote that Diodorus changed myths into facts and the writing should not be considered necessarily the truth.[40] The translator of Diodorus, C.H. Oldfather, in the 20th Century, was much kinder to Diodorus and reinforced what Voltaire had stated about myths, legends, and the unusual customs of foreign tribes.[41]

SALLUSTIUS

Sallust (Gaius Sallustius Crispus), 86-34 BC, was a Roman historian born at Amiternum, about 55 miles northeast of Rome. He was an elected tribune in Rome and later was awarded with the governorship of a province in Africa by Julius Caesar. With his accumulated wealth he retired to his famous gardens and wrote history. His several histories were written with political and social points of view, such as taking the leaders to task for their mistakes and misdeeds and warning about the effects of decadence and decay. It apparently did not bother his conscience that he had been a brutal governor. His most famous was *Histories,* which covered Roman history during the period 78-67 BC. Tacitus later spoke highly of him and Quintilian put him on a level with Thucydides. He endeavored to explain the connection and meaning of events and successfully delineated character. His model was Thucydides in imitating truthfulness and impartiality.[42] I found some quotations from Sallust that are worthy of repeating, based on my experience and knowledge. "Every man is an architect of his own fortune....Few men desire liberty:

The majority are satisfied with a just master....Small communities grow great through harmony, great ones fall to pieces through discord. The higher the station, the less your liberty....To someone seeking power, the poorest man is the most useful....Ambition drove many men to become false; to have one thought locked in the breast, another ready on the tongue. [politicians?]...The renown which riches or beauty confer is fleeting and frail; mental excellence is a splendid and lasting possession."[43] On the last quote, by definition, I've had to be satisfied with mental excellence.

Dionysius of Halicarnassus (Bodrum on southeast coast of modern Turkey), c. 60 BC-after 7 BC, was a Greek historian and flourished during the time of Caesar Augustus. His great work was *Roman Antiquities* which covered the history of Rome from the mythical period to the beginning of the First Punic War, 265 BC. His chief purpose was to convince the Greeks that the Roman rule was good by expanding upon the Roman's good qualities, who were the conquerors of the Greeks. Dionysius believed that history is philosophy teaching by examples.[44] The intertwining of philosophy and history will be explored later when we reach the 18th and 19th Centuries. Dionysius and Livy are considered the two best historians of the early Roman period.

Livy (Titus Livius), traditionally 59 BC-17 AD, was a Roman historian who wrote a monumental history of Rome, *Ab Urbe Condita (From the Founding of the City)*, from its founding (traditionally dated to 753 BC) through the reign of Augustus in Livy's time. Livy was born in modern Padua, northern Italy. He wrote in a mixture of annual chronology and narrative often having to interrupt a story to announce the elections of new consuls as this was the way that the Romans kept track of the years. He wrote the majority of his works, 142 books of which only 35 survive, during the reign of Augustus, 27 BC-14 AD. Livy's writing style was poetic and archaic in contrast to Caesar's. In keeping with his poetic tendencies, he did little to distinguish between fact and fiction. Although he frequently plagiarized previous authors, he hoped that moral lessons from the past would serve to advance the Roman society of his day.

Many of Livy's comments on Roman politics seem surprisingly modern today. For example, he wrote (of the year 445 BC):

St. Peters -Rome

"War and political discussion made the year a difficult one. Hardly had it begun, when the tribune Canuleius introduced a bill for legalizing intermarriage between the nobility and the commons. The senatorial party objected strongly on the grounds not only that the patrician blood would thereby be contaminated but also that the hereditary right and privileges of the *gentes,* or families, would be lost.... The senatorial party felt that if such a bill were to become law, it would mean not only that the highest office of state would have to be shared with the dregs of society but that it would, in effect, be lost to the nobility and transferred to the commons."[45]

I gathered 17 citations about Livy. Barnes calls Livy "...one of the greatest story-tellers of all time. His work was a massive prose epic of the growth of the Roman world-state. While he had a decent general appreciation of the value of accuracy in historical statements, he subordinated precision in statement to perfection in style....Livy wrote frankly to glorify Rome, to flatter national vanity and to inspire in Roman youth patriotic ardor and affection."[46]

Plutarch (Mestrius Plutarchus), c. 46 AD-c. 120 AD, was a Greek historian, biographer, essayist and Middle Platonist. He was born in Chaeronea, which is about 75 miles northeast of Athens. He led an active social and civic life while producing an incredible body of writing, much of which is still extant. His best known work is the *Parallel Lives*, a series of biographies of famous Greeks and Romans, arranged as dyads to illuminate their common moral virtues or failings. The surviving *Lives* contain twenty-three pairs of biographies, each pair containing one Greek and one Roman life, as well as four unpaired single lives. Plutarch was not concerned with writing biographies, as such, but in exploring the influence of character—good or bad—on the lives and destinies of famous men. Plutarch stretches and occasionally fabricates the similarities in order to write their biographies as parallels. In defense of Plutarch, he generally sums up all his moral anecdotes in a chronological sequence unlike his Roman contemporary Suetonius. In *On the Malice of Herodotus* Plutarch criticizes the historian Herodotus for all manners of prejudice and misrepresentation. It has been called the "first instance in literature of the slashing review."[47] I found eight citations on Plutarch.

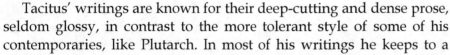

Publius (or Gaius) Cornelius Tacitus, c. 56 AD-c.117 AD, was a Roman senator and historian. He was born somewhere in the provinces, most likely around Narbonne, which is in southern France and slightly north of northeastern Spain. His two major works were the *Annals* and the *Histories.* The two works of some thirty books span the history of the Roman Empire from the death of Augustus in 14 AD to the death of Domitian in 96. Tacitus' major style was annalistic, and is distinguished by boldness and sharpness of wit, and a compact and sometimes unconventional use of Latin. He used official sources of the Roman state and collections of emperors' speeches. He was a scrupulous historian who paid attention to his historical works. He used a variety of historical literary sources; he used them freely and he chose from sources of varied positions.

Tacitus' writings are known for their deep-cutting and dense prose, seldom glossy, in contrast to the more tolerant style of some of his contemporaries, like Plutarch. In most of his writings he keeps to a chronological ordering of his narration, with only seldom an outline of the "bigger picture", and leaves the reader to construct that picture for himself. His prose style has been both derided as "harsh, unpleasant, and thorny" and praised as "grave, concise, and pithily eloquent." Tacitus' historical style combines various approaches to history into a method of his own (with some debt to Sallust): seamlessly blending straightforward descriptions of events, pointed moral lessons, and tightly-focused dramatic accounts, his historiography contains deep, often pessimistic, insights into the workings of the human mind and the power of nature.

Tacitus is remembered first and foremost as Rome's greatest historian, the equal—if not the superior—of Thucydides, the ancient Greeks' foremost historian; the *Encyclopedia Britannica* opined that he "ranks beyond dispute in the highest place among men of letters of all ages."[48]

I found 25 citations about Tacitus. Gay compares Gibbon's style, who wrote *The Rise and Fall of the Roman Empire*, with Tacitus' style, as Gibbon used much of Tacitus' material. "Tacitus was an outraged moralist, Gibbon an erudite cynic. Like all human beings, both historians had something to hide: Tacitus, a tormented politician's guilt; Gibbon, a professional bachelor's conflicts. Tacitus appears like a glacier concealing a volcano, Gibbon the glacier concealing an iceberg."[49] Acton writes, "Tacitus was an atheist;' but no historian has passed severer judgment on the morals of his age, none has a more earnest moral feeling."[50] Tacitus also wrote *The Germania*, which was about the Germans of that era, and which provided the basis for historians, particularly German historians, to write and analyze the relationship of the Germans and the Romans.

Schevill writes, "Tacitus was a man of senatorial rank who held high office under the Flavian emperors (Vespasian, Titus, Domitian) and under Trajan. He had the customary aristocratic prejudice. He hated the emperors as usurpers but hated them more when they were tyrants. He was a man of dour, severe temper, a kind of puritan who grieved over the public corruption of his day and the spread of private morality. Like every other author, he walks through his books: a man of high authority and dignity with a frown on his face, for he is out of tune with public and private

Rome-Castello di St Angelo

life....There is evidence of a monumental prejudice on the part of Tacitus."[51]

R.G. Collingwood's specialty (20th century) was the philosophy of history, not actual history, so his comments below on Tacitus must be tempered with that background.

> "As a contributor to historical literature, Tacitus is a gigantic figure; but it is possible to wonder whether he was an historian at all. He imitates the parochial outlook of the fifth-century Greeks without imitating their virtues. He is obsessed with the history of affairs at Rome, neglecting the Empire, or seeing it only as refracted through the spectacles of a home-keeping Roman; and his outlook on theses purely Roman affairs is narrow in the extreme....What is really wrong with Tacitus is that he has never thought out the fundamental problems of his enterprise."[52]

To have to type Collingwood's comments offends my sensibilities and makes me angry. The elitism of the Oxford historians has its place, I suppose, but I would really like to grab Collingwood by the throat and throw him back into the end of the first century and the beginning of the second century and tell him to write a history of the Roman Empire. Wonder how he would do writing a real history, not just criticizing others?

Gibbon wrote, "...the first of historians who applied the science of philosophy to the study of facts."[53] "Tacitus, also a historian of the decay of his country, was another ancient historian to indulge in extensive reflecxions on chance."[54] Tacitus wrote, "history's highest function is to let no worthy action be uncommemorated, and to hold the reprobation of posterity as a terror to evil hands and deeds."[55]

Tacitus' *Germania* was discovered by Enoc of Ascoli at Hersfeld (modern Germany) in the mid-15th century and was taken to Rome. It is "one of the most bitterly controverted historical documents of all time. Important historical sources were thus brought to light, and editing them gave birth to scientific practices in editing and criticism."[56]

When I started this inquiry I had no idea I would end up here in this chapter with a "holy cow, I did not know that" moment. The subject below, Justus of Tiberius, caused my first real turmoil on my way toward a nice clean and clear look at historians.

I am now forced to disclose more of my background than I had intended when I started. This might be called full disclosure of my beliefs and biases. I was born and raised on Toledo, Ohio and went to Sunday school and church through my high school years. My mother must have been a reasonably strong Protestant believer. My father was a cynic on the subject of religion, but he went to keep the peace with my mother. Beginning with college, I have only been inside a church for weddings and funerals for the last over-fifty years. Religion meant nothing to me.

Around the year 2000 I started to study history to teach courses at my lifetime learning group at a local university. About that time there were four new books out about the writing of the King James Bible. I devoured them and built a class on the subject, because the insights were absolutely fascinating. In parallel I built four and a half hours of lecture on the various aspects of the 600-year long Roman Catholic Church's Inquisition. From this I learned about the perceived biases against the Catholic Church, and developed my own historical feelings on that subject. History was suddenly fun to research and learn.

I usually avoid religion unless I can deal with it on a clinical basis, such as historically. The following discussion about Justus of Tiberius must necessarily take on a larger dimension. I will try to not get too wrapped up in this discussion, and hopefully it will satisfy for the remainder of the book. Perhaps that is just wishful thinking, considering the course that I've charted for myself, without any predetermined way stations.

Justus of Tiberius was a *Jewish historian* who flourished late in the 1st century AD. He wrote *Chronicle of the Kings of the Jews*. Tiberius is only six miles from the current location of Nazareth, yet Nazareth was not mentioned by two contemporary writers who mentioned over 30 towns in the area of Galilee. That evidence does not support the existence of Nazareth in the 1st century. Photius, a Christian scholar of the 9th century wrote, "He (Justus) makes not the mention of the appearances of Christ, of what things happened to him, or of the wonderful works that he did."[57] This same website provides the names of 41 historians who lived within Christ's lifetime or within a hundred years of it who did not mention Jesus. The site does mention two disputed passages in the works of Roman writers and two forged passages in the works of a Jewish writer. In other words, no contemporaries mentioned Jesus, and it was only after several hundred years that the Christian apologists started to write to make the case for Jesus. There is an old phrase, "Something was lost in translation." There seems to be a companion phrase, "Something was added in translation." Another website on this subject is www.dissidentvoice.org/Oct04.Salisbury1012.htm. I have just made up my mind on the historical truth about Jesus. To each his own! There is an old homily about letting sleeping dogs lie. Well, this controversy will go on forever and has plenty of bite. When you are in a hole, stop digging!

"…maps are like the Bible: Devotees of particular doctrines can always find support in them, but they are so vulnerable to emendation and forgery that no historian should ever rely on them without supporting evidence from other sources."[58]

Gaius Suetonius Tranquillus, c. 69/75-after 130, was a prominent Roman historian and biographer. He was probably born in the area of ancient Hippo, North Africa, now Annaba, Algeria. He is most remembered for his *Lives of the Caesars*, best known in English as "The Twelve Caesars." In case a few of my readers cannot remember the names or order of the twelve Caesars, I shall refresh memories: Julius Caesar, Augustus, Tiberius, Caligula, Claudius, Nero, Galba, Otho, Vitellius, Vespasian, Titus, and Domitian. The work tells the tale of each Caesar's life according to a set formula: the descriptions of appearance, omens, family history, quotes and then a history is given in a consistent order for each Caesar.[59] Barnes credits Suetonius with one of the earliest examples of historical muckraking and scandal mongering….Suetonius style of historiography became the model for historical biography during the period of Humanism (roughly 15th & 16th centuries).[60]

Cassius Dio, c. 155-c. 163/164, was a Roman historian and public servant born and raised in Nicaea, which is now Izmit in modern Turkey at the eastern end of the Sea of Marmara. This is about 50 miles east of Istanbul, and the site where the Nicene Creed was established in 325 by Emperor Constantine. Dio published *Roman History* in eighty books covering a period of 983 years from the arrival of Aeneas in Italy to 229. Aeneas supposedly founded Rome in 753 BC after getting away from Troy and the Trojan War.[61]

Troy-Turkey. My family. Tom, Diane, and wife, Margaret, c. 1974

Ammianus Marcellinus, c. 325/330-after 391, was a Greek historian born at Antioch, which is now the city of Antakya, in the south central segment of Turkey between Syria and the Mediterranean Sea. His *Res Gestae Libri XXXI* was originally in thirty-one books and covered the history of the Roman Empire during the period 96-378. Edward Gibbon, who made his name with *The Decline and Fall of the Roman Empire*, wrote, "…an accurate and faithful guide, who composed the history of his times without indulging the prejudices and passions which usually affect the mind of a contemporary." Ernst Stein praise Ammianus "the greatest literary genius that the world produced between Tacitus [120 AD] and Dante [1321]." Others were not so kind.[62]

Zosimus, fl. 490s-510s, was a Byzantine historian who lived in Constantinople during the reign of the Byzantine Emperor Anastasius I (491-518). Zosimus' work is the *Historia Nova*, (New History), in six books, the earlier books being mainly a compilation from previous authors. The fifth and sixth books, the most useful for historians, cover the period between 395 and 410, when Priscus Attalus was deposed. For this period, he is the most important surviving non-ecclesiastical source. The style is characterized by Photius as concise, clear and pure; other historians have judged his accounts confused or muddled, and valuable only because he preserves information from lost histories. The historian's object was to account for the decline of the Roman Empire from the pagan point of view. Zosimus is the only non-Christian source for much of what he reports.

Zosimus was a Pagan, and is by no means sparing of the faults and crimes of the Christian emperors. In consequence of this his credibility has been fiercely assailed by several Christian writers, and has been sometimes defended merely because his history tended to the discredit of many leading persons in the Christian party. It is not to be wondered at that one who held to the old faith should attribute the downfall of the empire in great part to the religious innovations attendant upon the spread of Christianity. The single good manuscript, in the Vatican Library (MS Vat.Gr.156) since at least 1475, was held unavailable to scholars until the mid-19th century.[63]

Zosimus' manuscript, described above, is an example of the situation regarding historical documents in Europe. From Constantine in 325 until Martin Luther's Reformation in 1517, the Roman Catholic Church was the most single dominate religious and economic power in Europe. It was usually triumphant in its "secular" battles with normal secular royalty as the two forces were in continual conflict/accord over the "little" people. It was able to easily squash competition, usually by excommunicating people or killing them during the 600-year long Inquisition. The Church had the motivation and resources to record, conceal, and distort history to its own benefit. It did this ruthlessly for almost twelve hundred years. After Luther it had serious competition from the Protestant churches and the rise of nation states. Thus, Zosimus' manuscript was a non-Christian history critical of Christianity held in the Vatican Library to prevent historians from learning another version of events. The Vatican seldom allows non-Catholics to enter its library. Who knows what other documents and revelations might be there?

Jordanes was a 6th century Eastern Roman Empire (Byzantine) bureaucrat and historian. His principal work was a continuation and a replacement of Cassidorus' *History of the Goths*. Jordanes was a secretary of a minor state on the northern reaches of the Byzantine Empire, now Bulgaria and southern Serbia, which was adjacent to the Goths' territory. It is valuable for the Gothic history, which had few historians documenting their period.[64]

Lesson Learned:

-Homer might not have been a real person. Those works were mostly theocratic legend.

-Hesiod was a Greek poet frequently paired with Homer.

-Hellanicus prepared the way for Herodotus and recognized the necessity of a comprehensive system of chronology.

-Herodotus is known as *the father of history*, and *the father of lies*.

-Thucydides is considered to be the founder of scientific and critical history and is frequently paired with Herodotus.

-Timaeus introduced the chronology of time from the Olympiads.

-Polybius was one of the first to look at history from cause and effects.

-Diodorus was defamed by the 1911 *Encyclopedia Britannica*.

-Livy was a great storyteller.

-Plutarch was a moralist by comparing a Greek and a Roman.

-Tacitus was the greatest Roman historian.

-Justus was one of over forty contemporary historians who failed to mention the name of Jesus until several hundred years later.

-Suetonius was an early historical muckraker and scandal monger. (It had to start some time.)

Chapter 3

Early Christian

This chapter is a short one dealing with the early Christian writers. I have purposely tried to not get involved in the writing of the Bible because I do not like to get into the never-ending who-wrote-what in the Bible controversies. This chapter covers historians from the 1st to the 7th centuries.

Josephus, 37-100(101) AD, was a Jewish historian and apologist who later became known as Flavius Josephus in his capacity as a Roman citizen. He was born in Jerusalem. He fought against the Romans, surrendered to them, and then went to Rome in 71. The works of Josephus provide crucial information about the First Jewish-Roman War. *Jewish War* was in seven books and his second effort, *Antiquities of the Jews* was in twenty-one volumes. He has been criticized for producing pro-Roman propaganda, having been on the losing side. He glorifies himself and blames other Jews for losing the war, but he is a strong apologist for Judaism. His passages about a fellow by the name of Jesus are also controversial.[1]

Jerusalem-Dome of the Rock

Sextus Julius Africanus, c. 160-c. 250, was probably born in Libya, hence his given name. He was a Christian historian known principally for one effort, *Chronografiai*, which was in five books and covered from the Creation to the year 221 AD. He calculated the period from the Creation to Jesus as 5500 years, placing the Incarnation on the first day of AM 5501, our modern March 25, 1 BC. This method of reckoning led to several Creation eras being used in the Greek Eastern Mediterranean, which all placed the Creation within one decade of 5500 BC. His work was used by Eusebius, our next historian, and lasted for centuries.[2]

Eusebius of Caesarea, c. 275-30 May 339, was the bishop of Caesarea, now on the coast of modern Israel. Caesarea is half way between Tel-Aviv to the south and Haifa to the north. His birth place is unknown. He wrote many religious tracts, which are outside the scope of this inquiry.

Eusebius is often considered as the father of the Roman Catholic Church history. His two greatest historical works are *Chronicle* and *Church History*. The first part of *Chronicle*, or *Universal History*, claims to give a summary of universal history from many sources, arranged by nations. The second part attempts to furnish a synchronism of the historical material in parallel columns, the equivalent timeline.[3] "Eusebius was fortunate enough to live and work near the most complete Christian library of his time, which had (also fortunately) somehow escaped the wholesome destruction of Christian literature which had been sanctioned under the order of the emperor Diocletian. Eusebius first produced a chronology, similar to those written by Sextus Africanus and others, which began, naturally, with the Creation and extended to 324 C.E. Unlike the earlier chronologies, which linked only the classical and Judeo-Christian calendars, Eusebius's work incorporated precise chronological systems of every civilization known to him, including the Assyrian and Egyptian calendars as well as the Greek Olympiads and Roman consulates."[4]

His *Church History*, or *Ecclesiastical History*, presents the history of the Church from the apostles to his own time, with regard to the following special points:

1. The succession of bishops in the principal sees;
2. The history of Christian teachers;
3. The history of heresies;
4. The history of the Jews;
5. The relations to the heathen;
6. The martyrdoms.

He grouped his material according to the reigns of the Roman emperors. This comprehensive approach would have taken considerable preparation and writing time. It must be remembered that monks or other religious historians tend to naturally favor their faith as they write about history. Eusebius blamed the calamities which befell the Jewish nation on the Jew's role in the death of Jesus. The following quotation has been used to attack both Jews and Christians,

> "...that from that time seditions and wars and mischievous plots followed each other in quick succession, and never ceased in the city and in all Judea until finally the siege of Vespasian overwhelmed them. Thus the divine vengeance overtook the Jews for the crimes which they dared to commit against Christ."

A chronicle is basically a story of events that have occurred, without much discussion of why the events happened. Historians separate themselves from the chroniclers by doing critical analyses of the events, based on other evidence and their own biases. The last sentence of the quotation above is dripping with religious bias from Eusebius, and has stood the test of time as a damming indictment of the Jews to this day. Such statements, for example, from the 4th Century, tend to be repeated by later historians, with their own biases, which continue to surface in many writings. Reinterpretations of that sentence satisfy some historians, but the basic meaning carries on and is available for every one to satisfy their own purposes.

We now arrive at one of the main reasons for exploring this subject, and the most fun to research, the criticism of historians by other historians. Eusebius was accused of dishonesty at various times and in various connections

Edward Gibbon, 1737-94, the English historian and author of the renowned *The Rise and Fall of the Roman Empire,* took Eusebius to task for several things, one of which was the statement, "We shall introduce into this history in general only those events which may be useful first to ourselves and afterwards to posterity." That statement reflects the way in which boundaries are set by historians as they write about a certain era of time or subjects. Joseph Lightfoot, 1828-89, an English theologian and Bishop of Durham, in an era one hundred years later, rebutted Gibbons remarks in several ways. One way was to comment that Eusebius was honest in saying what he was not going to cover because of his own limitations. That is most logical, and is the reason that I have neither the time nor inclination to go further into this controversy. G.A. Williamson, a prolific historian about Eusebius era wrote,

"Gibbon's notorious sneer…was effectively disposed of by Lightfoot, who fully vindicated Eusebius' honour as a narrator 'against this unjust charge.'"

There were attacks on Gibbon's comments during his lifetime and so he wrote a book which included his vindication for his statements about Eusebius. If you go on the Internet and Google or abebooks.com with "vindication, gibbon" that book will be found.[5]

Throughout this inquiry I've tried to stay out of the written arguments espoused by the religious writers because they have their own religious agendas. Their critical analyses and other comments must be assessed in light of their biases, and this sentence applies to non-religious historians. Please reread Lightfoot's statement above, now consider that in light of Lightfoot's analysis that the Creation of Adam was on Friday, October 289, 4004 B.C., at 9 A.M.[6] In retrospect, how much credibility should we give to Lightfoot?

Jacob Burckhardt, 1818-97, Swiss historian wrote about Eusebius, "the first thoroughly dishonest historian of antiquity." We will meet Burckhardt later, as he has a different, but enjoyable style in some of his writings. My Wikipedia article on Eusebius cites other historians' opinions about Eusebius and Burckhardt. Benedetto Croce, the Italian historian, placed Eusebius next to Herodotus as "father" of modern historiography.[7]

Eusebius wrote in Greek so few scholars in the Western Empire could read his works. Saint Jerome, c. 340-420, translated Eusebius' *Chronicle* into Latin, with certain revisions and additions.[8] Let me expand this point. Historians throughout history have taken others' works, and translated, edited, added and revised those works. How does a later reader know what were the original words and thoughts? The answer is only the person who did that work. Other experts would have to spend considerable time to compare the various works to determine the answer. Saint Jerome was the person who translated the Bible into the Latin Vulgate Bible, which remained until the first English translation by John Wycliffe in the 14th Century. Much later in this inquiry I will provide my effort on a 19th Century book revised by a 20th Century editor. I was unhappy with the liberties the editor took to change the original author's intend and meaning.

"As Professor Defarrari summarizes his [Eusebius] talents and contributions: 'Eusebius was the first to grasp clearly the concept of a Christian literature, and to employ with it the ancient methods, fixing the dates of writers and cataloguing their works. He translated the tradition of Alexandrian philology to Christian soil.'"[9]

Caesarea

Now I will provide my Chronicle of Caesarea. In March 1975 my wife and I were living in Ankara, Turkey and we took a week-long tour of Israel. We visited the ruins of Caesarea and I picked up a piece of sandstone as a souvenir. It weighs about 4/10 of a pound, is smooth as if by water action, and shaped like a distorted pyramid. I carried with me on our military tour to Germany from Turkey, and thence to Huntsville, Alabama where I now live. It was in with seashells collected from forgotten places, but I'd taped Caesarea on it. It now functions as a blocking device to keep my business-card notes upright as I work on this project. Thank you, Eusebius, for allowing me to feel wonderful about that very, very old stone.

Paulus Orosius, c. 384-420, historian and Christian apologist, was born in Gallaecia (possibly at Braga in northwest Portugal). He was well connected to two powerful historical Christian figures. He studied for five years under Augustine of Hippo, now known as Annaba (Bône) on the Algerian coast. Augustine sent Orosius to work with Jerome, the translator of the Vulgate Bible, in Palestine. Orosius' best known work is *Seven Books of History Against the Pagans*. The purpose of the effort, compiled between 415 and 418, was to refute the pagans who claimed there were more natural disasters in the world since Christianity became popular. His work was really a chronicle of calamities that have happened to mankind and provided "evidence" that the circumstances were not worse under Christianity. It became popular because it showed that God was guiding humanity and determining the destinies of nations.[10] The impact of Orosius' work is stated by Barnes:

"Despite the fact that it was intended as a polemical work in defense of the Christian faith, Orosius' book became the standard manual on profane history-that is, ancient pagan world history-during the Middle Ages. This was a highly unfortunate occurrence for students of history during the medieval period, for several very evident reasons. In the first place, the work was decisively biased against the pagan nations and culture. Second, it ignored the more peaceful and constructive elements in pagan life. Third, its treatment of ancient history was sketchy and inadequate as to countries and subject matter alike. Finally, even the sketchy materials were unreliable, having been compiled from secondhand abstracts and then fitted into a pre-determined scheme of historical interpretation.[11]

The "Orosius method" was used by Martin Luther in the 16th century to "prove" that the world had gotten worse under the leadership of the Roman Catholic Church.[12] Long live the "Orosius method" to be used by anyone against someone else. Think American politics.

Marseille-Notre Dame

Prosper of Aquitaine, c. 390-c. 455, was an enthusiastic Christian writer, although he was a layman. Aquitaine is an old region in southwest France. Prosper was apparently educated in Marseille. He was the author of numerous works, mostly theological. His principal historical work was *Epitoma chronicon,* which covered the period 379-455. Its early part was a careless compilation from St. Jerome, but the lack of other sources for the period 425-455 made it very valuable, as it is drawn from his personal experience. It covers the Attila's invasions of Gaul in 451 and Italy in 452.[13]

Gregory of Tours, c. 538-November 17, 594, was the bishop of Tours and a Gallo-Roman historian. Gallo means from Gaul, a Roman Empire territory which was now what is currently France and Belgium. He is the main contemporary source for Merovingian history, which refers to the first Frankish dynasty reigning during the period c. 500-751. The Dark Ages are generally considered to be the period between the fall of the Roman Empire in 410 A.D. and 1000. Tours is about 120 miles southwest of Paris, lies on the Loire River, and has long been a travel crossroads between Spain and northern France.

Gregory's major contribution to history was *Historia Francoruim,* which is in ten books. Books I to IV cover the world's history from the Creation, but moves quickly to the Christianization of Gaul, the life and times of St. Servatius, the conversion of the Franks and the conquest of Gaul under Clovis, and the more detailed history of the Frankish kings down to the death of Sigebert in 575. The second part, books V and VI, close with Chilperic's death in 584. This segment is biased as Chilperic arrested Gregory and tried him for treason for allegedly slandering Chilperic's wife. The third part, books VII to X, takes his increasing personal account to the year 594 when Gregory died. Gregory was the leading prelate in Gaul for 21 years, so naturally he was a prominent person in his history. Historians have taken different views of Gregory's history. Perhaps there is general agreement that he was trying to highlight the vanity of the secular life and contrast it with the miracles of the Saints. He was sainted.

Gregory's second major work was *Life of the Fathers*, which comprises twenty hagiographies of the most prominent religious men of the preceding generation. This collection of lives is structured to bring out the various good qualities of the subjects. Of course, this is to be expected of a religious tract. Both of his works are important contributions to that period of history known as the Dark Ages, which is a transitional period between the Roman Empire and what is now known as the Middle Ages.[14]

The Catholic Encyclopedia has an astute assessment of Gregory which is quoted:

> "Gregory relates, indeed, as stated above, the story of his age, but in the narrative he himself always plays a prominent part. The art of exposition, of tracing effects to their causes, of discovering the motives which influenced the characters he described, was unknown to Gregory. He tells a plain unvarnished tale of what he saw and heard. Apart from what concerns himself, he always tries to state the truth impartially, and in places even attempts some sort of criticism. This work is unique in its kind. Without it the historical origin of the Frankish monarchy would be to no small extent unknown to us. Did Gregory, however, correctly appreciate the spirit and tendencies of his age? It is open to question. His mind was always busied with extraordinary events: crimes, miracles, wars, excesses of every kind; for him ordinary
> events were too commonplace for notice. Nevertheless, to grasp clearly the religious or secular history of a people, it is more important to know the daily popular life than to learn of the mighty deeds of the reigning house. The morality of the people is often superior to that of its governing classes. In Gregory's day, great moral and religious forces, beloved by the people, must have been leavening the country, counterbalancing the brute force and immorality of the Frankish kings, and saving the strong new race from wasting away in civil strife. From Gregory's account, however, one could scarcely conclude that the people were altogether satisfied with their religion."[15]

One footnote needs to be added to Gregory from another footnote, which comes from the prologue to a work by William of Tyre, whom we shall meet later. "This recognition of the possibility – rather the certainty – of error in his work is a further tribute to the scholarly qualities of William's mind. Not infrequently medieval writers, like Gregory of Tours, invoked anathema on anyone who should change even a line of their writing."[16] Anathema, according to Webster, is "one that is cursed by ecclesiastical authority." In other words, the Catholic Church believed that it was always right and anybody who changed his writing to be more correct after uncovering more information was to be cursed. This is the legacy of the Roman Catholic Church. Some notable examples are:

- Refusal to accept the proofs of Copernicus in 1453 and Galileo in the early 1600s about the center of the solar system being the sun rather than the earth.
- The Church finally revoked its condemnation of Galileo in 1992, 359 years after it decided he was a heretic for his teachings and writings supporting the Copernican theory.
- William Tyndale, English religious reformer, was declared a heretic and burned at the stake in 1536 for translating the Bible into the English language. His real crime was translating from the original Greek and Aramaic languages instead of the Latin Vulgate Bible, which was translated by St. Jerome in the 4th century from Greek and Aramaic. The Church argued that the Latin Vulgate was more original that the original Greek and Aramaic.

Isidore of Seville, c. 560-April 4, 636, was the Archbishop of Seville, Spain for more than thirty years. He was born in Cartagena, about 300 miles east of Seville. His family was very influential in the political-religious maneuvering to convert the Visigoths to Catholicism. He was educated at the Cathedral school in Seville, where he studied the trivium of grammar, rhetoric and logic at the basic education. Then he studied the advanced quadrivium of arithmetic, music, geometry and astronomy. He wrote two significant tracts of history, the *Chronica majora* (universal history) and a *History of the Goths.* His most important and long-lasting work was *Etymologiae,* or *Origines,* which is the first known encyclopedia compiled in Western civilization.[17]

Isidore of Seville

The influential 20th Century historian, R. (Robin) G. (George) Collingwood credits Isidore with inventing the single universal chronology, which was popularized by the Venerable Bede a century later. This idea is based on dating everything backward and forward from the birth of Christ.[18] Barnes gives credit to Bede, and does not mention Isidore.[19] Dionysius Exiguus, ?-c. 544, is given credit for introducing the dating of Christ's birth and the method of computing Easter. There are, of course, several variants of this process and not all agree. My effort dares not to venture too far into the philosophy of Christian history, with all its entanglements, but Isidore's idea integrated history and Christianity. In an earlier chapter we met some of the historians who struggled to establish a time baseline for their chronicles.

Lessons Learned:

-Josephus was a Jewish historian and apologist.

-Sextus Africanus calculated the period from the Creation to Jesus as 5500 years.

-Eusebius is often considered as the father of the Roman Catholic Church history.

Chapter 4

A of B

This chapter is so titled because most of the chroniclers and historians of the 10th-13th centuries seem to have "of" as their middle name. Of course, the answer is that most people of that era had only a given name and the second was based on their birth place, or in the case of the many clergymen, the location of their ordination. In some cases it was the location where they became the abbot or some other powerful position. I have retained the alphabetical order in which I researched and then wrote as a matter of convenience. Occasionally two were made a pair, but generally there was not adequate linkage. During that era, the scattered writers were not in timely communication to make much difference. Later writers made use of earlier ones, but the connections appeared to have no special merit. This chapter could have also been labeled medieval or Middle Ages.

Adalberon of Laon, ???-c. 988, was the archbishop of Laon, a town about 80 miles northeast of Paris. He wrote a poem in the form of a dialogue in which he showed his dislike of Odilo, the abbot of Cluny, and his objection to persons of humble birth being made bishops. He also wrote a poem in which he identified three orders of society: the clergy ("praying church"); nobles and chivalry ("the fighting church"); and the laboring people ("church of toiling"). The laborers supported the other two classes, and all three groups supported mankind. Adalberon's idea of the three social orders was incorporated into the "three social orders" of the Ancien Régime in France.[1] Should Adalberon be considered a historian? He wrote in poetry instead of prose. Is that a disqualifying form of expression? He conducted a critical analysis of Odilo and his followers, which is a well-used technique throughout the ages by countless historians. He used a conceptual framework to describe elements of society, which had a life of at least 1,000 years. By all those criteria, he must be considered a historian. Does one have to be a full-time historian, or a professional historian to be recognized as a historian? Definitely not! But I have not answered the question as to who has the legitimacy to decide whether someone is or is not a historian. I can guess what historical associations might rule in that matter, but history is too important to be left to only the opinions of professional historians. They have a built-in bias to keep their club small, manageable, and in the modern day, lucrative.

Adam of Bremen, c. before 1050-12 October-c. 1081-85, was one of the most important medieval chroniclers. He was thought to have come from Meissen, a town about 12 miles northwest of Dresden, Germany. The Catholic Encyclopedia suggests that Adam's origin is mere conjecture based on evidence furnished by dialectic traces occurring during the work. Meissen is well known for its high quality china dinnerware and figurines, which have been items of distinction for the nobility across Europe. Meissen china is in the category, "If you have to ask the price,

Meissen

you cannot afford it." Meissen is about 270 miles south from Bremen. His best known work is *Deeds of the Bishops of the Hamburg Church*, which consists of four volumes. The first three are mainly historical and the fourth is purely geographical, which describes the Northern lands and the islands in the Northern seas. That work contains the earliest mention of America (Vinland) found in any geographical work. Adam bases his knowledge partly on written sources and partly on oral communication. He made diligent use of records and manuscripts in the archives of his church, as well as of the official document of popes and kings. Adam assures us repeatedly that he has taken great pains to make his account both truthful and accurate. "If I have not been able to write well," so he says in his epilogue, "I have at any rate written truthfully, using as authorities those who are best informed about the subject."[2] One can ask no more of a 12th Century chronicler.

Adémar (Adhemar) of Chabannes, c. 989-1034, was born in Chabannes, a village in southwestern France about 20 miles north northeast of Limoges. He was educated at the monastery of St. Martial at Limoges. It was common in that era that the highest calling was to be educated in a monastery, because there were essentially no other alternatives to the Roman Catholic Church as the dominant institution during those times. That dominance included legal, cultural, economic, as well as religious. Latin was the language of the few learned people in those days. Adémar spent most of his time doing what the other monks did, copying chronicles and doing additional writing. His principal work was *Chronicon Aquitanicum et Francicum* or *Historia Francorum*. In modern language that would be the history of the Franks. There were three books which covered Frankish history from the reign of King Pharamond, c. 370-c. 430, to 1028.

We should remember Adémar best for his skill and persistence as a forger.

He embraced the developing tale that Saint Martial, the 3rd century bishop who Christianized the Limoges district, had actually lived centuries earlier, and was in fact one of the original apostles. And he supplemented the less than scanty documentation for the alleged 'apostolicity' of Martial, first with a forged *Life* of Martial, as if composed by Martial's successor, Bishop Aurelian. To effect this claim, he composed an "Apostolic Mass" that still exists in Adémar's own hand (Paris *Bibliotheque Nationale* MS Latin 909), making it the **earliest autograph Western musical composition** that has survived. The local bishop and abbot seem to have cooperated in the project and the mass was first sung on Sunday, August 3, 1029.

Unfortunately for Adémar, the liturgy was disrupted by a traveling monk, Benedict of Chiusa, who denounced the improved *Vita* of Martial, as a provincial forgery and a new liturgy as offensive to God. The word spread, and the promising monk was disgraced. Adémar's reaction was to build forgery upon forgery, inventing a Council of 1031 that confirmed the 'apostolic' status of Martial, even a forged papal letter. The reality of this pathological tissue of forgeries was only unraveled in the 1920s, by a historian, Louis Saltet. Mainstream Catholic historians ignored Saltet's revelations until the 1990s.

In the long run, Adémar was successful. In the late 11th century Martial was indeed venerated in Aquitane as an apostle, though his legend was doubted elsewhere. In a very direct way, Adémar's Mass shows the power of liturgy to affect worship.[3]

There are several long-lasting lessons to be learned from the story of Adémar.
1. Many people naturally want to move up the hierarchy of large institutions. The Roman Catholic Church is such an institution. The lowest monastery cannot be considered in isolation because all dogma and canon law, etc., are created and maintained by the Pope and his councils in Rome.
2. The Church's power and importance were maintained and enhanced by the addition of holy people and relics generated from local areas. This provided the local populace with continuing

rationale to believe in the faith and, therefore, contribute their labor and other capital to support the church. Of course, in return, they hoped for everlasting life or salvation.

3. Adémar's creative efforts would have been enthusiastically supported by his immediate superiors, because they would have received more attention from the supervisory hierarchy all the way up to the Pope.

4. Adémar's persistence to build forgery upon forgery has been used through human history by institutions to enhance their organizations. In modern terms, this is the "Big Lie," which if repeated often enough, particularly in societies dominated by one institution, the lie becomes the truth for a long time, in some cases forever. Debunking the Big Lie reaches only some of the people, while others continue to believe it because it serves their aims and purposes.

5. Institutional historians, such as the Catholic Church historians above, and especially nationalistic historians, do not want to expose the truth from the falsehoods that benefit their organizations.

6. Can we trust this history?

Albert of Aachen (Aix la-Chapelle), floruit circa 1100, a historian of the First Crusade, was born during the latter part of the 11th century. *Floruit* means a period of flourishing and is frequently used by historians, which is abbreviated as "*fl*" in references. He was the author of a work of twelve books written between 1125 and 1150, which began at the time of Clermont when Pope Urban II initiated the First Crusade, covers the First Crusade and ends somewhat abruptly in 1121. This work was well known in the Middle Ages and largely used by William of Tyre, a later historian of the crusades. It was accepted unreservedly by many historians, including Edward Gibbon in the 18th Century, whose works carry great credibility. Some parts may be doubted, but general consensus seems to be that is a true record of the First Crusade.[4]

"His narrative is written with little order and less critical skill, his chronology is inexact, and his topographical references are often greatly disfigured. But the work is to be looked upon as the outpouring of a deeply religious and poetic heart, which saw in the contemporary Christian knighthood the salvation of the civilization of Christendom." Heinrich von Sybel, a German historian of the mid-19th Century, severely criticized Albert's work. Wilhelm Wattenbach, a German historian of the late 19th Century, "says that he (Albert) may have occasionally used good historical material; in general he is a panegyrist (eulogist) of an ideal Christian military service, a brilliant painter of scenes and events; his work and others like it served as bugle calls to summon to the Orient new multitudes of devoted soldiers of Christ."[5]

Now I will add that Albert never visited the Holy Land, but apparently learned much from returning crusaders and also had access to valuable correspondence.[6]

The above three paragraphs provide a wealth of material with which to discuss historians and historical writing.

1. Albert most certainly must have been a persistent and inquisitive pursuer of information about things of which he had no first hand knowledge. He was at Aachen, a town in northwest current Germany, which was the seat of Charlemagne's powerful reign of three centuries earlier, which now carries the title, the First German Reich. The crusaders came from many parts of current Germany, France and Italy. It must be assumed that the crusaders returned to their original home territories, therefore Albert's sources were probably geographically limited to those from northern Germany. The First Crusade was from 1096 to 1099. Information from other parts of

the European Continent may have eventually flowed his way, but undoubtedly filtered through many persons by the time Albert wrote his works over a century later.

2. The use of the material by many historians, especially one as Edward Gibbon, certainly gave great gravitas to the works. A general reader's book of the crusades in my library provides several passages from Albert describing the death of individual leaders, specifically Yaghi Siyan, the emir of Antioch. Such intimate, detailed passages from the confusion of battle and the heroic tales of the returning knights who are scattered around the continent may stretch the imagination about the full truth of those situations. But, who could dispute them? Later historians probably had little choice but to use the material in their own works, and thus the material gained validity over centuries.

3. The quote above, "His narrative…of Christendom" should be divided into two parts. The first part of this critiques Albert's organizational techniques and exactness by one who undoubtedly studied writing techniques in a university of an era 800 years later. In the modern vernacular, that would be called a "cheap shot." By what right does Wattenbach criticize Albert? That right is well established within the historical profession: **Because I went to a university, I am a better researcher of later materials and such a well organized writer that I must express my intellectual superiority over you of 800 years ago.** Oh, that Wattenbach had stood in Albert's shoes! The second part of that quote was similarly discussed previously. The members of the Roman Catholic Church had a responsibility and desire to further the interests of the Church by extolling the triumphs of the Christians over the infidels and the saving of Christendom for the salvation of all its members.

4. One might suspect that von Sybel's "severe criticism" of Albert may have been a little German one-upmanship over the Englishman, Gibbon, who had accepted Albert's work. Von Sybel will be discussed later.

5. Wattenbach's comment, "a brilliant painter of scenes and events" is a precursor to the religious allegorical paintings of the Italian renaissance several centuries later. Albert had the responsibility to his church to paint such scenes.

Alexander of Roes, ?-1289, was born in the village of Roes, which is in the western part of Germany. Roes is on the Elzbach River, which flows into the Mosel River. Roes is about 15 miles southwest of Koblenz, which is at the junction of the Mosel and Rhine Rivers. More significantly, Roes is about 70 miles southeast of Aachen, where Alexander eventually became a canon of the church there. Europe was divided in many ways during that period. The Roman Catholic Church was the most dominant institution and Latin was the principal language. There were many other vernacular languages and each became a focus for each community as its bonding means. The various groups were trying to establish its natural superiority over other groups by what might be labeled group genealogy. The Europeans felt superior by tracing their lineage back to the ancient Greeks, and specifically to ancient Troy, which is on the west coast of Turkey. Alexander of Roes deserves recognition because he taught and wrote that the Franks (now Germans) were the true leaders now that the Roman Empire disappeared during the 5th Century. By the same reasoning, the Franks were superior to the French, Spanish, and Italians. Alexander was first a religious person, and so used the rationale that the Franks were more Christian than the other groups.[7] Of course, Alexander was just following in the footsteps of Albert of Aachen, discussed above, to perpetuate the legacy of Charlemagne, from both the religious and secular perspectives. "God's Chosen People" was the key phrase describing the written and verbal efforts to establish superiority over other peoples.

Bede (Venerable Bede), c. 672-3-May 25, 735, was a Benedictine monk at the Northumbrian monastery of St. Peter at Monkwearmouth, which is on the North Sea coast near Newcastle Upon Tyne, 240 miles north of London. His most famous work, *The Ecclesiastical History of the English People*, gained him the title "The father of English history." Bede became known as *Venerable Bede* (Latin: Beda Venerabilis) soon after his death, but this was not linked to consideration for sainthood by the Roman Catholic Church. In fact, his title is believed to come from a mistranslation of the Latin inscription on his tomb in Durham Cathedral, intended to be *Here lie the venerable bones of Bede*, but wrongly interpreted as *here lie the bones of the Venerable Bede.*

Bede's works show he had at his command all the learning of his time. It was thought that the library at Wearmouth-Jarrow held between 300-500 books, making it one of the largest and most extensive in England. Bede's writings are classified as scientific, historical and theological. His scriptural commentaries employed the allegorical method of interpretation and his history includes accounts of miracles, which to earlier historians had seemed at odds with his critical approach to the materials in his history. His major work was in five books and 400 pages, covering both ecclesiastic and political activities from the time of Caesar to the completion date of 731. The noted historian of science, George Sarton, called the eight century "The Age of Bede", as Bede wrote several major scientific books. Bede was also instrumental in popularizing the time concept of BC and AD.[8]

I found eleven citations about Bede. Vincent sums up Bede's importance, "His masterpiece...stated its sources, named his authorities, some from Canterbury, one from Rome, invented [not true] dating by AD and BC instead of regnal years, wove a rich tapestry web of meaning, and gently ground an axe. In all this he was as modern as the moderns; but whereas once it was the precocity of his technique which most excited applause, today it is his art in going beyond technique, his construction of a personal vision of events, which reaches us across the centuries."[9] There are probably at least a dozen reasons to write history. Bede saw the historian's task as a social and moral one. In his preface, he pointed out that if history records the virtues of good men, then the virtuous reader is encouraged to follow the good. If it records the wickedness of

Bede

evil men, then the reader will be prompted to avoid similar sins.[10] That probably sounded good to Bede, but he did not realize that evil men will see the advantage of being powerful and evil, and thus go down that path, and history since Bede more than demonstrates that.

Bede is just the first of several medieval English historians you will meet in this chapter. Three books about medieval England included in my bibliography are worthy of note at this time if further reading is desired, and I recommend them for their history of England and the authors' cross-references among the historians and chroniclers of that period: *Chronicles*, by Chris Given-Wilson; *Dark Age Britain*, by Henry Marsh; and *The Medieval Foundations of England*, by G.O. Sayles.

Cassiodorus, Marcus Aurelius, c. 480-c. 570, was an Ostrogoth official serving at the court of Theodoric, the king of the Ostrogoths. Cassiodorus provided valuable information in *Variae*, which contained voluminous letters and state papers written primarily by him in his official duties. He also wrote a pretentious *History of the Goths* in twelve books between 526 and 533.[11]

Eadmer of Canterbury, c. 1060-c. 1124, was an English historian, theologian and ecclesiastic. He is best known as the contemporary biographer of Saint Anselm. Eadmer's circumstance is a mixture of religious and secular histories. Eadmer's birth in 1060 was six years before William I of Normandy invaded England in 1066 and defeated King Harold of England at the famous battle of Hastings. King William I was responsible for the famous Domesday Book of 1086, which was a complete inventory of all of England: people, land and livestock, etc. Eadmer became a Benedictine monk of Christ Church, Canterbury, which is located about 15 miles northwest of the English Channel port of Dover and on the main road to London, about 50 miles to the west.

Canterbury Cathedral

Anselm was the abbot of the Abbey of Bec, an important abbey between the English Channel ports of LeHavre and Rouen (now France), about 45 miles to the east, all of which were in the realm of William of Normandy. Eadmer became acquainted with Anselm when Anselm visited Canterbury. Anselm was appointed archbishop of Canterbury in 1093 and Eadmer became Anselm's secretary, confidant and biographer. Anselm died in 1109 and Eadmer devoted his time principally to writing and became one of the most important historians and biographers of the period after the Norman conquest of England. His *Life of Anselm* is well known. Eadmer's best known work is *Historia Novorum*, which deals mainly with the history of England between 1066 and 1122. During that era it was difficult to separate ecclesiastic history from secular history, so this is considered an ecclesiastic history but is regarded as one of the ablest and most valuable writings of its kind. Being a man of the cloth, Eadmer was naturally a defender of the faith and is known for his biographies of saints. I researched his name on the Internet and found one example, *Eadmer of Canterbury: Lives and Miracles of Saints Oda, Dunstan, and Oswald.*[12]

Einhard, c. 775-March 14, 840, was a Frankish monk and historian born in Seligenstadt, Germany, about 13 miles southeast of Frankfurt am Main. Einhard's most famous work was a biography of Charlemagne, which was modeled after Suetonius' *Lives of the Caesars.* His work was biased in favor of Charlemagne, but appears to be a fairly accurate description of events.[13] The preface to a book is the author's opportunity to tell why he wrote the book and things related to that. It is a way to get a sense of the author, in his own words. Prefaces should be relished by the readers, and I try to explain myself in them. I will now provide some excerpts from Einhard's preface to his biography on Charlemagne.

Abbey in Seligenstadt

"Since I have taken upon myself to narrate the public and private life, and in no small part of the deeds, of my lord and foster-father, the most lent and most justly renowned King Charles, I have condensed the matter into as brief a form as possible....Be this as it may, I see no reason why I should refrain from entering upon a task of this kind, since no man can write with more accuracy than I of events that took place about me, and

Einhard's Tomb

of facts which I had personal knowledge, ocular demonstration as the old saying goes, and I have no means of ascertaining whether of not any one else has the subject in hand….In any event, I would rather commit my story to writing, and hand it down to posterity in partnership with others, so to speak, than to suffer the most glorious life of this most excellent king, the greatest of all the princes of his day, and his illustrious deeds, hard for men of later times to imitate, to be wrapped in the darkness of oblivion."[14]

Ekkehard of Aura, c. 1050-c. 1125, was the Abbot of Aura, a monastery on the Saale River, about 25 miles north of Wuerzburg, Germany, and about 4 miles southwest of the well-known spa town of Bad Kissingen. It is in the northern part of Bavaria, for those readers who think of Bavaria as only in the extreme southern part of the country. Ekkehard was the first Abbott of Aura, and was originally from the

Aura Abbey

Benedictine order at Bamberg, about 40 miles to the east. The majority of the monks came from Hirsau Abbey, which was about 115 miles southwest of Aura. This geography lesson provides a sense of the distances traveled 12th Century by the Catholic orders to establish and populate new monasteries, and also gives a sense of the communications, by voice and writing, by the Church to spread the Gospel throughout the land. Now let us try to imagine the difficulty of trying to determine "facts" over such difficult conditions to be able to write history manuscripts. Of course, during that period much of the history was ecclesiastic history, which was inherent in the dogma of the Church when writing about saints and other Church stories.

Ekkehard is best known for his contributions to the *World Chronicle*, or *Universal Chronicle*, depending slightly on the translation from Latin into German or other languages. This chronicle is the chief source of the history of Germany during the years 1080-1124, which coincidently closely parallels the time-span of Eadmer's works of English history discussed immediately above. Ekkehard was a participant in, and a chronicler of, the First Crusade, as were several other personalities in this chapter, although not all participated. As a counterpoint to the distances described in the paragraph above, Ekkehard's travel to the First Crusade constituted a round trip of at least 4,000 miles from his monastery to Jerusalem and back. A *universal* history or chronicle will be identified numerous times as writers of the earlier eras used that term to describe their efforts to start with Biblical history and eventually arrive at events in their own times.

This period also contained the great controversy between Holy Roman Emperors King Henry IV & V and several popes, principally Gregory VII, over who had the right to name and invest officials of the Church. Ekkehard naturally sided with the pope so his writings would reflect such tendencies. The lesson learned is that historians bring their own biases to the writing desk, so the writer's background needs to be considered when reading such histories.[15]

Engelbert of Admont, c. 1250-12 May 1331, was the Abbott of the Benedictine Admont Abbey in Styria, Austria, which is almost in the exact geographic center of Austria, both north/south and east/west. My ESSO road map of Austria, circa 1970, shows the red-colored road to Admont, both east and west, with a green line beside it, indicating a picturesque route. That road follows the Enns River, which runs between the Ennstaler Alps and the Eisenerzer Alps. That means that the passengers in your car will have many scenic views, but the driver will be fighting curves and had better keep his eyes on the road.

Engelbert was born of noble parents at Volkersdorf, a very small community about 10 miles southeast from Linz, six miles from the Danube River, in northwestern Austria. Since Engelbert had noble parents, it might be assumed that Volkersdorf was a "bedroom community" to the much larger city of Linz. Today Volkersdorf has a population of over 27,000 and is probably even more of a bedroom community in the forested hills near Linz. As was the situation in the 13th Century, the Catholic Church provided the leading opportunity for a child to receive a good education and prepare for a respectable profession, as a monk. He enrolled in Admont at age seventeen and four years later he was sent to the Saint Vitus School in Prague, about 170 miles north of Admont, to study grammar and logic. After studying there for two years he went to study theology and philosophy for nine years at the University of Padua, Italy, which was founded in 1222, and is about 20 miles west of Venice in northeastern Italy. Padua is the sixth oldest university in Italy.

In 1297 Engelbert was elected Abbot of Admont and held that position for thirty years until he resigned at almost eighty years old. He was one of the most learned men of his time and he wrote on a variety of subjects, ranging from theology, philosophy and history to political science, natural sciences and music. He wrote 32 works, according to www.womenpriests.org, but the Catholic Encyclopedia cites 38 works. The best known of Engelbert's work is *Origin, Growth and Decline of the Roman Empire*. This work was written during the reign of King Henry VII, 1308-1313, and puts forth political principles, many of which would be contrary to those promulgated by Machiavelli early in the 16th Century. Another title was *Whether a Wise Man should marry a Wife*, but I'd better not go further on that one before I get into trouble.[16]

Admont Abbey today has the largest monastic library in the world, with more than 145,000 volumes, including 1,400 manuscripts and 900 incunabula (books written before the end of 1500 AD). The pictures of the interior of the library shown in *The Most Beautiful Libraries in the World* demonstrate the well-appointed art works and white shelf-facings with gold-leaf designs.

Florence of Worcester, ??-July11, 1118, was a monk at Worcester, England, which is about 25 miles south of Birmingham. He is given credit for the first attempt made in England to write a universal chronicle, but the universal part was based entirely on the work of Marianus Scotus, an Irish monk who died about 1082. Florence's *Chronicon ex Chronicis* added references to Bede's *Anglo-Saxon Chronicle*. Florence begins to be an independent authority in 1030 and his effort goes to 1117. A John of Worcester, ?-c. 1140, appears to have written parts of the same chronicle, so confusion exists.[17]

Frutolf of Michelsberg, ?-1103, was a monk and priest in the monastery Michelsberg at Bamberg, Germany, about 30 miles north of Nuremburg. Little seems to be known about him, but his world chronicle is considered as the most comprehensive and best organized chronicle of the Middle Ages. It goes from the Creation to 1099, and was continued by Ekkehard of Aura.[18] I am surprised that so little information is available about him, considering the description of his chronicle.

Fulcher of Chartres, c. 1059-c. 1127, was born in or near Chartres, a well-known cathedral town about 50 southwest of Paris. He was probably trained as a priest and was part of the entourage of Count Stephen of Blois and Robert of Normandy who participated in the First Crusade. In 1095 Pope Urban II announced the First Crusade at the Council of Clermont in 1095. Fulcher's details of the council led historians to believe that Fulcher attended the council or knew someone who did. Fulcher was eventually appointed chaplain to Baldwin of Boulogne and followed him when Baldwin founded the county of Edessa, which in southeastern modern Turkey north of the current Syrian border. The town of Edessa is now Urfa, about 30 miles north of Syria. Fulcher followed when Baldwin later became king of Jerusalem in 1100. Fulcher's *Gesta Francorum* is a lively description of many activities.

Fulcher's work was used by many chroniclers who lived after him. William of Tyre and William of Malmsbury used part of the chronicle as a source. Fulcher's work was mostly accurate, but not entirely so. (Wikipedia) Barnes characterized Fulcher's work as "egotistical and partisan."[19]

Gennadius of Marseille (of Massilia, Scholasticus), ?-c. 496, was a Christian priest and historian. He was a contemporary of Pope Gelasius I, 492-96, who was the second pope of African descent, but born in Rome. Gennadius's best known work is *Of Famous Men (De Viris Illustribus)*, a biography of over 90 contemporary significant Christians, which continued a work of the same name by Jerome, c. 340-420, the translator of the Vulgate Bible, the first Latin language Bible. Little is known of Gennadius's life, except what he tells us himself in the last of the biographies he wrote, "I, Gennadius, presbyter of Massilia, wrote eight books against all heresies, five books against Nestorius, ten books against Eutyches, three books against Pelagius, a treatise on the thousand years of the Apocalypse of John, this work, and a letter about my faith sent to blessed Gelasius, bishop of the city of Rome." He was on the whole an honorable and scrupulous writer.[20]

Geoffrey le Baker, ?-c. 1360, English chronicler, is also called Walter of Swinbroke, and was probably a secular clerk at Swinbrook, about 15 miles west of Oxford. He wrote chronicles about Edward II and Edward III, which deal with the history of England from 1303 to 1356. From the beginning until about 1324 this work is based upon Adam Murimuth's *Continuatio chronicarum,* but after this date it is valuable and interesting, containing information not found elsewhere, and closing with a good account of the battle of Poitiers on September 19, 1356.[21] The English won this hard-fought battle, but both sides were exhausted. This followed the highly significant battle at Crecy ten years earlier, when the English beat a force three times its size, principally through the use of the long bow, which revolutionized warfare of the period. These two battles were early in the Hundred Years War between England and France, which ran from 1337 to 1453 (120 years). Two excerpts from Geoffrey follow:

> "A.D. 1342: Then [after his Scottish campaign] the king [Edward III] returned to the southern parts and celebrated an exceptional tournament at Dunstaple, with 230 knights; and the same year he allowed a behourd to take place at Northampton.
>
> A.D. 1349: Meanwhile [while war was taking place in Flanders] on the feast of the Nativity of St. John the Baptist, in conjunction with the purification of the Queen, hastiludes were celebrated at Windsor, in which David, king of Scots, the Count of Eu, the lord of Tankerville, Lord Charles of Blois and many foreign captives were present, and they took part in the hastiludes by the permission of the king and their captors; the Count of Eu was given first place for his performance on the field. Afterwards, in hunting season, the same captives, along with the lord king and other leading men of the kingdom, gave themselves to the pleasurable pursuit of hunting at Clarendon and in the forests."[22]

Geoffrey of Monmouth, c. 1100-c. 1155, was a clergyman and one of the leading figures in the development of British history and the popularity of the tales of King Arthur. His birthplace is unknown, but may have been in Monmouth, a town just west of the Severn River in southeast Wales, England, and about 120 miles west of London. He was educated by his uncle Uchtryd, afterwards Bishop of Llandaf. He studied at Oxford University, about 60 miles east of Monmouth. On February 21, 1152 Archbishop Theobald consecrated Geoffrey at Lambeth, which is the home of the Archbishop of Canterbury and is directly across the Thames River from the Parliament Buildings, as bishop of St. Asaph, having ordained him as a priest just ten days before. St. Asaph is on the Irish Sea about 193 miles northwest of London and about 120 miles north of Monmouth. Appointments such as this were common practice by the Roman Catholic Church throughout its history. The appointment allowed the recipient to receive benefices (part of the revenues) from the diocese or estate. There is no evidence that Geoffrey ever visited St. Asaph, which was also a common circumstance in many cases. These appointments were strictly to provide a source of income for members of the Church as they moved up the hierarchy.

Geoffrey's earliest work was *The Prophecies of Merlin,* which he wrote some time before 1135. His best known work is *History of the Kings of Britain,* which was completed in 1147. It purports to relate the history of Britain, from its first settlement by Brutus, a descendant of the Trojan hero Aeneas, to the death of Cadwallader in the 7th century, taking in Julius Caesar's invasions of Britain, two kings, Leir and Cymbeline, later immortalized by Shakespeare, and one of the earliest developed narratives of King Arthur. Geoffrey claims to have translated it from an ancient book written in Welsh, although few take this claim seriously. Much of it is based on the *Historia Britonum,* a 9th century Welsh-Latin historical compilation, Bede's *Historia ecclesiastica gentis Anglorum* and Gildas' 6th century polemic *De Excidio Britanniae,* expanded with material from Roman histories, Welsh legend, genealogical tracts, and Geoffrey's own imagination. It contains little trustworthy historical fact, and many scholars are tempted to agree with William of Newburgh, who wrote around 1190 that "it is quite clear that everything this man wrote about Arthur and his successors, or indeed about his predecessors from Vortigern onwards, was made up, partly by himself and partly by others, either from an inordinate love of lying, or for the sake of pleasing Britons."

Geoffrey's "History" has been one of the great influences in English literature, making it especially felt in the national romance from Layamon to Tennyson. Shakespeare, Milton, Dryden, Pope, and Wordsworth have all used his legends, while many of the early chroniclers followed him as an historian. But the twelve books of his "History", recounting how Brut, great-grandson of Aeneas, founded the kingdom, and narrating the adventures of subsequent kings, are in truth not history at all but the beginning of English story-telling.[23]

I have used considerable material from Wikipedia.com. Using Geoffrey as an example, I want to demonstrate how Wikipedia operates as a free encyclopedia which anyone can change the words or substance of the article. The basic page has a tab, "discussion." This tab contains the changes and the discussion about those changes. I have quoted that entire tab below so you can gain a sense of the process and draw your own conclusions about its usefulness and validity. I did not edit it, so misspellings, etc. remain. I have used double brackets in bold to identify the entire "discussion" tab from the previous and following writings.

[[Removed from article:

> And all of it together is now recognized as a deliberate spoof--one which succeeded in fooling many historians and other writers for centuries.

I'm unaware of any scholar who has said *Historia Regum Britanniae* was a spoof or hoax. Can you cite some published studies that say this? If they can be furnished, then this sentence can be restored as reporting the POV of some scholars. -- llywrch 00:34, 13 Mar 2004 (UTC)

> The spoof thing seems to have crawled back into the article, but once again without the slightest shred of justification. HRB is pretty elaborate for a spoof; however, it fits well into the medieval search for documented connections -- even spurious ones -- between the present and the legendary past. I doubt that HRB is "spoofier" than the Aeneid. I've changed "spoof" to "fiction", which ought to cover just about any interpretation of the material (except for those who think

that Geoffrey really was working from a reliable ancient British history!) 68.100.18.183 05:24, 22 January 2006 (UTC) Random Critic

Two things I'd comment on

1. All learned books of the period were not in Latin. All "English" may be. The world is a larger place and the sentence misleads. Even in the British Isles other learned books were in Welsh, outside the UK they were in many languages

2. It might be worth making it clearer that the "Merlin = Myrddin" thing was an invention of Geoffrey and not one that there is evidence for surviving and recorded. (from IP 81.2.110.250)

Removed from article:

> John Morris writes in *The Age of Arthur* that Geoffrey warned aware readers of his time that his work stemmed from Walter Map of Oxford, "who was then well known as a satirist, a wit, and a literary practical joker." Consistent with this, Geoffrey makes numerous statements that historians of the time readily knew to be satirical, such as that Constantius married the daughter of Old King Cole. "It ought not to be necessary to warn," concludes Morris, "that no word or line of Geoffrey can legitimately be considered in the study of any historical problem; but the warning unfortunately remains necessary."

John Morris has apparently confused the "Walter, Archdeacon of Oxford" that Geoffrey of Monmouth referred to with Walter Map -- who was, indeed, archdeacon of Oxford -- but not until 1197, long after Geoffrey was dead. Map is (falsely) cited as a source for Arthurian "histories", but in the Vulgate Cycle of the early 13th century, not in HRB. The linkage between Constantius I Chlorus and Coel Hen, while doubtless an invention of Geoffrey's, is hardly more satirical than other elements in HRB; Coel was not at that time the subject of a nursery rhyme! I have not read Morris, but based on these extracts he seems untrustworthy as a source. (from IP 144.92.184.38)

> > I've removed the "spoof" thing again, as well as the assertion that the Historia is a work of fiction (it may not be true, but that's not the same thing) and added a bit about his sources. -- Nicknack009 21:05, 12 July 2006 (UTC)]]

You will notice that several editors were identified by their Internet Protocol (IP) numbers. There is also another tab, "talk," which provides a chronology of the revisions and an opportunity to look at the version on any particular date. Some folks may criticize this approach, but after reading about the "sins" of Geoffrey, one would have to conclude that Wikipedia provides more truth than Geoffrey.

John Vincent wrote, "Bad history perhaps made a greater mark on medieval culture than good. Its greatest practitioner was Geoffrey of Monmouth (1100-1154), a poorly educated Welshman, willing to try his hand at anything, whose eventual reward was the see of St. Asaph. Geoffrey's historical value was nil, his popularity was enormous, and his influence on subsequent writers great."[24] Harry Barnes wrote, "The unmatched fakir of medieval England was Geoffrey of Monmouth…"[25] Henry Marsh, in his *Dark Age Britain,* wrote a sixteen page chapter on Geoffrey of Monmouth, and concluded, "Had Geoffrey been born in modern times, he might have been a successful novelist. If Bede can be called the father of English history, perhaps Geoffrey is entitled to be known as the father of historical fiction."[26] William of Newburgh, c. 1136-c. 1198, who was 3-4 decades after Geoffrey, was one of the first to criticize Geoffrey's work, such as "weaving a web of fiction,"[27] and "only a person ignorant of ancient history would have any doubt about how shamelessly and impudently he lies in almost everything."[28] Chris Given-Wilson's *Chronicles, The Writing of History in Medieval England* is a superb book about the historical writers of that era.

We should now stop flogging Geoffrey of Monmouth, although there are many more details available. Suffice it to say, when you see "Geoffrey of Monmouth," be prepared to disbelieve almost everything he wrote, but he provided a great service to English literature and the national ancestry.

Geoffrey de Villehardouin, c. 1160-c. 1213, French, was one of the leaders of the Fourth Crusade, 1202-1204. His *Conquest of Constantinople:*

> "was one of the more notable historical works of the Middle Ages. It was the first medieval historical book of importance written in the vernacular. While modest in speaking of his own deeds, the book was somewhat of an apology for Villhardouin's own policy in the Fourth Crusade. It is still the best source from which to learn of the spirit of the Crusaders on this holy sacking expedition. It was written in a vigorous and concise style, full of personal touches and throbbing with virile human interest. Gustave Masson observes that: 'the slightest study of Villehardouin's prose will convince the reader that no medieval French author can be named more noteworthy for clearness of style, neatness of composition, and admirable delination of character.' In his political philosophy, Villehardouin was an apologist for chivalry and feudalism."[29]

An example of Geoffrey de Villehardouin's style is below, recognizing that translations are sometimes open to considerable interpretation themselves:

> "Afterwards the barons held a parliament at Soissons, to settle when they should start, and whither they should wend. But they came to no agreement, because it did not seem to them that enough people had taken the cross. So during all that years (1200) no two months passed without assemblings in parliament at Compiègne. There met all the counts and barons who had taken the cross. Many were the opinions given and considered; but in the end it was agreed that envoys should be sent, the best that could be found, with full powers, as if they were lords in person, to settle such matters as needed settlement. ... To these six envoys [Geoffrey one of them] the business in hand was fully committed, all the barons delivering to them valid charters, with seals attached, to the effect that they would undertake to maintain and carry out whatever conventions and agreements the envoys might enter into, in all sea ports, and whithersoever else the envoys might fare."[30]

Gerald of Wales, (Giraldus Cambrensis, Gerallt Gymro in Welsh), c. 1146-c. 1223, was a medieval clergyman and chronicler of his times. Note "of his times" because most of our previous chroniclers wrote of much earlier times and forward. He was born at Manorbier Castle in Pembrokeshire, the castle being on the northern shore of Carmarthen Bay in southwest England. His original name was Gerald of Barri and he was of mixed Norman and Welsh blood. Gerald received a church education at Gloucester, about 125 mile east as the crow flies, but probably further by the natural travel routes of that era. He then studied in Paris, which is about 350 miles to the southeast of Gloucester, and includes a boat ride across the English Channel. Crossing the channel sometimes took a long time, not so much the actual trip, but waiting for the weather to calm sufficiently. Later on in his life, after becoming an established historian, he made three trips to Rome to try to become a bishop. Rome is 900 straight-line miles from London, so going to Rome was a tough trip, particularly since one had to go over the Alps. I repeatedly measure the distances to demonstrate the lengths that people went to in that era to obtain a good education or to rise in the Roman Catholic Church hierarchy.

Gerald's Welsh background was a significant deterrent to rising in the church hierarchy. He became chaplain in 1184 to King Henry II of England, who reigned 1154-89. Gerald was chosen to accompany John, one of the king's sons on an expedition to Ireland. This was the catalyst for his literary career. His account of his finding during that trip was published in 1188 as *Topographia Hibernica*, the Latin name for Ireland. He followed it up shortly afterwards, with an account of Henry's conquest of Ireland, the *Expugnatio Hibernica*, (Taking Ireland by Storm). Gerald was selected to accompany the Archbishop of Canterbury, Baldwin of Exeter, on a tour of Wales to recruit people for the Third Crusade, 1189-91. Jerusalem had fallen to the forces of Saladin at noon, Friday, October 2, 1187. Gerald's account of his journey with the Archbishop was published in 1191 as *Itinerarium Cambriae* and was followed in 1194 with *Descriptio Cambriae*, Cambria being another name for Wales. Gerald's two works on Wales remain incredibly valuable historical documents of Welsh and Norman

Gerald Of Wales

cultures, however untrustworthy and inflected by ideology, whimsy and his unique style. Gerald finally gave up his attempts in 1203 to gain benefices by becoming an archbishop. He spent the rest of his life in academic study, producing works of devotional instruction and politics. Given-Wilson described Gerald's work, more sophisticatedly, as having reinvented a form of literature, the "ethnographic monograph, which had not been attempted in the West for a thousand years." Included in this category are such things as language and appearance, dress, marriage and inheritance practices, social structure, and religious and burial customs.[31]

A long quotation from Wikipedia follows to provide addition insight into Gerald's "whimsy and unique style":

"This nation, O King, may now, as in former times, be harassed, and in a great measure weakened and destroyed by your and other powers, and it will also prevail by its laudable exertions, but it can never be totally subdued through the wrath of man, unless the wrath of God shall concur. Nor do I think that any other nation than this of Wales, nor any other language, whatever may hereafter come to pass, shall on the day of severe examination before the Supreme Judge, answer for this corner of the earth."

It was Giraldus who also wrote (of the Welsh) that "If they would be inseparable, they would be insuperable," and that, unlike the English hirelings, who fight for power or to procure gain or wealth, the Welsh patriots fight for their country. He had pleasant things to say about the poetic talents of his people, too:

"In their rhymed songs and set speeches they are so subtle and ingenious that they produce, in their native tongue, ornaments of wonderful and exquisite invention both in the words and the sentences... They make use of alliteration in preference to all other ornaments of rhetoric, and that particular kind which joins by consonancy the first letters or syllables of words."

Giraldus could not have predicted the later perfection of cynghanedd, the complex system of sound correspondence that has characterized the strict-meter poetry of the Welsh for so many centuries and that is still practised today, especially in competitions for the eisteddfod chair. Cynghanedd did not become a formal system with strict rules until the fourteenth century, but its uniquely Welsh forms had been honed for centuries before that. Finally, in *Descripto Cambriae*, Giraldus penned the following words that give so much pride to Welsh singers of today, especially those who participate in the immensely popular Cymanfaoedd Canu (hymn-singing festivals) held throughout Wales and North America:

> "In their musical concerts they do not sing in unison like the inhabitants of other countries, but in many different parts... You will hear as many different parts and voices as there are performers who all at length unite with organic melody."[32]

Notice several of the Welsh words above. In my opinion, they defy the translation by guessing of the Welsh language, contrary to Latin, German, and French, which at least offer the opportunity to make an intelligent guess as to the meaning.

Gerald, a half century behind Geoffrey of Monmouth, along with William of Newburgh, openly denounced Geoffrey's work as fiction masquerading as fact.[33]

Gervase (Gervaise) of Canterbury, c. 1141-c. 1210, was a monk at Christ Church, Canterbury. In 1178, he took the depositions of five monks of Canterbury who had witnessed a spectacular flash of light on the moon, which today is known to be the meteoric impact that formed the Giordano Bruno crater. Gervase wrote a chronicle covering the period 1100-1199; the *Gesta Regum*, which is in part an abridgement of an earlier chronicle, and from the year 1199 an independent source of great value for the early years of King John, 1199-1216, the signer of the Magna Carta in 1215; a history of the archbishops of Canterbury to the death of Hubert Walter in 1205; and *Mappi Mundi*, a topographical work with lists of bishoprics and ecclesiastical foundation in the various counties of England, Wales, and part of Scotland.[34] Barnes assesses Gervase "Though lacking stylistic brilliance, the writings of Gervase are laborious and conscientious compilations which contain a large fund of information."[35]

Gervase seems to have been credited by many later historians as the first one to identify what separated historians and chroniclers from other writers of literature. The single idea was the claim to be presenting the truth. Given-Wilson identified "what is probably the most frequently-cited prologue to any English chronicle—should 'instruct truthfully (*veraciter edocere*) concerning deeds, manners, and the life which he describes'; the chronicler, on the other hand, should reckon by true computation (*supputatione veraci*) the years of the Lord and the events listed under them'. The chief point of Gervase's prologue was to explain the differences between the historian and the chronicler. Fundamentally, however, he conceded that 'The intention of each is the same'—for, he declared, 'each seeks the truth' (*uterque veritati intendit*).[36] In my introduction I mentioned about not having too many manuscript titles in a foreign language. There is some merit to having both English and Latin words as above, so readers can check their Latin skills against the English translations. Maybe by the end of the book you will become proficient.

Gervase wrote, "I have no desire to note down all those things which are memorable (*memorabilia*), but only those things which ought to be remembered (*memoranda*), that is, those things which are clearly worthy of remembrance (*digna memoriae*)"[37] Shades of Senator Moynihan. Gervase, in the 12th century, was selecting his own facts, based on his humble (?) judgment on what was important or not. Shades of Professor Kennedy. Gervase undoubtedly left enough facts laying around his cutting table that others could go back, look at the same source documents, select different facts for different themes, and write about the same events, with little similarity to Gervase's version. Thus historians write.

Godfrey of Viterbo, c. 1120-c. 1196, was a Roman Catholic chronicler, but no one is sure whether he was Italian or German born. He spent his early life in Viterbo, which is about 70 miles north of Rome, but he was educated in Bamberg, Germany, which is almost 600 miles north of Rome. Godfrey was active in both government and ecclesiastical offices. In 1140 he became chaplain to the German king, Conrad III. He spent most of his life as a secretary in the service of the Holy Roman Emperor, Frederick I Barbarossa. He was apparently well trusted by Barbarossa as he was sent on diplomatic missions around Europe, which included over 40 trips to Rome. Poor guy had to make 40 trips over the Alps. During these times he collected historical material, which must have been a rare resource for his later writings.

One of his well known works was *Speculum regum,* which translates to Mirror of Kings, which was works suitable for the education of kings and their sons. Godfrey was a favorite of Frederick's son, Henry IV, who followed Barbarossa as king when Barbarossa drowned in a river in southern Turkey on June 10, 1190 during the 3rd Crusade. This history of the world beginning with the deluge was intended to reconcile the Romans with the Germans.[38] I have no idea what was in that history or how it was written, but the stated theme would be an example of slanted history. In other words, only use selective facts and weave them into a mosaic to prove the desired point. Godfrey also wrote *Liber universalis* 'universal book," which chronicled world history from the creation down to the time of Henry VI. Godfrey's *Memoria seculorum,* or *Liber memorialis,* was a world chronicle dedicated to Henry VI, which professes to record the history of the world from the creation until 1185 when it was completed. Godfrey later did a revision, which enjoyed unmerited fame during the Middle Ages, but it was full of imaginary occurrences.[39] We have now built up quite a collection of universal histories, so that was obviously a popular activity by historians during many centuries.

Gregory of Catino, 1060-?, was a monk at the Abbey of Farfa, which is about 25 miles north of Rome. He was an archivist, the first one we've met so far, which provided him with his historical background. Let me digress slightly to set the stage for Gregory the archivist. The Catholic Church has been a wealthy church for well over one thousand years. During the Middle Ages the Church owned 30-40 percent of the land in France, Britain, and Italy. It utilized the land for agriculture and livestock operations. The Church dominated the economic landscape of those countries because it was by far the largest and most proliferated organization of any kind. There were no nation-states, as the land belonged to nobles, etc., which were much smaller and not organized. The monks of Farfa of Gregory's era are credited with owning 683 churches or convents; two towns, Civitavecchia, 50 miles west of Farfa and now Rome's main seaport on the Tyrrhenian Sea, and Alatri (40 miles southeast of Farfa; 132 castles; 16 strongholds; 7 seaports; 8 salt mines; 14 villages; 82 mills; and 315 hamlets. That is an impressive conglomerate worthy of any today.

Gregory arranged the archives, and to substantiate Farfa's claims and the rights of its monks, edited the *Regesto di Farfa,* composed of 1324 documents, which were all very important for the history of Italian society in the 11th century. Ugo Balzani, a 19th century historian on the early European chroniclers, praised the accuracy and exactness of Gregory's work, "planned along the lines quite in harmony with the best critical efforts of our own times." In 1103, Gregory wrote the *Largitorium,* a lengthy list of all the concessions, or grants, made by the monastery to its tenants. Having collected all this detailed information, he set to work on a history of the monastery, the *Chronicon Farfense.* He compiled an index in order to reference his earlier works. Gregory was a man of real learning and wrote with remarkable accuracy for someone in the 11th century.[40]

Henry of Huntingdon, c. 1080-1160, was the archdeacon (not a clergyman) of Huntingdon, which is about 65 miles directly north of London. He is best known for his *Historia Anglorum (History of the English),* which covers the period from the Roman invasion of England in 43 BC to the accession of Henry II in 1154. It has been estimated that about seventy five percent derives from others' work through direct quotation, translation or summarization. About forty percent comes from Bede's *Historia ecclesiastica gentis Angloruim.* It is 'original' for the years 1126-1154, some of the events of which he was often a personal witness, including the reigns of Henry I and Henry II, and the anarchy of King Stephen.

Henry's history is full of dramatic stories and was extremely popular and influential with other historians. Yet his work's popularity should not diminish the sense of the Historica as rigorous history, nor of its careful crafting as a contribution to ongoing political debates about ethnicity, nationality, and the justification of rule over England and Wales. Henry divided English history according to the five great invasions by the Romans, Picts and Scots, Anglo-Saxons, Viking and Normans. The Historia was divided, in its 1135 version, into seven books entitled"

1. The Rule of the Romans in Britain
2. The Coming of the English
3. The Conversion of the English
4. The Rule of the English
5. The Danish Wars
6. The Coming of the Normans
7. The Rule of the Normans

Henry is credited with the periodization term Heptarchy: a hypothetical confederacy of seven Anglo-Saxon kingdoms of the 7th and 8th centuries.[41] Creating the name for a period is probably something all historians dream of doing. Unfortunately most will be disappointed. The name usually comes considerably after the period started when folks recognize that there has been a shift of events in some way, many times around a specific event.

The Catholic Encyclopedia cites Henry's death as 1155, not 1160 in Wikipedia. It picks this date because a new archdeacon of Huntingdon was chosen that year. It also notes that Henry's details are occasionally invented and his chronology is not reliable.[42] Barnes cites Henry's years as 1084-1157, and calls him an accurate and well-balancer chronicler. He had unusual poise and skepticism for his time in rejecting both legends and the marvels of the supernatural. In this category are the 'miracles,' which are one of the backbone dogmas of the Roman Catholic Church. Henry writes that care needed to be taken in authenticating miracles,

> "Simple people especially, and some clever ones in the name and under the guise of religion, seem to err in assenting to instant belief in miracles which are either fictitious or are not susceptible of certain proof; indeed, ordinary people for the sake of stupid novelty, and men in religion either for money or so that their saint's resting-place may be properly enriched, mendaciously and falsely go along with these customs… However, if miracles are narrated to me in this way I do not openly contradict them unless they are obviously frivolous, nor give them constant affirmation unless I observe them to be fully corroborated by well-known proofs and trustworthy persons."

Henry accepted Bede as a "completely secure" authority.[43]

Herman of Reichenau, July 18, 1013-September 24, 1054, was a historian, composer and music theorist. He also goes by Hermannus Contractus and Hermannus Augiensis. Contractus is translated as lame or twisted, because Hermann was crippled from early childhood by a paralytic disease. His father was the duke of Altshausen, about 30 miles north of the well-known Abbey of Reichenau, which is on Reichenau Island in the middle of the southwestern finger of Lake Constance, the boundary between Germany and Switzerland. Hermann wrote a detailed chronicle from the birth of Christ to his own present day, for the first time compiling the events of the 1st millennium AD scattered in various chronicles in a single work, ordering them after the reckoning of the Christian era.[44] "He was one of the ablest historians of his time and his work was particularly valuable as a survey of his own period. On the previous century also, his book was important, for it relied upon a highly valuable source which has since been lost."[45] Hermann was sent by his father to Reichenau at the age of seven to be educated, which was common in those days, but especially because of Hermann's physical condition. He developed a fully rounded education in music, mathematics and astrology. The Abbey of Reichenau claims to have been the largest and artistically most influential center for producing lavishly illuminated manuscripts in Europe during the late 10th and early 11th centuries.[46] The headwaters of the Rhine River flow past Reichenau from Lake Constance.

Hermann of Reichenau

Berthold of Reichenau, ?-1088, was a Benedictine monk and chronicler who continued the work of Hermann of Reichenau, when Hermann died. Berthold worked on the chronicle capturing the troubled time immediately preceding the troublesome times of Hildebrand, who became Pope Gregory VII, 1073-1085. Berthold was succeeded in these efforts by Bernold of Reichenau. This case provides an example of the later works of the 18th century German historians. Wilhelm von Giesebrecht, 1814-1889, and Georg Heinrich Pertz, 1795-1876, were just two of several historians who sometimes agreed and sometime disagreed over the writings and overlaps of Berthold and Bernold, as to which one should get credit for certain passages.[47]

Jacobus de Voragine, c. 1230-July 13 or 16, 1298, was an Italian chronicler and archbishop of Genoa. He was born in Varazze, a coastal town about 20 miles west of Genoa, Italy. His major work was the *Golden Legend (Legenda Aturea)*, a collection of the legendary lives of the greater saints of the medieval church. The preface divides the ecclesiastical year into four periods corresponding to the various epochs of the world's history, a time of deviation, of renovation, of reconciliation and of pilgrimage. The saints' lives are full of fanciful legend, and in not a few cases contain accounts of 13th century miracles wrought at special places, particularly with reference to the Dominicans, of which Jacobus was one. This work was one of the most popular religious works of the Middle ages.[48] The people in the chronicle undoubtedly existed, but the rest seems to be totally religious pabulum for the church masses. I have included Jacobus for another reason. The statement below is from the prologue to the *Golden Legend,* circa early 20th century.

Genoa-Cathedral

"Though it does not appear to have been among the earliest of printed books, the Legenda Aturea was no sooner in type than edition after edition appeared with surprising rapidity. Probably no other book was more frequently reprinted between the years 1470 and 1530 than the compilation of Jacobus de Voragine. And while almost innumerable editions appeared in Latin, it was also translated into the vulgar tongue of most of the nations of Europe, usually with alterations and additions in accordance with the hagiological preferences of the concerned nationalities. It is with an early French translation that we are chiefly concerned, of which Caxton's version is a close rendering."[49]

There are several points to be made with the above quotation.

1. Johann Guttenberg invented the movable-type printing press and printed his first book, the Bible, in 1454 in Mainz, Germany. His press was rapidly proliferated throughout Europe during the next forty years. This invention not only allowed for more copies to be made of any book, but also created a demand for more reading because there were more books available. There were many different genres of books being printed, and so the process became a self-reinforcing cycle of enlightenment for the populations of several countries.
2. The first printed edition of the *Golden Legend* was in 1470, probably in the original Latin.
3. Each country's presses would have been busily engaged in getting translations to press because of the profits involved.
4. The first English version was in 1483, by William Caxton, the first English printer, whose office was quite close to Westminster Abbey in London.
5. Each country had its *hagiological preferences*, therefore it could highlight the many good points of its favorite sons. "When Bede or Jacobus of Voragine wrote the biography of a saint, it was not at all in order to give an accurate rendition of that particular man's character, in our sense; it was with the idea of showing the general character of a holy man, so that the reader might imitate him, and achieve sainthood too."[50]

Joachim of Fiore (Flora) (Gioacchino da Fiore in Italian), c. 1135-March 30, 1201, was a mystic, theologian and esoterist (limited to a small circle). He was the founder of the monastic order of San Giovanni (now Jure Vetere). His followers are called Joachimites. He was born in the small village in the vicinity of Cosenza, Italy, which is a medium size town about 300 miles south of Rome, and is on the main road between Rome and the Straits of Messina, the crossing to Sicily.

Joachim, as a historian, presents an opportunity to discuss the mixture of theology and history. This inquiry is not about theological arguments, disputations, or whatever term is used to identify the endless controversies of and over religion. Joachim was trained as a secular clerk, but went on a pilgrimage to Jerusalem and converted to a life within the church. He played a role in many different aspects of the Roman Catholic Church. His study and interpretation of the Book of Revelations led to his legacy as a historian. He believed that history, by analogy with the Trinity, was divided into three fundamental epochs:

- The *Age of the Father*, corresponding to the Old Testament, characterized by obedience of mankind to the rules of God;
- The *Age of the Son*, between the advent of Christ and 1260, represented by the New Testament, when the Man became the son of God;
- The *Age of the Holy Spirit*, impending (in 1260), when mankind was to come in direct contact with God, reaching the total freedom preached by the Christian message.[51]

Joachim must be looked at in the context of his age, when the Roman Catholic Church dominated all thinking. Everything in his historical model was based on interpretations of the Bible. But there were many religious persons we have previously visited who wrote strictly about actual events, to include the Crusades. I am somewhat mystified why four other historians commented on Joachim, since he does not fit the criteria that seems to be applied to history by other historians. Their comments will be provided for you to make your own judgments about Joachim as a historian.

Mark Gilderhus, a 20th century academic historian, cites the three periods by Joachim and that "each period would endure for forty generations, and the passage from one to the next would signify advancement toward a condition of greater wisdom, love, spirituality, and happiness. The prophecy ironically took on revolutionary political implications after Joachim's death in 1202 by sparking interest among poor and humble people who aspired to a better life and promoted an upsurge of religious millenarianism, that is, the expectation of 1,000 years of joy, serenity, prosperity, and justice."[52] I see nothing there but pure religious ideology and prophecy, not history.

Benedetto Croce, a highly respected Italian historian of the early 20th century, mentioned Joachim in the context of *history of things future* and *allegorical interpretation*.[53] There does not seem to be much history there without a serious stretch of the definition.

Page Smith, a middle 20th century historian, mentioned Joachim as an example of the Christian notion of an expectation of a really impending transformation of the Christian world.[54] It seems as if Christians have had a never-ending belief in a better world for well over a millennium, which means that they have a history of unsuccessfully predicting the future.

Pardon Tillinghast, a late 20th century academic historian, cites Joachim in the logical context as one of the four categories dealing with the relationship between history and Christianity. This one is chiliasm: the Kingdom of God will come very soon. It thrives in times of crisis and is still alive today, but it has little relevance to most present-day historical writing.[55] Chiliasm, millenarianism, apocalyptic, and other similar words mean essentially the same thing and are used to avoid repetition. Of course, *crisis* is in the eye of the beholder.

Joceline of Brakeland, flourished c. 1200, wrote a chronicle of the St. Edmundsbury (also Bury St. Edmunds) monastery, which is about 75 miles north of London. "This was a veritably unique memoir on English social and monastic life in the 12th century. It was invaluable as a description of monastic administration. Joceline was highly autobiographical in his writing, and he thus gives us much insight into the thoughts and actions of a lively, entertaining and able monk."[56]

Joceline's chronicle is on the Internet under Medieval Sourcebook. The modern-day abbot who wrote the introduction to the document said that this is a new translation. As historians we do need to question how the new compared with older translations. Perhaps there is not much significant difference, but it makes one wonder. Joceline became a novice in the Church under Samson of Tottingham, who later became Abbot of St. Edmundsbury. Joceline was Samson's chaplain for six years and held other positions, which gave him access to many documents and observations with which to write his chronicle. The author's preface follows:

> "I have undertaken to write of those things which I have seen and heard, and which have occurred in the church of Saint Edmund, from the year in which the Flemings were taken without the town, in which year also I assumed the religious habit, and in which Prior Hugh was deposed and Robert made Prior in his room. And I have related the evil as a warning and the good for an example."[57]

Istanbul-Blue Mosque

John of Ephesus (of Asia), c. 507-c. 588, was a leader of the Monophysite Syriac-speaking Church in the 6th century, and one of the earliest and most important of historians who wrote in Syriac. He was born in Amida, now Diyarbakir in southeastern modern Turkey. He traveled to Constantinople, back to Amida, and finally back to Constantinople (Istanbul). The distance between the two towns is about 650 miles. I flew that terrain in a small airplane in the 1970s, looking out the window the entire time. The landscape is mostly barren with not many recognizable landmarks. It would not be fun to walk, if that is what John did.

Ephesus-My family on the march

John's main work was his *Ecclesiastical History*, which covered more than three centuries from the time of Julius Caesar to 588. The third part of John's history was a detailed account of the ecclesiastical events which happened in 571-588, which survives in a fairly complete state in the British Museum. It forms a contemporary record of great value to the historian. Its somewhat disordered state, the want of chronological arrangement, and the occasional repetition of accounts of the same events are due, as the author himself informs us (ii. 50), to the work being almost entirely composed during times of persecution. The same cause may account for the somewhat slovenly Syriac style.[58] It was of special significance for its account of the last struggles and extinction of paganism and for the political and cultural history of the Eastern Empire in the sixth century.[59]

John of Salisbury, c. 1120-1180, author, historian, diplomat and philosopher, was born at Salisbury, England, which is about 70 miles southwest of London. He received his religious studies in France. He was secretary to the Archbishop of Canterbury and crossed the Alps many times conducting diplomatic missions to Rome. He was at Canterbury when Thomas Becket was assassinated for displeasing King Henry II. He ended his life as the Bishop of Chartres in France.

Salisbury Cathedral

John was one of the most cultured scholars of his day. His two principal works were *Policraticus* and *Metalogicus*, writings invaluable as storehouses of information regarding the matter and form of scholastic education, and remarkable for their cultivated style and humanist tendency. The *Policraticus* also sheds light on the decadence of the 12th century court manners and the ethical lowness of the royalty. His fine taste and superior training made him the most elegant Latin writer of his time. He is equally distinguished as an historian and as a philosopher: he was the first medieval writer to emphasize the importance of historical studies in philosophy and in all other branches of learning.[60] He is not the usual historian, which is the theme of this effort. Later on we will encounter many other examples of the mixture of history and philosophy, of which I will tread lightly, since philosophy is not within my field of thought or work.

Lambert of Hersfeld, c. 1024-c. 1088, was a monk from Thuringia, a region in current central Germany, and during the divided Germany of the second half of the 20th century was in the western part of East Germany. He became a monk at Hersfeld, which is about 70 miles northeast of Frankfurt. He was ordained at Aschaffenburg, about 65 miles south of Hersfeld. His principal work was *Annals*, which is a universal history from the creation of the world until about 1040, in which he used others' works for the segments up to their life and then wrote in detail the events during their lifetime. His own accounts range from 1042 to 1077. He was openly hostile to Henry IV, the Holy Roman Emperor. Lambert was superbly educated for his day and wrote in a fine, classicizing Latin peppered with references and allusions to Roman authors. Like many of the classical authors he admired, Lambert fancied himself a cynical observer of elite society, casting a critical eye on the political melodramas and scandals of his day and chronicling the way which power and pride corrupted rulers and perverted society, raising up the unworthy and punishing the good and decent. [Could he have been writing about the 20th century?]

Aschaffenburg Castle

In the 19th century the German historians trained in the positivistic method of historical source criticism taught that Lambert was strongly biased and a partisan writer that could not be trusted for an objective account of the reign of Henry IV. Leopold von Ranke, possibly the greatest German historian (19th century) was the first to discredit Lambert. Other German historians tried to rehabilitate Lambert. The results are mixed, and as usual, which century's standards are to be used for grading?[61] "In the last portion Lambert sometimes dropped the annalistic method and rose to the level of an original historian. He succeeded far better than his contemporaries in attaining a respectable notion of time perspective in history, and he chronicled events but discussed intelligently the problems of cause and effect in the flow of historical scenes. … Yet, his work possessed distinct historical value and it far surpassed that of any contemporary as polished historical literature."[62]

Liutprand of Cremona, c. 922-972, was a Lombard historian and author and bishop of Cremona, which is about 45 miles southeast of Milan in northern Italy. He was well educated and became a confidential secretary to a ruler of Italy. He learned Greek, as his father and stepfather were both ambassadors to Constantinople, and also became an ambassador to Constantinople. It was here that he accumulated information about the court activities, and wrote his most important work, *Relations of the Constantinople Legation*. The detailed description of Constantinople and the Byzantine court is a document of rare value, though highly colored by his ill reception and offended dignity.[63] "He also had a tendency to overcolor his materials, and his judgments were at times rash. But he stood head and shoulders above the other chroniclers of his day."[64]

Marianus Scotus, 1028-1082, was an Irish-born chronicler who is credited with *Universal Chronicle*, a history of the world, year by year, from the beginning of the Christian era to 1082. This Marianus Scotus should not be confused with Marianus Scotus, an Irish monk who migrated to the continent and ended up as the abbot of Saint Peter's in Regensburg, Germany. Marianus became a monk in 1052 and in 1056 he went to Cologne, Germany where he entered the Irish monastery of Saint Martin. He tells us that in 1058 he traveled to Fulda, 120 miles southeast of Cologne, visited Paderborn, 80 miles northwest of Fulda and then went to Wuerzburg, 130 miles south, where he was ordained priest in 1059. (Wikipedia &

Fulda Dom

Catholic Encyclopedia) In 1060 Scotus became a hermit, or recluse, at Fulda, and from there in 1070 he moved to Mainz on the Rhine River, about 75 miles west. I do not suggest that he did, but he could have floated down the Main River from Wuerzburg to Mainz, since the Main runs into the Rhine across the river from Mainz. These travels demonstrate the mobility of many monks, probably the ones who showed great promise to Church authorities, and allowed them to observe the lives of the common folks in different areas. This would have broadened their perspective, versus those of monks who stayed in the same monastery for long years.

Wuerzburg-Marienberg

Marianus' "chronicle was in three books, the first devoted to ancient history, the second to the life and times of Jesus, and the last to the Middle Ages. The first portion of the last book was based on Cassioodotus and early medieval annals. The work was of real value only for the period of the author's life. It contained much information on Irish history and still more on the history of Mainz. Marianus was a mathematician as well as a historian, and his books included interesting discussions of chronological problems in history."[65] For example, Marianus contended that a chronological approach was preferable, and was based on his contention that the date of Christ's birth given by Dionysius Exiguus (circa 6th Century) was twenty-two years too late. This was not generally accepted, but Marianus worked with both systems.[66]

Martin of Opava (Martin of Poland, Martin von Troppau, Martinus Polonus), ?-after June 1278, was an important Dominican chronicler. He was born in Opava, Silesia (Czech Republic), which is about 140 miles east of Prague. Martin's Latin chronicle, the *Chronicon pontificum et imperatorum*, is especially interesting for its layout; each double page covers fifty years, with fifty lines per page. The left-hand pages give the history of the papacy, with one line per year, and the right-hand pages give the history of emperors, the two accounts being kept strictly parallel. This was a revolutionary new approach in graphic design, which was not appreciated by all his contemporaries: many manuscripts simply copy the text without retaining the page layout, which results in a rather chaotic

Martin of Troppau

chronology. The chronicle was enormously influential; over 400 manuscripts are known, and the influence on many dozens of chroniclers is palpable. Translations were made into many vernaculars, including Middle English. Martin's *Chronicon* is the most influential source for the legend of "Pope Joan."[67]

Matthew of Edessa, 12th century, was an Armenian historian born in the city of Edessa. Location was provided under Fulcher. The literary and historical knowledge of Matthew was limited; however, the accuracy of his work has not been disputed. He remains the primary source of information about the political and ecclesiastical events of his time and area. A man of strong convictions, he was a determined opponent of the Greek church and as well as the Latin church. He was especially bitter against the Frankish settlers, whose avaricious and imperious rule and ingratitude he condemned. He left a record of two important documents, a letter from the Byzantine Emperor Tzimisces to King Ashot III Bagratuni and a discourse delivered in the cathedral of Hagia

Sophia, Constantinople, in the presence of the Emperor Constantine X Ducas by Gagik II, the exiled Bagratid king, concerning the doctrinal divergence between the Greek and Armenian churches.[68]

Matthew Paris, c. 1200-1258, English chronicler and Benedictine monk, was based at St. Albans Abbey, which is about 20 miles west of downtown London. His last name probably comes from having studied in Paris during his youth and learned French. Paris was highly unusual among the chroniclers of the A of B era because he illuminated his own works, mostly drawings partly colored with water-colored washes. Paris was admitted to the order in 1217 and in 1236 he succeeded Roger of Wendover as the abbey's official recorder of events. He revised Roger's work and added new

Matthew Paris

material during his tenure, which became his *Chronica Majora (Greater Chronicle)*, an important historical source document, especially for the period 1235-1259. This work is significant because his revisions of Roger are with a strong English nationalistic and anti-clerical bias.[69] This allowed him to wander over the landscape of personalities and institutions at will with whatever feelings he had, defending and criticizing at the same time.

Henry III, King of England 1216-1272, knew that Paris was writing a history, and wanted it as exact as possible. In 1257, in the course of a week's visit to St. Albans, Henry kept Paris beside him day and night and "guided my pen with much good will and diligence," wrote Matthew. Matthew wrote unfavorably about the king's policies.[70] In addition to being a breakthrough historian, Matthew deserves a medal for bravery, because in those days, and for centuries after, criticism of the king could bring one to the unfavorable situation known as, "being hanged, drawn, and quartered," or losing your head, literally. Wait a minute, I think we have to withdraw that medal from Paris. Given-Wilson cites the story of Paris attending a ceremony at Westminster Abbey, at which King Henry invited Paris to set on the steps below to insure that the religious miracle was firmly impressed in his mind. Paris said that it was firmly in mind. Henry replied, "I entreat you, and in entreating I command you, to write a clear and detailed account of all these proceeding to be entered indelibly in a book, lest memory of them be in any way lost to posterity through the passing of time." Henry then invited Paris and three companions to dinner. It may be even the reason why Paris ordered the expurgation of a number of passages offensive to Henry from his manuscript of his *Chronica Majora* because he was planning to present a copy of it to the king. Apparently the expurgation did not happen.[71] Just how does a historian write about a king, when the king might choose to look at the document?

Gilderhus points out the issues of the medieval writers of rendering verdicts and judgments, while at the same time telling the truth. Matthew Paris wrote about untruthful historians, "If they commit to writing that which is false, they are not acceptable to the Lord." We have Matthew making judgments about the king's policies, good or bad, so where is the truth in the good or bad?[72] It is one man's opinion of the truth. Dare I disagree?

Barnes said that there was general agreement that Matthew was the ablest historian of medieval England. Better than any historian of the age, he freed himself from religious and mythical interests and devoted himself to the story of political development. He was the incomparable authority on English constitutional developments between the Magna Carta (1215) and the rise of Parliament. He was a plain and direct writer and showed plenty of capacity for independence of judgment, even on the acts and policies of the kings of England.[73] It appears that Matthew's significance is that he was among the first to be free with his judgments, instead of just recording events and facts. This is one of the underlying themes of this inquiry, what is the truth in histories, this man's bias or another man's bias. Everybody can have an opinion. Is that history? It certainly makes reading history more fascinating, and keeps other historians employed by providing targets for criticism (their opinions).

Matthew of Westminster is the name given to the supposed author of a well-known English chronicle, the "Flores Historiarum". The misunderstanding regarding this imaginary personage originated in the title of a rather late manuscript of this history (Cotton, Claudius, E, 8) which describes the work as "liber qui Flores Historiarum intiulatur secundum Matthaeum monachum Westmonasteriensem". This seems to be due to the blunder of some copyist, who, perceiving that the latter part of the chronicle was written at Westminster while the greater portion followed the history of Matthew Paris, concluded that the said Matthew was himself a monk of Westminster. The "Flores Historiarum" in its fullest form extends from the Creation to 1326, but many manuscripts stop short at 1306. From 1259, where Matthew Paris ends, it possesses considerable historical value. The compilation from 1259-65 was made at St. Albans; from 1265-1325 it bears evident signs that the various writers who contributed to it lived at Westminster. The chronicle was printed for the first time by Archbishop Parker in 1567 and was attributed by him, following Bale and Joscelin, to "Matthew of Westminster". It was re-edited by Luard for the Rolls Series in 1890 with an introduction containing the fullest investigation of the genesis of the work."[74] Matthew had almost 600 years of fame until the error was first discovered in 1826 by Francis Turner Palgrave. Henry Richards Luard later proved the falsity of Matthew.[75]

Nithard, 790-844, was a Frankish historian and the grandson of Charlemagne. His work consisted of four books on the history of the Carolingian empire under the turbulent sons of Emperor Louis I, especially during the period 840-843. The Carolingian empire relates to the Frankish dynasty dating from about 613 AD and including among its members the rulers of France from 751 to 987, of Germany from 752 to 911, and of Italy from 774 to 961.[76] The work recites in rather uncouth language the causes of the quarrels and describes, minutely and clearly, the unjust behavior of Lothair, sometimes a little partially, but with understanding and a clear insight into the conditions. He was the only layman of his time who devoted himself to the writing of history, and he reported earnestly and truthfully what he had seen and heard.[77] Barnes cites that Nithard's writings have stood up well under the critical examination of the specialists of the 19th and 20th centuries. Even his harsh judgments of Lothar are now generally accepted.[78]

Ordericus Vitalis, 1075-c. 1141-43, was a monk born at Atcham, a village 3 miles southeast of Shrewsbury, which is 140 miles northwest of London. His father was Norman and his mother English. This is significant because he was born just nine years after the Norman prince, William of Normandy, conquered England by defeating King Harold at the Battle of Hastings in 1066. The following information demonstrates the integration of the Norman influence on England. Odericus was sent to St Evroul Abbey in Normandy at age ten. He eventually returned to England and founded his own monastery at Shrewsbury. Later he returned to Normandy where he spent the rest of his life. Odericus' principal work was *The Ecclesiastical History*, which he wrote between 1123 and 1141, and mainly dealt with the rule of William the Conqueror. Orderiucus was inspired by Bede. He used original documents, interviews and literary sources to write his

Ordericus Vitalis

books, He started to write a chronicle of his abbey, but it developed into a general ecclesiastic history in 13 books.[79] [He apparently was bitten by the same bug as me, writing a little history leads to the urge to write even larger histories.]

Ordericus was not well organized, did not work systematically, and was careless with his chronology. His strengths were comprehensive scope and breadth of interests. Barnes quotes Charles W. David,

> "No other historian of his time had his breadth of human interest or his zeal for full and detailed knowledge. All things modern and human interested him, whether the local affairs of his abbey or distant events in England, Italy or the Orient, whether military, ecclesiastical, religious, or literary and artistic. Especially was he interested in people....He saw and comprehended the life of all classes....No other writer of his time is so rich in local color."[80]

Otto of Freising, c. 1114-1158, was a German chronicler and bishop of Freising, which is about 20 miles north of Munich, Germany. Otto studied in Paris and became the Abbott of Morimond, in east central France. He then became Bishop of Freising.

"The most noted and influential German historian of the Middle Ages was Bishop Otto of Freising (ca. 1114-58), uncle of the Emperor Frederick I [Barbarossa]. He was not only an able chronicler of events but also the first medieval philosopher of history of any proportions. His two most important books were his *Chronicle* or Book *of Two Cities,* and his *Deeds of the Emperor Frederick l.* The *Book of Two Cities,* which came down to 1146, was the first important medieval philosophy of history. The historical method was that of Orosius and the historical philosophy that of Augustine. The book rested upon the Augustinian antithesis of the City of God and the City of the Devil. Otto illustrated their struggles, after the manner of Orosius, from Creation to his own time. The work was carried on to 1249 by another monk, Otto of St. Blaisen. The treatise was in eight books, the final one of which was devoted to the Last Judgment and the world to came. It was the first attempt of a medieval historian, says Balzani, to force "the whole story of humanity into a foreordained system of causes and effects." Otto's philosophical approach lessened the historical value of his work in two ways. In the first place, it biased him against secular and pagan affairs. In the second place, his primary interest in the philosophy of history led him to be careless at times in his handling of details. This carelessness with respect to facts was also intensified by his striving for rhetorical effects and for dramatic contrasts-the form was as important as the content to him. His account of the important Concordat of Worms in 1122 was, for example, both wrong-headed and shaky in details. Despite all this, Otto's material was very valuable as he approached his own time. He used reliable sources, depending especially on Ekkehard. And no other historian of his day gave as much attention to cause and effect or so earnestly endeavored to explain the present by light from the past.

Otto of Freising

The *Deeds of the Emperor Frederick* was a less impressive book but more important for contemporary history. It was an invaluable source for the relations of Frederick and the Church. Otto was an eyewitness and fully informed for his task. His premature death prevented him from carrying the work beyond 1158. He was sympathetic with German imperialism at the expense of the Italians, but his churchly background often led him into partisanship in behalf of the pope. This work was completed and continued by Otto's assistant, Rahewin. Otto also is supposed to have written a work on the history of Austria, which has been lost. As a stylist

Otto was polished and dramatic, but somewhat rhetorical and affected. A sympathetic Catholic critic, Franz X. van Wegele, pays the following tribute to Otto:

'A writer possessing such extraordinary literary talent as Otto of Freising did not appear again in German historical writing for many a century. However much Lambert of Hersfeld may have excelled him as a polished narrator, Otto more than made up for this by the deep seriousness of his world-philosophy and by the loftiness of the viewpoint which he invariably maintained. Whatever one may think of his philosophy, he was the only medieval German historian who was able to grasp in a philosophical manner the march of world history and who sought to give its progress a judicious exposition. And he occupies no less conspicuous a position as a narrator of the history of his times.'[81]

Otto of St. Blasien, c. mid-12th cent-July 23, 1223, was a German Benedictine chronicler. St. Blasien is in the heart of the German Black Forest and is about 20 miles southeast of Freiburg. Otto is known as the writer who continued the chronicles of Otto of Freising, discussed immediately above. Like many of his contemporaries, he liked to apply the fixed formulas of Justinian to the German emperors, probably on the assumption, then widespread, that the Holy Roman Empire was only a continuation of the Roman Empire of the Caesars. St. Blasien is about 170 miles southeast of Freising.[82]

Paul the Deacon, c. 720-April 13, probably 799, and probably in Monte Casino, Italy. Before we go on, let us look at the first sentence. Both the Catholic Encyclopedia and Wikipedia have his death for certainty on April 13th, and say probably 799, but the Wikipedia article claims it could have been one of the years between 794 and 800, and Barnes cites 800. Apparently the sources are consistent on the month and day, it just seems strange to have the year so flexible. Paul was a Benedictine monk and historian of the Lombards. He was also known as Paulus Diaconus (Deacon), Paul of Wornefred and Paul of Cassinensis (Monte Cassino).

Paul's principal work was the *History of the Lombards*, which covers the period 747-794 and contains much information about the Byzantine Empire, the Franks and others. It is especially valuable for the relations between the Franks and the Lombards. His sources included Secundus of Trent, Bede, Gregory of Tours and Isidore of Seville.[83]

Barnes writes, "He had little critical power in sifting and assessing this mass of source material, and he was especially uncritical in his treatment of early Lombard legends."[84] I mentally wince when I read such statements. Paul had a mass of material from which he thought were well regarded and reliable sources. Should he have spent his time and energy trying to critically analyze those sources, and what would have been his reference points on which to make comparisons? Did Paul have the capability and capacity to discriminate between the legends and the truth? What would have been his standards and sources? "But he was apparently intellectually honest and sincere, and his handling of more recent Lombard history seems to have been relatively reliable. Even his myths of early times may have accurately reflected the spirit and culture of those times." A major weakness in Paul's history was its careless and sloppy chronology, which led to much confusion in the narrative. The book was written in clear, fluent and unpretentious style, and certain passages possess high dramatic interest. It was popular in the Middle Ages and not the least of its value resides in the fact that it preserved many sources which have subsequently been lost."[85] Imagine being a writer in 760, using a quill pen in some dark and musty stone building, using a candle for light, having a few manuscripts strewn about or stored in his armoire (storage), and no heat trying to critically analyze the Venerable Bede's work. Who could have done better? What should we expect from writers of the era? We display our arrogance as we stand on the shoulders of our giant historical predecessors and criticize them!

Paul of Bernried, was an Italian priest of whom I found no personal background information. Bernried is a Benedictine monastery in southern Germany on the western side of the Starnberger Sea about 20 miles south of Munich. Paul is well known for his biography of Pope Gregory VII, which was completed in 1128. Gregory was Pope 1073-1085, and got into a dispute with the Holy Roman Emperor, Henry IV, over whether the pope or the emperor had the right to appoint bishops (investiture conflict). "Paul prepared himself carefully for his work by much study and the questioning of many eyewitnesses. The result was a very able book--the best Italian historical work on the investiture conflict. Paul used good sources and studied many official documents. He was, to be sure, not exceedingly critical in his handling of sources, but he made few major blunders save in his proclivity to admit the miraculous and the legendary. Even here the reader is able to distinguish between what Paul took from legends and what he derived from substantial historical sources. The work was strongly biased in favor of Gregory, whose great moral strength was emphasized in the book."[86]

Procopius of Caesarea, c. 500-c. 565, was an Eastern Roman scholar, and is commonly considered to be the last major ancient historian. His *History of the Wars* was published as a unit in seven books and covered the wars of Justinian, the Byzantine emperor for thirty eight years. Justinian's principal general was Belisarius and Procopius accompanied him on many campaigns. These books are called, in fancy terms, a panegyric (eulogistic or praiseful). Procopius also wrote an eighth book, known as *Secret History*, which was discovered in the Vatican archives centuries later and published in 1623.[87] Justinian's reign was a brilliant period, and the word justice comes from Justinian's successful effort to codify many ancient laws into a cohesive body. Now for the rest of the story. Following is an excerpt of chapter 8 of *Secret History*, the Character and Appearance of Justinian:

"Now such was Justinian in appearance; but his character was something I could not fully describe. For he was at once villainous and amenable; as people say colloquially, a moron. He was never truthful with anyone, but always guileful in what he said and did, yet easily hoodwinked by any who wanted to deceive him. His nature was an unnatural mixture of folly and wickedness. What in olden times a peripatetic philosopher said was also true of him, that opposite qualities combine in a man as in the mixing of colors. I will try to portray him, however, insofar as I can fathom his complexity.

This Emperor, then, was deceitful, devious, false, hypocritical, two-faced, cruel, skilled in dissembling his thought, never moved to tears by either joy or pain, though he could summon them artfully at will when the occasion demanded, a liar always, not only offhand, but in writing, and when he swore sacred oaths to his subjects in their very hearing. Then he would immediately break his agreements and pledges, like the vilest of slaves, whom indeed only the fear of torture drives to confess their perjury. A faithless friend, he was a treacherous enemy, insane for murder and plunder, quarrelsome and revolutionary, easily led to anything evil, but never willing to listen to good counsel, quick to plan mischief and carry it out, but finding even the hearing of anything good distasteful to his ears."[88]

So Justinian was known for his justice? Just your average nice guy emperor? But in those days the people on top had to be ruthless to survive their many enemies. What Procopius wrote about Empress Theodora was more titillating.[89]

Ralph the Bald, ?-c. 1050, wrote *Chronicle*, which covered the period 900-1046. It was often inaccurate and was notorious for legend-mongering. Barnes cites Ralph's work as important because it was one of the few sources that the end of the first millennium, and started the famous legend of a panic that was supposed top come over Christendom as the year 1000. Several much-later historians carried on that idea. In our own time there was considerable concern, but most of that was over the computer clocks turning over into a new millennium.[90]

Ralph of Diceto, c. 1120/1130-c. 1202, was dean of St. Paul's Cathedral in London and a chronicler. The background of Diceto has not been accurately determined. He was a scholar and his position allowed him the opportunities to collect materials for his own works, chiefly *Abbreviationes Chronicorum* and *Ymagines Historiarum*. They cover the history of the world from the birth of Christ to the year 1202. The first is built primarily on existing sources, while the second becomes an original authority about 1172 and a contemporary record about 1181. He was careless in his chronology and his documents are select by no principle. His style is limited, but demonstrates insight when discussing a political situation. The best edition of Ralph's historical works is that edited by Bishop William Stubbs in 1876. The prefaces to the two volumes contain an admirable account of the historian, of the society in which he moved, and of the writings themselves.[91] A new and important point needs to be made here. I have not read these prefaces, but have read others during my research, but such prefaces provide a much more meaningful look at the man and his works than one could get by just reading the original works. Prefaces are invariably worth your time to read, especially prefaces by the editorial historians.

Richard of San Germano, c. before 1170- c. after October 1243, was a notary at the monastery of San Germano, now called Monte Cassino, about 70 miles southeast of Rome. His work, *Chronica regni Siciliae*, which covered the death of William II of Sicily in 1189 to 1243, is the chief source of information on the Hohenstaufen (Germanic dynasty) in Italy. Richard's work focused on the lands of the Abbey Monte Cassino, which included visits by popes, and included many events in which Richard was personally involved.[92]

London-St Paul's

London-Westminster Abbey

Richard of Cirencester, c. 1335-c. 1401, was an English historical writer and a member of the Benedictine abbey at Westminster, London. He is known for two works, one he wrote and one he did not write. Richard's *Speculum Historiale de Gestis Regum Angliae, 447-1066* was written in four books. Its contribution to our historical knowledge is minimal, as it came mainly for others' works, and he made many careless errors. It was used extensively, until it was critically analyzed for its slight contributions. Richard's second work, *De Situ Britanniane*, appeared in 1747, three and a half centuries after he died. It was actually an elaborate forgery by Charles Julius Bertram, professor of English in the academy of Copenhagen. The forgery was accepted as genuine by a well-known 18th century antiquarian, Dr. William Stukeley, as a sanction under his authority. Based on that, it was accepted in the same light by numerous scholars and antiquaries, including Gibbon and Lingard. Professor J.E.B. Mayor, the editor of Richard's real work, masterfully exposed the entire fraud.[93] There are two lessons: one, beware of professors of English editing histories; and two, a big lie is more easily accepted than a small one. The second lesson has been well known and utilized by nations and politicians for centuries.

Wikipedia and the Catholic Encyclopedia gave credit to two different persons for exposing the fraud.

Richard of Devizes, c. late 12th century, was an English chronicler and a monk of St. Swithin's house in Winchester, about 60 miles southwest of London. His principal work was the *Chronicle of King Richard I* (Lionheart), in 1992, which covered only the first three years of Richard's reign. Richard's accounts of the First Crusade are poor, but his writings on the crusade preparation and the events in England after Richard the Lionheart departed are considered valuable, even with some inaccuracies.[94]

Richard of Durham, c. early 13th century, was an English Franciscan monk. Durham is about 240 miles north of London near the east coast. He is credited with writing the first part of the *Lanercost Chronicle*, which covers northern English and Scottish history during the period 1201-1346. Much of the work consisted of preternatural (existing outside nature or inexplicable by ordinary means) events and dream interpretation. These things were apparently real to folks in that era as part of the Roman Catholic religion. Source identification seemed to be lacking, but that is the way religious beliefs are.[95] Richard

> "included many stories about promiscuous rustics, incompetent ploughmen, parish priests and their concubines, herdsmen, farmers, and so forth, but the reason why he did so was not out of any desire to preserve folk memories; it was because they provided good material for morality tales, the sort of tales that might be used in sermons top discourage drunkenness or unchasity, for example, or to encourage attendance at mass. Hardly anyone believed that there was anything about the lives or deeds of the poor which was worth remembering for its own sake."[96]

The above material today might become the basis for a nice steamy novel or actually make a contribution to understanding human behavior of a thousand years ago, and how much human behavior has not changed over that period.

Richerus of Reims, c. late 10th century, was a French monk. Reims is about 80 miles northeast of Paris. In 991 Richerus made a visit to Chartres, which is about 50 southwest of Paris. His major work, *History of France,* was written circa 998, and discusses the conflicts among the French, a dispute between two claimants to the office of an archbishop, among other things. In spite of his violent partisanship in support of the Carolings (Frankish dynasty) and French, great defects in style, and utter disregard of truth and accuracy, his work has a unique value as giving us the only tolerably full account by a contemporary of the memorable revolution of 987, which placed the Capets (next French dynasty) on the throne of France.[97] Richerus' work was discussed, and cussed, at some length by a 20th century historian of literary criticism, whose name I shall not mention here, but will much later in this inquiry. The unnamed person thrashed Richerus 1,000 years later, but one must ask whether we are richer for Richerus' accounts than not having them at all.

Robert of Clari, c. late 13th-c. early 14th century, was a knight from Picardy, a region in northwest France, who participated in the Fourth Crusade. He wrote a 120-chapter chronicle of the crusade, but perhaps he is more famous for having seen the Shroud of Turin in 1203.[98]

Robert of Auxerre, c. 1156-1212, was a French chronicler and inmate of the monastery of St. Marien at Auxerre, which is about 90 miles southeast of Paris. He was now one of many who wrote a universal history, a *Chronicon.* It covered the period between the creation of the world and 1211.

Like all the others, he depended on others for the early parts, which then became an original authority during years of their lives, in Robert's case, 1181-1211. It is one of the most valuable sources for the history of France during the reign (1180-1223) of Philip Augustus. Robert displayed great diligence and sound judgment, and is credited with being one of the best historians of the Middle Ages.[99]

Robert of Avesbury, c. 1350, was the keeper of the registry of Canterbury and one of the few lay historians of medieval Europe. Edward III was King of England during this period.

"Robert devoted his book chiefly to military history, especially the wars with France from 1339 to 1356. He gave little attention to matters of internal political or constitutional history or to the religious history of England. As a historian of military affairs he was accurate and painstaking and relatively impartial. His work is particularly important because of the many original documents and letters which he incorporated in his narrative."[100]

Examples of Robert's documents were dispatches from the various theaters of war, treaties, truces, royal proclamations, formal exchanges between Edward and his continental allies or opponents, and newsletters from the war zones.[101]

Robert of Gloucester, flourished 1260-1300, was possibly a monk of St. Peter's Abbey in Gloucester, about 100 miles northwest of London. His chronicle apparently does not have a title, as do most others. Robert's fame came from writing a vernacular metrical chronicle. Vernacular means in the Middle-English language and metrical means that it was written in measured verses. It covered the period from *Brut*, the legendary Roman Brutus who vanquished the giants inhabiting the island and thus establishing the beginnings of Britain, to 1270. It was possibly written by more than one person. It is important both for philological (language origin) and as a historical source for the Barons' War in the reign of Henry III.[102] There is some doubt that Robert was a monk because his chronicle in English verse was a century ahead of other English writers writing in Middle-English verse.[103] An example of Robert's verse regarding the struggle between the barons and Henry III follows:

"So that at last, they persuaded the king
To remove the Frenchmen to live overseas
On their lands here and there, and not to return.
And to grant good laws, and the old charter,
So often granted, so often ignored."[104]

Robert of Reading, c. 1270-1325, was a monk at Westminster Abbey in London. He was probably born at Reading, which is about 35 miles west of central London. Robert was the author of the portion of the *Flores Historiarum* from 1307 to 1325. Luard said "this must rank of equal authority with other chronicles of the time. It appears to me independent of them all. The feeling, on the whole, is against the King (Edward II); the writer is strongly opposed to Gaveston, strongly in favor of Thomas of Lancaster."[105]

Robert of Torigni, ?-23-24 June 1186, was a Norman monk and chronicler. He was born at Torigni-sur-Vire, about 210 miles west of Paris and 25 miles south of the World War II Normandy beach. He was one of three co-authors of the *Gesta Normannorum Ducum*, along with William of Jumièges

Mont Saint Michel

and Orderic Vitalis. He was elected abbot of Mont-Saint-Michel in 1154, which is that famous abbey off the western French coast and which is also an island at high tide.[106] A causeway now eases access. Robert also wrote an *Appendix to Sigebert*, covering the period 1154-1186, which is good for its chronology and valuable for ecclesiastic history. It was one of the most important sources for the reign of King Henry II of England.[107]

Roger of Hovedon (Howden), fl. 1174-1201, was an English chronicler. Howden is about 160 miles north of London and 16 miles southeast of York. He apparently was a royal clerk, as he was sent on missions as a negotiator for King Henry II. His first primary work was *King Henry II and King Richard*, which included some official documents and provides information from sources not named. Roger went on the Third Crusade with King Richard I in 1190. Upon his return in 1192 he started his *Chronica*, a general history of England from 732 to his own time. Up to 1192 his narrative adds little to our knowledge. He was very impersonal, and made no pretense to literary style. In both foreign affairs and domestic policy he is usually well informed. He was particularly useful on points of constitutional history.[108]

Roger of Wendover, ?-13 May 1236, was a monk at St. Albans Abbey 20 miles northwest of downtown London. Wendover is just 10 miles west of St. Albans. He was the first of the important chroniclers who worked at St. Albans. Roger's best known work was *Flowers of History*, which covered from the Creation to 1235. The name comes from Roger selecting "from the books of catholic writers worthy of credit, just as flowers of various colors are gathered from various fields." It was based on the works of others before 1188, when Roger revised and continued it up to 1235. His work was continued by Matthew Paris, whom we met previously. Roger was less prejudiced and less picturesque than Matthew.[109] Barnes cited Roger as the best original source for the reign of King John (1199-1216), who signed the Magna Carta in 1215.[110]

Sigebert of Gembloux, c. 1030-5 October 1112, was born in what is now modern Belgium in the village of Gembloux, which is about 20 miles southeast of Brussels. He was a monk in the Gembloux Abbey and spent a long time as a teacher at the Abbey of St. Vincent at Metz, France, about 150 southeast of Gembloux. There Sigebert became a violent partisan of Emperor Henry IV in the battle with Pope Gregory VII. His best work is *Chronographia (Universal Chronicle)*[111] "His chronicle, which he completed about 1106, began with the Creation and became more voluminous when it reached the year 381. It ended with the year 1101, and was based in large part on the earlier work of Marianus Scotus. The earlier portions are worthless as history, but later sections are rather valuable as a chronological guide. It was easily the most popular summary of universal history."[112]

Abbot Suger

Suger of St. Denis, c. 1081-13 January 1151, was one of the last French abbot-statesmen, a historian and the influential first patron of Gothic architecture. St. Denis is on the northern edge of Paris. Suger advanced through a series of higher church positions, eventually becoming the abbot of St. Denis in 1122. He was friends with King Louis VI, the Fat, and during Louis VII's participation in the Second Crusade, Suger was named regent (temporary ruler) of France. Suger became the foremost historian of his time. He wrote a panegyric (eulogistic writing, elaborate praise) on Louis VI ands collaborated in writing the more impartial history of Louis VII. Suger's works served to imbue the monks of St. Denis with a taste for history, and called forth a long series of quasi-official chronicles.[113] The beginning of chapter 1 of Suger's writing about Louis VI follows:

"The glorious and famous king of the French Louis, son of the magnificent king Philip, in the first flower of his youth, barely then twelve or thirteen years old, was elegant and handsome, and had achieved such progress, by praiseworthy development both of his character and of his fine body that he gave promise of a swift and honourable enlargement of his future kingdom and encouraged warm hopes that that he would defend the churches and the poor."[114]

Sulpicius Severus, c. 363-c. 420/425, was an aristocrat born in Aquitaine (modern southwest France). His wife died early and he became a monk. His principal work was a biography of St. Martin of Tours who died in 397. Severus' other work was a world chronicle from the creation of the world to 400 AD. Barnes cites the latter work as possessing real literary merit.[115]

Symeon (Simeon), ?-after 1129, was a monk at Jarrow, which is about 7 miles north of Durham, which is about 240 miles north of London. His first notable work was *The History of the Church of Durham*, which is valuable for original information about the northern part of England. Symeon's second work is the *History of Kings,* which traced the Northumbrian history from the end of Bede's work in 731. It is mostly compiled from other authors, but does contain valuable material.[116] How valuable is a copyist? If he prepares compilations of authors several hundred years earlier, he is at least preparing another copy in case earlier information is lost through burning (accidental or purposeful), bookworms, or some other mishap that causes the manuscript to cease to exist and thereby preserving the information. If he adds information from new/later sources, then he has enhanced, hopefully, the material for posterity.

Istanbul-Hagia Sophia

Theophanes the Confessor, c. 758-17 March 818, was an aristocratic but ascetic Byzantine monk and chronicler. He was born in Constantinople, Istanbul in modern Turkey. His chronicle preserves a vibrant childhood memory of icebergs created from the thawing of the frozen Black Sea, and floating past Constantinople in February 764. His chronicle of world events covers the time of the accession of Emperor Diocletian in 284 to 813, and is valuable for preserving accounts of lost authorities on Byzantine history that would have otherwise been lost for the seventh and eighth centuries. It was much used by later historians. Perhaps the most valuable part was the Iconoclastic Controversy. Iconoclasm is the destruction of icons and has taken many forms over many centuries. This particular controversy was emperor Leo V's (813-820) continued destruction of religious icons started earlier by Leo II (717-740).[117]

Vincent of Beauvais

Vincent of Beauvais, c. 1190-c. 1264, was a Dominican friar and encyclopedist. His name comes from the town about 40 miles north of Paris, where a Dominican abbey was founded by King Louis IX in 1228. Vincent did visit the Abbey of Royaumont, another abbey founded by Louis IX, which is about 20 miles north of Paris. Vincent wrote a massive work, *The Great Mirror*, which was a compendium of all the knowledge of the Middle Ages and which consisted of three parts, *The Mirror of Nature, The Mirror of Doctrine,* and *The Mirror of History. The Mirror of History* was a history of the world to Vincent's time. It was divided into 31 books and 3,793 chapters, which would run to about 20 volumes of the size of an ordinary present-day book. It ran to nearly 1,400 large double-column pages in the 1627 printing. Barnes labeled it a monument to medieval writing. Vincent's two other *Mirrors* filled 32 books and 3718 chapters, and 17 books and 2374 chapters respectively.[118] He was a busy, industrious and dedicated individual, and must have had a good supply of quills and ink.

William of Jumieges, c. 1000-c. 1070-1090, was a Norman monk at the royal abbey of Jumieges, which is about 95 miles northwest of Paris. It is further located in a tight horseshoe bend of the Seine River about 20 miles east of the port city of Le Havre. His work, the *Deeds of the Dukes of the Normans,* is the primary authority for the history of the Norman people from 851 to 1137, which includes the invasion of England by William the Conqueror in 1066. The Catholic Encyclopedia ends its article on William with an **incredibly inane** statement, "The style is considered passable for the age in which the writer lived, though it does not come up to the requirements of modern criticism."[119]

William of Malmesbury, c. 1080/1095-c. 1143, was an English monk and historian. Malmesbury Abbey is about 85 miles west of London. William modeled his history after Bede's approach, to recount events so as to show cause and effect of events. William received the classical education of the time, and spent most of his time on moral philosophy. He considered history a branch of moral philosophy. About 1120 William produced his first major work, *Deeds of the English Kings,* (449-1127), now considered by modern scholars to be one of the greatest histories of England. In 1125 William produced *Deeds of the English Bishops.*[120] William was cited in six books from which I extracted historians' names. Barnes cites him as apparently looking up every extant (in existence) source before writing his book.[121] Henry Marsh devotes a twenty-page chapter in his *Dark Age Britain* to the content, description and an analysis of William's first work.[122] Chris Given-Wilson's *Chronicles, The Writing of History in Medieval England* cites William on 24 pages.

"...William of Malmsbury well deserves a place among the bibliomaniacs of the Middle Ages. As an historian his merit is generally well known and acknowledged to require an elucidation here. He combines in most cases a strict attention to fact, with rare attributes to philosophic reflection, and sometimes the bloom of eloquence. But simplicity of narrative constitute the greatest and sometimes the only charm in the composition of the monkish chroniclers. William of Malmsbury is a genuine historian, not a dry compiler of annals like the writers who had preceded him. He aimed at a more ambitious style, and attempted to adorn, as he admits himself, his English history with Roman art; this he does sometimes with tolerable elegance, but too often at the cost of necessary detail. Yet we must place him at the head of the Middle Age historians, for he was always diligent and critical, though perhaps not always impartial; and in matters connected with Romish doctrine, his testimony is not always to be relied upon without additional authority; his account of those who held opinions somewhat adverse to the orthodoxy of Roman is often equivocal; we may even suspect him of interpolating their writings, at least of Alfric, whose homilies had excited the fears of the Norman ecclesiastics."[123]

I have a small collection of books about books. I have two copies of the above book by Merryweather, but they are not exactly the same. As I transposed the paragraph quotation above from my 1933 version, I was enthralled once again by the smell of musty paper from an old book. Wonderful. This inquiry about historians is really about historians rewriting history to suit their tastes. Merryweather's *Bibliomania* was partially rewritten by another fellow who did not like what Merryweather wrote. This irked me and I wondered by what right he did it, but that is what historians do. This story will be at the end of my chapter, First Half, Twentieth Century.

William of Newburgh, c. 1136-c. 1198, also known as Nubrigensis, was a monk from Yorkshire in northern England. York is the capital and is 183 miles north of London. William was born in Bridlington, on the east coast of England, 38 miles east of York. He apparently spent his entire adulthood at the Priory of Newburgh, 16 miles north of York. His major work was *History of English Affairs*, which covered the period 1066 to 1198. The work is valued for detailing The Anarchy under King Stephen, 1135-54, of England. For hundreds (?) of years William was considered "the father of historical criticism," but that position is no longer accepted. He had taken Geoffrey of Monmouth to the proverbial "woodshed" by saying, "only a person ignorant of ancient history would have any doubt about how shamelessly and impudently he lies in almost everything." He used Bede as a model in producing an accurate, clear and interesting book with discerning judgments.[124] Vincent cited William's death as 1201.[125]

William of Puylaurens, c. 1200-c. 1275, was apparently born in Puylaurens, which is in southern France, and about 30 miles east of Toulouse. William served in the households of two bishops of Toulouse, as well as Count Raymond VII of Toulouse. William is best known for his coverage of the Albigensian Crusade, 1209-1229, which was the start of the 600-year long Catholic Inquisition. This crusade was against the heretical movement of the Cathars. Albi is 25 miles north of Puylaurens. His account is evenhanded and in the words of one historian, "the product of an intelligent and reasonable man."[126]

William of Rubruck, c. 1220-c. 1293, was a Flemish Franciscan born in Rubruck, northern France. He accompanied King Louis IX on the Seventh Crusade in 1248. In May 1253, on Louis' orders, he set out from Constantinople on a missionary journey to convert the Tartars. The Tartars were nomadic Turkic people of North-Central Asia. They were conquered by Genghis Khan in the early 13th century and became assimilated to the Mongols. After that the Mongols were frequently known as Tartars. He traveled to the east as far as the Mongol capital at the time, Karakorum, in the vicinity of the Orkhon River, about 150 west of Ulaanbaatar, the current capital of Mongolia, in north central Mongolia. The Orkhon Valley Cultural Landscape is part of a World Heritage

Site, in case a reader might like to visit. William described many peculiarities of China, discovered the surprise presence of Islam in that area, and was the first to report that the Caspian was an inland sea that did not flow to the Artic Ocean. William's work is considered one of the great masterpieces of medieval geographic literature. It was comparable to Marco Polo's descriptions 50 years later, but in a different way.[127]

William of Tyre, c. 1130-c. 1185-90, was the archbishop of Tyre and a chronicler of the Crusades and the Middle ages. Tyre was an important port city during the Crusades, and is located in southern modern Lebanon with the current name of Sūr. William was born in Jerusalem, a child of the First Crusaders in the new Kingdom of Jerusalem. He was educated in Jerusalem, then in 1146 went to Europe to receive further education. He studied liberal arts and theology at several locations, and then civil law and canon law at Bologna University. He returned to the Holy Land in 1165 and served in several religious positions. One should remember that religion and politics were almost synonymous during that era. In 1175 William was named archbishop of Tyre. William's great work was a chronicle of twenty-three unfinished books, which he did not name, but later English translators labeled it *History of Deeds Done Beyond the Sea.* Most of it deals with the advent of the First Crusade and the subsequent political history of the Kingdom of Jerusalem. He used older works, but it is also valuable as a primary source itself. It was widely translated and circulated throughout Europe after his death.[128]

William of Tyre

Four authors in my bibliography cited William. Barnes states, "He gathered his information carefully and widely, was cautious in his statements, and was reasonably impartial."[129] His account was remarkable for its literary charm and the author had broad views. (Catholic Encyclopedia) The 49-page introduction to the 1943 Morningside Press translation of William's *Deeds* cites 22 historians who contributed to this reconstruction of William's career. He was indeed a popular fellow.

Smith wrote that William included the legend of Peter the Hermit, which was accepted for six centuries without question because William wrote it, such was William's reputation. Smith also wrote:

> "wrote eloquently of the pitfalls that threaten the historian. If he passes in silence over certain events, for fear of arousing popular resentment, 'he is not without fault.' Historians who deliberately flatter the prejudices of their readers 'are so detestable that they ought not to be regarded as belonging to the ranks of historians.' The first obligation of the historian was to God, the second to His truth."[130]

The single quotation marks in the paragraph above are from William's prologue to his *Deeds.*

Please refer back to the sentence in the middle of the opening paragraph on William, about religion and politics. Now look at the last sentence of the indented paragraph above: "The first obligation of the historian was to God, the second to His word." Almost all the chroniclers and historians in this chapter were an official of the Roman Catholic Church. Their "truth" was the dogma promulgated by the Church. The secular leadership of princes, counts, etc. was also

Roman Catholic and worked closely with clerical authorities at the top of society's elite. Yes, there were many, many, issues between the two groups, but most of the time they worked hand in glove together for their common benefit. Notice the capital "His" above. Catholic dogma was dominant, as there were few alternatives, which were smothered, such as heretics by the Inquisition. God and His word were the truth. Yes, the chroniclers wrote history, but it was almost always about the Church leadership or the combined secular/church leadership.

Lessons Learned:

-Adalberon wrote in poetry. Was he a proper historian?

-Adam said he tried to be truthful and accurate.

-Adémar was a superb forger.

-Albert was a panegyrist (eulogist) for Christian military service.

-Bede (Venerable Bede) is probably the most famous and most cited of all historians between 400 and 1000 AD.

-Diodorus traded in myths for facts?

-Eadmer wrote an important history of England after the Norman conquest.

-Einhard was the biographer of Charlemagne.

-Ekkehard is best known for his contributions to the *World Chronicle*, or *Universal Chronicle*.

-Engelbert of Admont lived in the center of mountainous Austria.

-Marianus dealt with the chronological problems of history.

-Fulcher participated in the First Crusade.

-Geoffrey of Monmouth was a great storyteller, especially about King Arthur, and I use Geoffrey as my explanation of Wikipedia.

-Geoffrey de Villehardouin participated in the Fourth Crusade, which only got as far as sacking Constantinople.

-Gervase seems to have been credited as the first one to identify what separated historians and chroniclers from other writers of literature.

-Joachim did a study and interpretation of the Book of Revelations.

-John of Salisbury was the first medieval writer to emphasize the importance of historical studies in philosophy and in all other branches of learning.

-Matthew of Westminster was a fictitious person based on a copyist's blunder.

-Richard of Cirencester was the victim of a forgery in his name four centuries after he died.

-Richard of Durham had all the material to become a successful writer of pulp fiction.

-Robert of Torigni was elected abbot of Mont-Saint-Michel, which has a nice view of the sea.

-William of Newburgh once was considered the father of historical criticism, but no longer.

-William of Puylaurens is best known for his coverage of the Albigensian Crusade.

-William of Rubruck traveled as far east as Mongolia and wrote one of the masterpieces of medieval geographic literature.

Chapter 5

Renaissance

The historians in the previous chapter were arranged in a haphazard manner, and their lives ranged over a thousand years. The most recent ones died in 1331, 1360 and 1401. Harry Barnes, in his *A History of Historical Writing*, started a new chapter, Humanism and Historical Writing. The humanism idea represents a break from the ecclesiastical and scholastic writers of the earlier past into a more secular theme, which became known as the renaissance and eventually the reformation. There was not a clear break, and we will meet some of the people who identified the eras which we now accept as logical decisions. "The negation of Christian transcendency was the work of the age of the Renaissance, when, to employ the expression used by (Eduard) Fueter, historiography became 'secularized.'"[1] The folks in this chapter are ordered by birth date.

Giovanni Villani, c. 1275-1348, was an Italian chronicler born in Florence. He was the greatest Italian chronicler of his times with his *Florentine Chronica*, which was the cornerstone of early medieval history in Florence. His interest in economic details makes him the most modern of the late medieval chroniclers (not a historian). He is perhaps unequaled for the value of the statistical data he has preserved.[2] Schevill observes Villani had a "feeling for factual reality which no medieval writer before his time possessed in the same degree."[3]

Francesco Petrarca (Petrarch), July 20, 1304-July 19, 1374, was an Italian scholar, poet, and early Renaissance humanist. He was born in Arezzo, which is 60 miles southeast of Florence. He spent much time in Avignon, France, for this was the time of the French popes during the Great Schism. Petrarch is often popularly called the "father of humanism." He is credited for perfecting the sonnet, making it one of the most popular art forms to date. His first major work, *Africa*, was about the great Roman general Scipio Africanus, for which Petrarch became a European celebrity. He traveled widely and collected manuscripts and other items that were not known. Disdaining what he believed to be the ignorance of the centuries preceding the era in which he lived, Petrarch is credited with creating the concept of a historical "Dark Ages."[4]

I found seven citations for Petrarch. He believed that the Roman experience incorporated the best attributes of mankind. He wrote, "What else, then, is all history, if not the praise of Rome?"[5] A sense of Petrarch's perspectives on history is encapsulated in a letter he wrote to Livy, who lived 1300 years earlier,

> "I would wish either that I had been born in your age, or you in ours. I should thank you, though, that you have so often caused me to forget present evils and have transported me to happier times. As I read, I seem to be living amidst Scipio, Brutus, and Cato. It is with these men that I live at such times, and not with the thievish company of today, among whom I was born under an evil star."[6]

Petrarch

Jean Froissart, c. 1337-c. 1405, was one of the most important of the chroniclers of medieval France. He was from Valenciennes, which is about 110 miles north of Paris and only 6 miles from the modern Belgian border. For centuries, *Froissart's Chronicles* have been recognized as the chief expression of the chivalric revival of the 14th century Kingdom of England and France. His history is also one of the most important sources for the first half of the Hundred Years' War. The text of Froissart's Chronicles is preserved in more than 100 illuminated manuscripts, illustrated by a variety on miniaturists.[7]

> "Froissart wrote with self-conscious detachment and endeavored to tell the truth in an age of chivalry. He stirringly depicted battles and heroic deeds by knights in combat. He also assumed that the divine played a role in human affairs but worked hard to obtain accurate information. As a historian mainly concerned with the aristocracy, he took little interest in the mundane lives of the lower classes."[8]

Adam of Usk, c. 1352-1430, was a Welsh priest, canonist and early historian and chronicler. He was born at Usk, Monmouthshire, South Wales, which is about 125 miles west of London. For my readers who understand Welsh, his name is Adda Brynbuga. He was educated at Oxford to receive his doctorate and became extraordinarius in Canon law, whatever that is. Most monks of that era were homebodies and didn't have a chance to travel much. They had to rely on documents and word-of-mouth for their chronicles. Adam moved around, was at Canterbury for seven years, sat in Parliament and was on a commission to find legal grounds for the deposition of King Richard II. He later went to Rome and met Popes Boniface IX and Innocent VII. He was, therefore, a player and close observer of many events, which enhanced the credibility of his chronicles. His Latin chronicle of English history from 1377 to 1421 was edited and published in 1876 as *Chronicon Adœ de Usk*.[9] *Chronicles, The Writing of History in Medieval England*, by Chris Given-Wilson, one of my references, has many citations from Adam.

Thomas Walsingham, ??-d.c.1422, was an English monk chronicler who lived most of his monastic life at St. Albans Abbey, which is about 20 miles north northwest of scenic Westminster Abbey in downtown London. Walsingham is the main authority for the history of England during the reigns of Richard II, Henry IV and Henry V, including the Peasants' Revolt rising under Wat Tyler in 1381. He shows considerable ill will toward John Wycliffe and the Lollards (Wycliffe's followers), for which he is the best source. Walsingham's most important work is his *English History*, covering the period between 1272 and 1422.[10]

Leonardo Bruni

Leonardo Bruni, c. 1370-March 9, 1444, was a leading humanist, historian and a chancellor of Florence. He was born in Arezzo, the same as Petrarch above. Must be something in the water. His most notable work is *History of the Florentine People*, which has been called the first modern history book, and so Bruni has also been called the first modern historian. He was the first historian to write about the three-period view of history: Antiquity, Middle Age and Modern, a concept from which the term Middle Age was coined by a contemporary, Flavio Biondo, whom we shall meet shortly. Bruni laid the conceptual groundwork for the three-period history, although the same times are not used by historians today. It was Bruni who used the phrase *studia humanitatis*, meaning the study of human endeavors versus those of theology and metaphysics, which is where the term humanists came from.[11] A major part of the secularism of historical writing was to reject miracles as part of history, except to satirize them, and Bruni was a leader in this respect.[12]

Gian Francesco Poggio (Poggius) Bracciolini, February 11, 1380-October 30, 1459, was one of the most important Italian humanists. He was born in the village of Terranuova, just 20 miles northwest of Arezzo, which is in the direction of Florence. There was definitely something in the water that brought forth those humanists from the same area. Poggio recovered a great number of classical texts, mostly lying forgotten in German and Italian monastic libraries, and disseminated copies among the educated world. He even bribed a monk to abstract a Livy and an Ammianus from the library of the Hersfeld Abbey in central modern Germany. He is also known for *Eight Books of Florentine History*.[13] He was a great traveler as he searched for misplaced manuscripts. I wish I could have been with him and visited those places. He wrote many letters, and an excerpt follows:

"While I was fleeing from the plague, I saw the cathedral of Salisbury and I hunted for the books about which you have written me so many times. What Manuel saw long ago I cannot imagine; I know only this, that there are no books of Origen there now. I did not make a careless search, but there was no one who could say that he had ever seen them. We can find plenty of men given over to gluttony and lust but very few lovers of literature and those few barbarians, trained rather in trifling debates and in quibbling that in real learning. I saw many monasteries, all crammed with new doctors [not medical], none of whom you even have found worth listening to. There were a few volumes of ancient writings, which we have in better versions at home. Nearly all the monasteries of this island have been built within the last four hundred years and that has not been an age which produced either learned men or the books which we seek; these books were already sunk without trace."[14]

"On this trip of mine I visited a monastery that is older than all the others in England and more magnificent. I inspected the library thoroughly; there were many books but none for us. I saw other libraries besides in many places, all full of nonsense, as I wrote you before; there is no supply of good books here for reasons that I explained to you. I shall go to Oxford as soon as I can, and before I go home, and if there is anything of value I shall let you know."[15]

Poggio Bracciolini

"For good luck, as much ours as his, while we were doing nothing in Constance, an urge came upon us to see the place where he was being held prisoner. This is the monastery of St. Gall, about twenty miles from Constance. And so several of us went there, to amuse ourselves and also to collect books of which we heard that they had a great many. There amid a tremendous quantity of books which it would take too long to describe, we found Quintilian still safe and sound, though filthy with mold and dust. For these books were not in the Library, as befitted their worth, but in a sort of foul and gloomy dungeon at the bottom of one of the towers, where not even men convicted of a capital offense would have been stuck away. As I know for certain, if there had been any other men who explored these prison houses of the barbarians where they confine such men as Quintilian and if they had recognized them after the custom of our ancestors, they would have found a treasure like ours in many cases where we are now left lamenting. Beside Quintilian we found the first three books and half a fourth of C. Valerius Flaccus'

Argonauticon, and commentaries or analyses on eight of Cicero's orations by Q. Asconius Pedianus, a very clever man whom Quintilian himself mentions. These I copied with my own hand and very quickly, so that I might send them to Leonardus Aretinus and to Nicolaus of Florence; and when they had heard from me of my discovery of this treasure they urged me at great length in their letters to send them Quintilian as soon as possible."[16]

Flavio Biondo (Latin Flavius Blondus), 1392-June 4, 1463, was an Italian Renaissance humanist historian, and is the historian who coined the term Middle Ages. He was born in Forli, which is about 60 miles northeast of Florence near the Adriatic coast. He published three encyclopedic works that were systematic and documented guides to the ruins and topography of ancient Rome, for which he has been called one of the first archaeologists. Subsequent antiquaries and historians built

Flavio Biondo's Grave

on the foundations laid down by Flavio and by his older contemporary, Poggio Bracciolini. Flavio's greatest work is the *Decades of History from the Deterioration of the Roman Empire,* which has thirty-two books. Using only the most reliable and primary sources, it was highly influential in furthering the chronological notion of a Middle Age that lay between the fall of Rome and Flavio's time. He also wrote *Italy Illuminated,* which is a geography, based on the author's travels, and the history of eighteen Italian provinces.[17] Perhaps by now you have perceived that Florence was the focus and center of the era known as the Renaissance.

Lorenzo Valla, c. 1406-August 1, 1457, was an Italian humanist, rhetorician and educator. His family was from Piacenza, which is about 35 miles southeast of Milan and about 110 miles northwest of Florence. He was priest, a professor of eloquence, and was summoned before the Inquisition for his public statements about theology. Remember, a humanist, by definition, usually disagrees with much of theology's dogmas and beliefs, etc.

Lorenzo Valla

Readers, now is the time to ask you an important question, is philology history? Ha, gotcha. Philology is the study of language in literature, and by default, becomes the history of languages and words. And that is why we should remember Valla. He became an expert in philology. Emperor Constantine made the Christian religion the Roman Empire's religion in 325 at Nicaea. The *Donation of Constantine* was a purported document by Constantine in 324 which granted Pope Sylvester I, and his successors, imperial sovereignty and spiritual authority over Rome, Italy and the entire Western empire. Constantine withdrew to Byzantium, which became the Eastern Roman Empire's center of power as the capital city of Constantinople. Papal powers and territorial claims were deduced from the *Donation* throughout the Middle Ages. Valla's study of the Donation ending in 1440 showed that it was a forgery from the ninth century. The Church ostracized Valla's effort, and it was not published until the Protestants did in 1517. Valla's proof still holds true today. He wrote other works, including documentation showing that a letter from Christ to Abgarus was another forgery, and was frequently in trouble with the Church faithful because of his humanist writings.[18]

I found seven citations about Valla. Croce writes about forged documents and their role in historical writing, and citing Valla's work.[19] Barnes quotes Ephraim Emerton,

"The most interesting thing about the exposure is the amazing ease of it. It does not prove the great learning or cleverness of the author, for neither of these was needed. The moment that the bare facts were held up to the world of scholars the whole issue of absurdities fell to pieces of its own weight."[20]

The Roman Catholic Church was the most powerful institution during the Middle Ages. It was essentially unchallenged, because there were no nation-states as we know them today, and the individual kings, princes, duke, etc. were all in loose coordination with the church because the two institutions supported each other in controlling the people and benefiting from their labor. The Church also owned 30-40 percent of the land in England and France, so the Church was also the most powerful economic institution. So the question arises, who had the most to gain from writing false histories and other similar falsehoods. The logical answer is the Roman Catholic Church, and it had a multitude of scholars/church officials who stood to gain from false histories. The Protestant Reformation brought on a new set of theologians who had a vested interest in discrediting the Catholic Church at the same time promulgating a new set of histories to support their churches. The literature about historical writing is filled with this theme. I shall not beat this dead horse anymore. Praise be to Valla!!!

Venice-St Marks & Ducal Palace

Marcus Antonius Coccius Sabellicus, 1436-1506, was a scholar and historian from Venice who authored a history of the world in 1504 entitled *Enneades sive Rhapsodia historiarium.*[21] Barnes labels it the first important humanist excursion into world history. He took his chronology of events from Eusebius and Jerome, but he provided a broader perspective including other nations. He was skeptical of biblical miracles, but was weak in its treatment of social, economic and cultural history.[22]

Hartmann Schedel, February 13, 1440-November 28, 1514, was a German physician, humanist and historian born in Nuremberg. He was one of the first cartographers to make use of the printing press. Schedel is best known for his writing the text for the Nuremberg Chronicle (1493), which has 2,000

Nuremberg Chronicle

woodcut illustrations of towns and the characters of history.[23] The woodcuts of towns are used several times with different titles, since wood cuts are difficult to make. I have a facsimile copy of this wonderful 9&1/2 by 13&1/2 inch book, which is almost two inches thick and has 680 pages. The words are a combination of Latin and Gothic German. There are English explanations (not translations) in the front and back. It has fake leather or suede covers with gold lettering, but I had to make my own slipcase for its preservation. It fits the category of a universal history, since it starts at the Creation and goes to the publication date.

Niccolò di Bernardo dei Machiavelli, May 3, 1469-June 21, 1527, was an Italian political philosopher, musician, poet, and romantic comedic playwright. He was born in San Casciano in Val di Pesa village, which was fifteen miles, by winding road, south of Florence in Machiavelli's day. Currently it is about eight miles by autostrada. His most significant works were *The Prince* and

Discourses on Livy.[24] Neither one of these works is considered history in the normal sense, but they provide the lessons to be learned about politics and political systems from history, without speaking about particular persons. The leader of Florence at that time was Cesare Borgia. Machiavelli also wrote *History of Florence* in eight books.[25] Croce states, "Machiavelli is a historian in

so far as he tries to understand the course of events; he is a politician, or at least a publicist, when he posits and desires a prince, founder of a strong nation state, as his ideal, reflecting this in his history….Thus Machiavelli belongs partly to the history."[26] Eighteen citations were found for Machiavelli, as he provides a well-known figure in history that historians like to include. Gilderhus writes, "…depicted human behavior as motivated by opportunism and aggrandizement."[27] Machiavelli's ideas became the baseline for political power analysis. The German historians of the 19th and 20th centuries used Machiavellianism as a rationale to explain the rise of the German nation during those times. Schevill wrote a chapter about Machiavelli, and immediately takes him to task in the opening sentence and paragraph, "Whatever his genius and literary purpose — and their definition is the aim of this essay — Machiavelli was not a historian….with the result that what he offers as history is

Machiordli

largely a free invention lacking a solid and indispensable substructure of tested events and, consequently, irritating, annoying, and meaningless."[28]

Polydore Vergil (also known as PV Castellenis), c. 1470-1555, was a naturalized English historian (of Italian extraction). He was born in Urbino, Italy about 75 miles east of Florence. He went to England in 1501. His major work was *Historia Anglica*, which was in twenty-seven books, ending with the birth (1537) of Edward VI, the son of Henry VIII.[29] Barnes states, "He showed critical powers in all parts of his history. He not only devastatingly attacked the myths of Geoffrey of Monmouth's history of British origins, but also produced the best narrative history of the reign of Henry VII."[30] Vergil destroyed the old story about the foundation of Britain by Brutus the Trojan and laid the foundations of a critical history of England.[31] Nations, and some individuals, pride themselves on how far back their history goes, thereby giving greater legitimacy to their existence and the power of tradition.

Sir Thomas More, February 7, 1478-July 6, 1535, was an English lawyer, author and statesman. He was born and beheaded in London. His primary historical work was the *History of Richard III*, which he worked on between 1513 and 1518, but it was unfinished. It is a skilled piece of Renaissance historiography, remarkable more for its literary skill and adherence to classical precepts than its historical accuracy. In 1515 More wrote his most famous and controversial work, *Utopia*, a novel in which a fictional character describes the political arrangements of an imaginary island. More contrasts the contentious social life of European states with the perfectly orderly and reasonable socials arrangements of the Utopia. Is the European description considered history? Even though the book is fiction, an accurate

Thomas More

description of the existing European life should be considered history, though no actual names are used. More refused to recognize King Henry VIII's divorce from Catherine and the remarriage to Anne Boleyn. All the machinations surrounding Henry eventually led to Thomas More's death as a traitor. He was granted mercy and allowed to be beheaded rather than suffer the usual penalty of hanged, drawn and quartered, such as was the quaint English custom of that era.[32]

Paulus Jovius, April 19, 1483-December 10, 1552, was an Italian historian and prelate born in Como, which is in north central Italy almost on the Swiss border. His two major works were about the lives of famous men, one of which has the title, *Praise of Men Illustrious for Courage in War*.[33] I like his first name. Ranke writes, "When I next turned to the two most reputable writers dealing with the beginnings of modern history, Guicciardini [below] and Jovius, I found in comparing them so many unresolved discrepancies that I did not know on which I could chiefly depend. Jovius is by far more objective, and reveals a variety of good information about details. In contrast, Guicciardini is far more informed and informative about the politics of the period. But it was no more possible to choose between them than to reconcile them, if truth itself were to be my first consideration."[34] Notice that last phrase, could truth not be the first consideration for a historian?

Francesco Guicciardini, March 6, 1483-May 22, 1540, was an Italian historian and statesman born in Florence. A friend and critic of Niccolò Machiavelli, he is considered one of the major political writers of the Italian Renaissance. Guicciardini is considered as the Father of Modern History, due to his use of government documents to verify his *History of Italy*, which covered the period 1494-1532. Before I go further into Guicciardini's works, note that he is only 14 years younger than Machiavelli, and they both lived and worked primarily in Florence. Later historians to this day consider them a matched pair insofar as their writings about political history, even though they had different approaches. The major part of his life was in the service of the Medici family and/or the pope, which I will not discuss.[35] He is honored in Florence by the naming after him the street one walks on immediately after coming off the south end of the Ponte Vecchio, the

Francesco Guicciardini

famous bridge over the River Arno, which flows through the southern part of Florence. His palace is along that street, about 200 meters from the bridge. That bridge has jewelry stores on both sides and is always crowded. What is little known is that the second story of the bridge houses an art gallery of self-portraits by famous artists, and is connected directly to the Uffizi Art Gallery. My wife and I walked on the bridge and Via de' Guicciardini in June 2007. Machiavelli has a much longer street named after him further south and up the hill, which turns into Galileo Street and then Michelangelo Street as it works its way north back to another Arno bridge.

The Ponte Vecchio runs north northeast to south southeast over the Arno River, but for all practical purposes it goes north to south. This picture was taken, circa 1978, from the northwest bank of the river. Although not very clear with my old film camera (remember those?), the general shabbiness of the bridge is noticeable, at least before I shrunk the picture. The continuous second story is on the opposite (east) side and it will be shown clearer under Giorgio Vasari shortly.

Florence-Ponte Vecchio

There were fifteen citations for Guicciardini. Gilderhus compares the two historians,

"A better historian than Machiavelli, Guicciardini carried out more research, notably in the papal archives, understood more subtly the diversity of human nature, and espoused a less provincial outlook. He examined the history of a larger geographic area, strove to provide a broad, interpretive framework, and showed some of the connecting features in various aspects of Italian experience."[36]

The great German historian of the 19th century, Ranke, got his start by demonstrating that Guiciardini,

"had to a large degree extracted his factual substance from feeble, secondary sources. This work had long enjoyed an immense reputation as marking the emergence of a modern as distinct from a medieval type of historical writing. Since it had never occurred to anyone to examine it in respect to its constituent elements, Ranke's demonstration of its insecure base created a professional sensation."[37]

Ranke's *The Secret of World History* has a chapter on his critique of Guicciardini.

Guiciardini wrote,
"Past events throw light on the future, because the world has always been the same as it is now, and all that is now, or shall be hereafter, has been in time past. Things accordingly repeat themselves, but under changed names and colors, so that it is not everyone who can recognize them, but only he who is discerning and who notes them diligently."[38]

Such observations have been made many times since Guicciardini, and history is full of events that prove him right on the money.

Joachim Vadian or Vadianus (actually Joachim of Watts), November 29, 1484-April 6, 1551, was a Swiss humanist, physician, and scholar as well as mayor and Reformator of St. Gallen, a Swiss city just south of the eastern end of Lake Constance, which separates Germany and Switzerland. He is noted for a chronicle of the abbots of the monastery of St. Gall.[39] Barnes cites that Vadian is often considered superior to Blondus, discussed above, and was especially skilled in tracing out and exploding ecclesiastic legends. As a humanist he traced the evolution of religious and political organizations and to sense the idea of social development.[40]

IOACHIMUS VADIANUS.
Med. Doct. Reip. Singallen as Consul
nat. 1484. ob. 1551.

Beatus Rhenanus, August 22, 1485-July 20, 1547, was a German humanist, religious reformer, and classical scholar. He was born in Sélestat, Alsace, the territory along the west bank of the Rhine River between Basel and Strasbourg, which has been disputed and moved between France and Germany for a long time. Sélestat is about 40 miles south of Strasbourg, now all in France. One of his major claims to fame is being a good friend of Desiderius Erasmus, c .1466-1536, the famous Dutch humanist, scholar and theologian, about whom he wrote a nine-volume work. Rhenanus wrote *A History of German Affairs*. Barnes assesses him:

"He examined the sources of early German history with the same objective, philological scholarship that Erasmus had applied to the ecclesiastical records and doctrines. His labors in research represented the highest level of scholarship to which the historiography of German

Humanism attained. Beatus always went back to the original sources, examined them carefully and cited them with exactness. He rejected classical fables as relentlessly as he did the ecclesiastical legends. He had a real love for historical research and good judgment in sizing up his discoveries. Though nationalistic in sympathies, his patriotism did not notably warp his judgments. His main defect was inability to weld his materials into a coherent and complete narrative. His history of Germany was fragmentary. It came down only to the Saxon Emperors, and it was reasonably complete only for the period of Roman domination and the invasions."[41]

Beatus Rhenanus

I discovered Rhenanus several years ago while reading Alberto Manguel's *A History of Reading*. Manguel, which included a photo of Rhenanus' adolescent school book open to a page demonstrating a new concept attributed to the humanists. The margins and between the lines are filled with writings by the student. Before that era, students learned by reciting from a common book without further explanation. Writing and questioning for one's self what was written was a breakthrough from the olden days when one did not question the instructor.

George Buchanan, February, 1506-September 28, 1582, was a Scottish historian and humanist scholar born in the area west of Stirling, about 40 miles west of Edinburgh. This era was full of religious turmoil, both in England and the Continent. Buchanan was just one of tens of thousands caught up in the conflict between Catholicism and Anglican/Protestantism. His chief historical work was the *History of Scotland*, which covered from the earliest times to 1580. Few of the best Italians equaled him in the purity of his Latin diction and the vigor and clarity of his narrative. He moved around Europe in teaching positions, as well as getting caught up in the Roman Catholic Inquisition which lasted for 600 years.

George Buchanan

Buchanan, in 1529, was elected "Procurator of the German Nation" in the University of Paris, and was re-elected four times in four successive

Giorgio Vasari

months.[42] Let me digress on this last point. While working on this effort, I've been reading Hastings Rashdall's *The Universities of Europe in the Middle Ages*. I do not recommend this to anyone. In the early centuries of the European universities, students picked their own professors in many cases. Buchanan's title above was the result of the organization of students at any university into groups by their national origin. Frequently there were four "nations;" German, French, English, and Italian.

Giorgio Vasari, July 30, 1511-June 27 1574, was an Italian painter, architect, and biographer of Italian artists. He was born in Arezzo, which by now you should know where it is. He was consistently employed as a painter by patrons of the Medici family in Florence and Rome. In discussing Guicciardini above, I described the Ponte Vecchio over the Arno. Its second-story passage/art gallery is called the Vasari

Corridor as Vasari built the long passage from the Pitti Palace on the south of the river to the Uffizi Museum on the north side. The total length of the passage is about 500 yards. As the first Italian art historian, he initiated the genre of an encyclopedia of artistic biographies that continues today. Vasari coined the term "Renaissance" (rinascita) in print, though an awareness of the ongoing "rebirth" in the arts had been in the air from the time of Alberti (1404-72).[43] "Everything was grist for his mill. And the indiscriminate information he gathered accounts in part for both the charm and the weakness of his work. The first edition came out in 1550. He traveled and interviewed still more and brought out an improved version in 1568."[44]

The continuous second story of the Ponte Vecchio shows clearly in this digital photo. The second story Vasari Gallery continues from the bridge, turns right toward us for about 100 yards where the people are standing and connects to the Uffizi, which is to the immediate right. My original color picture shows the

Florence-Ponte Vecchio

neatness and the pastel yellow color of the bridge from the northeast bank. A barred window is seen above the people.

Jean Bodin, 1530-1596, was a French jurist and political philosopher born in Angers, which is about 150 miles southwest of Paris. He wrote, "Of history, that is, the true narration of things, there are three kinds: human, natural and divine."[45] His principal historical work was *Method for the Easy Understanding of History,* "He wanted to create a new kind of universal history comparing and contrasting the laws and customs of all nations. He employed complex categories, establishing distinctions among divine, natural, and human history and organizing the material according to the chronological and geographic criteria. He also insisted upon the preeminence of primary over secondary sources."[46] Bodin divided history into Oriental, Mediterranean and north European stages.[47] I discovered ten citations on Bodin.

William Camden, May 2, 1551-November 9, 1623, was an English antiquarian and historian born in London. In 1577 he began his great work *Britannia*, a topographical and historical survey of all of Great Britain. The first edition, in Latin, was published in 1586, and had gone to seven editions by 1607. The first English translation was in 1610. Please ponder those dates. It was a hot item in Latin for twenty years before being translated into English. This speaks to the importance of Latin in the elite circles. *Britannia* is a county-by-county description of Great Britain. It is a work of chorography: a study that relates landscape, geography, antiquarianism and history. Rather than write a history, Camden wanted to describe in detail the Great Britain of the present, and to show how the traces of the past could be discerned in the existing landscape. By this method he produced the first coherent picture of Roman Britain. He did not simply accept older authorities unquestioningly, but traveled through Great Britain and looked at documents, sites and artifacts for himself. His firsthand research set new standards for the time. He even learned Welsh and Old English for the task. The result is one of the great achievements of sixteenth century scholarship. I'm sure by now that none of my readers are planning to learn Welsh.

In 1597, Lord Burghley suggested that Camden write a history of Queen Elizabeth's reign, 1558-1603. Lord Burghley's (William Cecil) history was almost synonymous with that of Queen Elizabeth's and England's from 1558 for almost forty years. Burghley was Elizabeth's closest advisor, secretary of state, for most of that time. Burghley gave Camden free access to his personal papers as well as a range of state archives. Camden began his work in 1607. Cecil's son had succeeded him in this important position and continued under King James I from 1603. As you can see from these connections, Camden had the historians' dream, free access to official documents and the personal papers of the man closest to the queen for over thirty years. The first part of the *Annales of English and Irish History in the Reign of Elizabeth*, covering the reign up to 1597, appeared in 1515. The second part was completed in 1617, but was not published until 1625 (Leiden) and 1627 (London), after Camden's death.

The *Annales* were not written in a continuous narrative, but rather in the style of earlier annals, giving the events of each year in a separate entry. Though sometimes criticized as being too favorably disposed towards Elizabeth and the future James I, the *Annales* are one of the greatest works of English historiography. Camden's access to source material is unparalleled; the *Annales* are the basis for later histories of the period and are still consulted by historians.[48]

Sir Walter Raleigh, 1552 or 1554-October 29, 1618, was a famed English writer, poet, courtier and explorer born in Devon, England. His exploits are too many to recount here. He was imprisoned for treason in the Tower of London from 1603 until1616. There he wrote many treatises and the first volume of *The History of the World*, about the ancient history of Greece and Rome. The Tower is an austere place in the best of conditions and with little natural light. It stretches the imagination how Raleigh could write such a volume, even if he had access to reference material. Of course, in such a time there is little to do except try to stretch ones mind to make the time pass quicker.[49] Barnes writes that Raleigh's history combined the humanist love for the classics with the Puritan relish for the Bible and liberty. His work was well written and interesting, but added nothing to our knowledge.[50] What does one expect from someone stuck in the Tower of London for thirteen years?

Walter Raleigh

Samuel von Pufendorf, January 8, 1632-October 13, 1694, was a German jurist, political philosopher, economist, statesman, and historian. Who can match that resume in the modern era? He was born at Dorfchemnitz, about 45 miles southwest of Dresden, southeast Germany. He wrote tracts attacking the Roman Catholic Church, found a home in Sweden where he studied the law according to Hugo Grotius, the Dutch founder of international law.[51] Barnes writes:

> "His works included a *History of Sweden*, a *History of Charles Gustavus [X]*, a *History of Frederick William the Great Elector* and *An Introduction to the History of the Leading Powers and States of Europe*. Pufendorf maintained a lofty tone and possessed a distinguished and lucid style. Unfortunately, this was the best thing about his historical writing. Since he often arranged material according to the date and nature of the documents he used, he failed to present a clear and consistent narrative of events. He was given to an extreme form of the personal and biographical interpretation of

Samuel von Pufendorf

history. The emperors, kings, and electors were his heroes, and, to Pufendorf, their acts accounted for the trend of historical events. He did not interpret historical events in relation to the general historical movements of the times or indicate clearly the inter-relation between internal political policies and foreign affairs. As a semi-official historian, he concealed much relevant material. He depicted Germany as a unified and coherent empire and said little about the very diversified and complicated internal politics of the many German states. There is much truth in Fueter's observation that he wrote for the empire rather than about it."[52]

Humfrey Wanley, March 21, 1672-July 6, 1726, was an English librarian, scholar and antiquarian born in Coventry, which is about 80 miles northwest of London. He was instrumental in the study of medieval manuscripts and in building up the largest private library in the country. In 1695 he was appointed an assistant at the Bodleian Library, Oxford University, and he used this access to great effect studying handwriting, compiling indexes of manuscripts and collating texts in Greek and Latin. He laid down the principles of paleography which are still followed today. He later worked for Robert Harley and his son, expanding the Harleian Library from 3,000 manuscripts and printed books in 1715 to about 7,600 manuscripts, 50,000 printed books and 14,000 charters, rolls and deeds by the son's death in 1741. This collection became one of the foundation collections of the British Museum, now the British Library.[53] Such *fun* Wanley must have had during those years.

Lessons Learned:

-Villani was noted for his early collection of statistical data.

-Petrarch is often popularly called the "father of humanism."

-Froissart was an important French chronicler.

-Adam of Usk was a participant and observer of much of his chronicle material.

-Bruni has been called the first modern historian.

-Bracciolini was a great traveler looking for misplaced manuscripts.

-Biondo is credited with coining the term Middle Ages.

-Valla used philology to disprove The *Donation of Constantine*.

-Machiavelli wrote *The Prince* and established a leadership adjective, Machiavellian.

-Sir Thomas More lost his head over Henry VIII.

-Guicciardini is considered as the Father of Modern History.

-Rhenanus wrote his own thoughts in the margins of his school books.

-Vasari coined the term "Renaissance" in print and was a biographer of artists.

-Camden produced the first coherent picture of Roman Britain.

-Raleigh wrote a history of the world while imprisoned in the Tower of London.

-Wanley built a library and laid down the principles of paleography.

Chapter 6

Reformation and Counter-Reformation

In 1517 Martin Luther posted his ninety-five theses of the door of the church in Wittenberg, Germany, about 55 miles southwest of Berlin. The Protestant Reformation had begun. There have been heretics in the Roman Catholic Church for centuries as the Inquisition started early in the thirteenth century. Now the Church had a new type of heretic, one with its own dogma going head-to-head with it in its own backyard. This chapter covers the efforts of the Protestants to discredit the Catholics, and the counter-reformation with the Catholics trying to discredit the Protestants. Please refer back to the Early Christian chapter and read about Orosius. He tried to prove, with history, that the world had less calamities and disasters under Christianity than paganism. Now it's the two Christian groups doing the same thing.

Martin Luther door, Wittenberg, my wife Margaret

Just like two armies or two football teams, both sides needed to get God on their side. "Protestant historians were 'aided by the God of Saint Paul' in the search for evidence that would prove, beyond a shadow of a doubt, that the elaborate ritual and dogmas of the Roman Catholic church had been wholly an extra-scriptural and semi-pagan growth, and that the pope was the real antichrist. Catholic investigators were 'guided by the Blessed Virgin' in their counter-demonstration that the Church and all its appurtenances were but the rich and perfect fulfillment of Scripture, and that the Protestants were inviting a most dreadful and certain punishment by their presumptuous and sinful defection from the organization founded by Saint Peter in direct obedience to the words of Christ."[1] Pope Leo X dismissed Luther as another drunken German monk and didn't take the threat seriously. By default, the Protestants won the coin toss and went on offense first.

Robert Barnes, 1495-July 30, 1540, was an English reformer and martyr. His major contribution to this controversy was *The Lives of the Popes of Rome*. It was composed under Luther's direct supervision and endeavored to prove the popes and the Catholic Church responsible for the disasters of the Middle ages and praised the virtues of their secular opponents. This was Orosius' procedure in reverse. We are not sure of Barnes' exact birth date, but we know his death date exactly because he was burnt at the stake for heresy under the Anglican Church.[2]

Much earlier in this book I explained Wikipedia. The Internet has provided the historical researcher with a multitude of tools. For example, at the end of each Wikipedia article is a list of sites associated with the information in the article. The Barnes article has the following sites available at the click of your mouse: 1495 births/1540 deaths/Protestant martyrs of the Early Modern era/Protestant reformers/English Lutherans/Martin Luther/Tudor people/English executions/People executed for heresy/People executed by burning at the stake/People executed under the Tudors. What more could you ask for?

Heinrich Bullinger, July 18, 1504-September 17, 1575, was a Swiss reformer and the successor of Zwingli as head of the Zurich church. He wrote three significant historical works: a history of Zurich from the Roman times to the Reformation; a history of the Swiss confederation; and a history of the Reformation.[3] Barnes labels Bullinger as one of the ablest Protestant writers of the Reformation. His *History of the Reformation, 1519-32*, dealt with the early years of the movement. Barnes calls Bullinger's effort an apologetic treatise and not a polemic like Knox's, see below.[4]

Heinrich Bullinger

Johannes Sleidanus, 1506-1556, was a German historian, the annalist of the Reformation, and was born in Schleiden, 25 miles southeast of Aachen, Germany. His major work was *Commentaries on Political and Religious Conditions in the Reign of the Emperor Charles V, 1517-1555*. He was a humanist scholar and a student of late medieval historical writings. Sleidanus' work was the first primarily political analysis of the Reformation movement. He was the official constitutional apologist of the Lutheran states in northern Germany, and his task was to justify at the bar of public opinion the entire legality of the secession of the Protestant princes from the Catholic Church. He limited himself mainly to legal documents, so he mixed political, constitutional and theological points of view. His *Commentaries*

Johann Seidanus

exhibited great power in the organization and presentation of material and in a dignified tone to make the case to the learned public of Europe. He was bitterly attacked from both sides of the religious argument, because they only wanted to hear their own biased histories. Later historians have seen great value in his arguments about the political issues involved in the Reformation.[5] Ranke was known for his rigorous investigations of sources, and he writes, "One result was that the famous report by Sleidanus about the imperial election of Charles V proved to have been taken from a biased, largely fictional, account, and that this author was not even acquainted with the authentic documents which would allow him to gain a solid knowledge of events."[6] The religious attacks on Sleidanus' work nicely sum up the atmosphere of the Reformation and Counter-Reformation. Only the beliefs and dogmas counted in the battle for men's minds and money. Don't bother me with any facts of a non-religious nature. My belief is correct, and yours is heresy!!!!

John Knox, c. 1514-November 26, 1572, was a Scottish religious reformer who took the lead in reforming the Church of Scotland along Calvinist lines. He is widely regarded as the father of the Protestant Reformation in Scotland and of the Church of Scotland. The generally accepted location for his birth is about 16 miles east of Edinburgh, Scotland. His major historical work was the *History of the Reformation of Religion Within the Realm of Scotland*, which was begun about 1559 and completed over the next six to seven years.[7] Barnes states, "Despite its obvious Protestant bias, and the ever-evident egotism of the author...From the standpoint of literary quality, his history was a work of genius, 'displaying a marvelous precision and sureness in the selection of the significant and striking details.' For a polemic-writer

John Knox

78

of the time he showed an unusual mastery of and reliance upon humor, sarcasm and irony....saw his facts through decidedly partisan eyes he did not consciously falsify or suppress facts."[8]

Knox is also well known for a treatise which he published anonymously in 1558 while in Geneva, *The First Blast of the Trumpet Against the Monstrous Regiment of Women*, which was primarily against women rulers. To stir up my women readers, please read the following (admittedly Old English is hard to read):

Geneva-Knox

"For who can deie but it is repugneth to nature, that the blind shall be appointed to leade and to conduct such as do see? That the weake, the sicke and impotent persons shall norishe and kepe the hole and strong? And finallie, that the foolishe, madde and phrenetike shal governe the discrete and give counsel to such as be sober of mind. And suche be al women, compared unto man in bearing of authoritie. For their sight in civile regiment is but blindness; their strength, weaknes; their counsel, foolishness; and judgment, phrensie, if it be rightlie considered."[9]

Needless to say, Knox did not get along well with Mary, Queen of Scots, who was a strong Catholic and schemed to replace Queen Elizabeth. Mary finally lost her head, literally, in 1587. However, her son eventually became King James I of England in 1603, of King James Bible fame of 1611.

John Foxe, 1517-April 8, 1587, was an English martyrologist born in Boston, about 100 miles north of London. His life-span was an exciting and dangerous time in England and Europe. Luther's action in 1517, Henry VIII's and Parliament's establishment of the Anglican Church in 1534, the reign of Catholic Queen Mary, 1553-1558, and the supremacy of the Anglican Church again under Queen Elizabeth all contributed to turmoil at all levels of society and government. Were you Catholic, Anglican or Protestant? The wrong answer might mean your life, but that might change in another year or two. In 1554 Foxe published in Strasbourg, France, the draft of *Acts and Monuments*, a Latin history of the Christian persecutions. On March 23, 1563, Foxe's English version of *Acts and Monuments* was published as *Foxe's Book of Martyrs*. But that was the short name and I want to be fully correct, sometimes, in this book, so I will provide the full title. Before I do that, remember the old saying, "You can't tell a book by its cover." Can you tell a book by its title? Well, the title of my book tries to provide the potential reader with a good idea what he/she will encounter. Now I am ready to give you the full title to Foxe's book.

John Foxe

"Actes and Monuments of these latter and perilous Dayes, touching matters of the Church, wherein are comprehended and described the great Persecution and horrible Troubles that have been wrought and practiced by the Romishe Prelates, especiallye in this Realme of England and Scotland, from the yeare of our Lorde a thousande to the time now present. Gathered and collected according to the true Copies and

Wrytinges certificatorie as well as of the Parties themselves that Suffered, as also out of die Bishop's Registers, which were the Doers thereof, by John Foxe."[10]

There now, you know exactly what you are going to read, 1800 pages!!! Vincent pointed out that the Protestantism writings established the idea that Catholicism meant cruelty.[11] My readers in Huntsville will be able to read Foxe's work at the Salmon Library, University of Alabama in Huntsville under the Library of Congress system, BR1600.F6 1841R.v. 2-8. For my relatives in Toledo, Ohio, the public library uses the Dewey Decimal system, so look under 272 Fox.

Matthias Flacius

Matthias Flacius Illyricus, March 3, 1520-March 11, 1575, was a Croatian born in Istria, which is that arrowhead shaped projection at the northeast corner of the Adriatic Sea. We will call him Flacius, since all the other historians do. He was a Lutheran reformer who spent most of his adult life in Germany, Switzerland and Belgium. His major work was the *Magdeburg Centuries*, a thirteen-volume polemic against the Catholic Church. Flacius was the planner and editor, and received contributions from four other prominent Protestant scholars. All the facts that could be used against the Catholic Church were gathered and the history of Christianity was reviewed toward establishing the historicity of the Lutheran position.[12] Regardless of his motives, his work is the beginning of scientific church history.[13]

Pula, Istria

Caesar Baronius, October 31, 1538-June 30, 1607, was an Italian cardinal and ecclesiastical historian born in Sora, about 55 miles southeast of Rome. His major work was the *Ecclesiastical Annals*, which was intended to counter the *Magdeburg Centuries* by Illyricus (above). Preserved Smith, a Reformation authority, writes:

> "However poor was the work of the authors of the *Magdeburg Centuries*, they were at least honest in arraying their sources. This is more than can be said of Caesar Baronius, whose *Annales Ecclesiastici* was the official Catholic counterblast to the Protestant work. Whereas his criticism is no whit better than theirs, he adopted the cunning policy, unfortunately widely obtaining since his day, of simply ignoring or suppressing unpleasant facts, rather than of refuting the inferences drawn from them. His talent for switching the attention to a side-issue, and for tangling instead of clearing problems, made the Protestants justly regard him as 'a great deceiver.'"[14]

Baronius is given credit for coining the term *Dark Ages* to describe the state of European civilization from about 500 to about 1100.[15]

Paolo Sarpi, August 14, 1552-January 15, 1623, was a Venetian patriot, scholar, scientist and church reformer, and the author of the *History of the Council of Trent*, published in 1619. The Council of Trent, intermittently 1545-1563, was the major event in the Catholic Reformation, an attempt to solidify Catholic thinking to respond to the Protestant Reformation. Sardi has been described as a Catholic overall and sometimes a Protestant in detail, but he was really a Venetian patriot first. He was deeply involved in Venice's disputes with Pope Paul V, who excommunicated the city. His history of Trent was published under the name of Pietro Soave Polano, an anagram of Paolo Sarpi Veneto. For several centuries it could be dangerous to publish anti-Catholic tracts in your own name. In 1607 he was attacked by religious gangsters on a bridge in Venice, but survived.[16]

His *Council of Trent* denounced the council as an example of papal bulldozing and Jesuit intrigue and manipulation. His major weakness was his inability to see the council in the proper historical perspective because he was wrapped up in the details. He had a vivid writing style and ever defended liberty and enlightenment. Macaulay, a 19th century liberal, called him the best of the early modern historians, while Lord Acton, a 19th century Catholic historian, said he was no better than a jailbird.[17] This is one more beautiful example how religious beliefs drive any writings about religious events.

Pietro Sforza Pallavicino, November 28, 1607-June 5, 1667, was a Jesuit cardinal born in Parma, about 90 miles north of Florence, Italy. His major historical work was the *History of the Council of Trent*. That is strange. It has the same title as Sarpi's effort (above) There is nothing strange, because this is Pope Innocent X's-directed effort to counter Sarpi's history. Let's look at some selected quotes from the Catholic Encyclopedia, which naturally has a vested interest in Pallavicino's work:

> "The *odious and hostile account* of the Council of Trent by Sarpi had appeared as early as 1619 under a fictitious name…Several Catholic scholars had already begun to collect the material for a refutation of this work, but none had been able to finish the gigantic undertaking…. Pallavicino by order of the pope was now to take up the work anew….The reports of the council in the secret archives of the Vatican were at his unrestricted disposal…Pallavicino's work is *more copious, more conscientious,* and more *in accordance with the truth* than that of his adversary Sarpi. But it is *an apologetic treatise,* and for that reason *not free from partiality* as it is *not without errors*…In any case, however, Pallavicino *did not purposely falsify* the history of the council, and he has *reported much that proves his frankness and objectivity* in the recital." [Italics mine]

The first part of this work initially came out in 1656, and a new edition in three volumes was published in 1664. Pallavicino was elevated to cardinal in 1659.[18]

Although their works of the same title were about forty years apart, Sarpi and Pallavicino should be considered as a matched pair of bookends and the truth lies somewhere in between. Leopold von Ranke, who wrote *History of the Popes*, examined the use they made of their manuscript materials. The result was not highly favorable to either: without deliberate falsification, both colored and suppressed. They write as advocates rather than as historians. Ranke rated the literary qualities of Sarpi's work very highly.[19] The above observations are obvious. They both wrote to prove religious points, and made no disguise of their biases. That was easy for Ranke to observe from his 19th century position. I wonder what he would have written as a proponent for only one position?

Louis Maimbourg, 1610-August 13, 1686, was a French Jesuit and historian born in Nancy, about 190 miles east of Paris. His numerous works include histories of Arianism, the iconoclastic controversy the Greek schism, Lutheranism, Calvinism, and the pontificates of Leo I and Gregory I; they are mere compilations, written indeed in a very lively and attractive style, but inaccurate and untrustworthy.[20]

Veit Ludwig von Seckendorf, December 20, 1626-December 18, 1692, was a German statesman and scholar born at Herzogenaurach, about 12 miles northwest of Nuremburg.[21] He wrote several treatises, but his *Historical and Apologetic Commentary on Lutheranism and the Reformation* (1688-92) is germane here. Its sheer volume overwhelmed Maimbourg's book.

Louis Maimbourg

"Seckendorf was of the school of Sleidanus and produced little that was original. But his work was a dignified and sound historical summary of the Protestant position. Seckendorf desired to combat not only Maimbourg but also a more dangerous enemy, namely, skepticism and indifference to the basic issues of the Reformation. The Saxon princes opened their archives to Seckendorf and he was thus able to use many sources not hitherto touched by Protestant historians. His major work was a paragraph-by-paragraph refutation of Maimbourg by recourse to the sources, with the addition of much in the way of elaboration and comment."[22]

Jacques-Benigne Bossuet, September 27, 1627-April 12, 1704, was a French bishop and orator born at Dijon, about 170 miles southeast of Paris. His major work associated with the Reformation was *History of the Differences Among Protestant Churches*. He tried

"to convince the Protestants of the error of their ways by showing them that there could be no logical end to sectarian divisions, once the crucial initial break has been made with unifies ecclesiastic authority. The ultimate result would be inevitably atheism, anarchy and immorality, and Bossuet tried to find ample justification for this prediction in the historical course of the Protestant movement to his own day. His importance here lies in the fact that he alone of the controversialists, Protestant or Catholic, was able to get beneath personalities and events and to view the conflict in its deepest philosophical aspects as a struggle between liberty and authority, in which the victory of liberty meant to him indifference, atheism and religious anarchy. Bossuet made an honest effort to be fair in this work, for he was appealing directly to Protestant readers whom he sought to convert and restore to the Catholic fold. He admitted there had been bad popes, that the Church needed reform in Luther's day and that Luther had some decent qualities. But he was only too eager to exploit any charges against Protestants which served to support his thesis."[23]

I found ten citations for Bossuet. Almost all of these are references to his *Discourse on Universal History*, which was a treatise on the role of God on everything that happens on earth. Frankly, I do not have the stomach to take on that subject, because it has no ending and is totally religious in nature and argument!!!

Pietro Giannone, May 7, 1676-March 27, 1748, was an Italian lawyer and historian born in Ischitella, on the spur of the Italian peninsula's boot on the Adriatic Sea about 110 miles northeast of Naples. In 1723 he published a four-volume "work which caused a great sensation, especially on account of its bitter anti-ecclesiastical bias, which led to its repeated translation into English and German. In it Giannone combined a narrative of political matters, founded on historical sources, with an interesting description of the juridical and moral condition of the country; but as he ascribes all existing evils to the malignant influence of the Church, especially the Roman Curia, we *may justly assume* it a compilation of *biased attacks and misstatements*. It was *immediately put on the Index* and its author excommunicated and forced to leave Naples."[24] [Italics mine]

Barnes states that the importance of Giannone's work was "that he was the first historian to make the history of law and institutions a legitimate field of general historical research and exposition. In order to prove his case with respect to the political usurpations of the Church and to show them illegal, Giannone was compelled to go into the history of law, administration and constitutions. Incidentally, this helped to make clear the primarily political character of the Catholic Church, whether legitimate or not. Giannone very ably assembled the researches of specialists in the history of law and administration into a general historical treatise. He wrote clearly and spiritedly with aim of reaching a large body of readers."[25]

Note the Catholic Church's response was to put the book in the *Index of Forbidden Books* and excommunicated the author, a typical response. Fifty-five years ago I did not fully understand why the Catholics were characterized as "Don't confuse me with the facts, my mind is made up."

Lesson Learned:

-Sleidanus' work was the first primarily political analysis of the Reformation movement.

-Knox wrote about the Reformation in Scotland, and did not like women.

-*Foxe's Book of Martyrs* was long (1800 pages) and gruesome.

-Flacius wrote a thirteen-volume polemic against the Roman Catholic Church.

-Baronius is given credit for coining the term *Dark Ages*. If you have the Middle Ages, you need something before it.

-Sarpi wrote a (Protestant) history about the Council of Trent, which was the Catholic attempt to counter the Reformation.

-Pallavicino wrote a (Catholic) history of the Council of Trent to counter Sarpi's history.

Chapter 7

Social and Cultural

Harry Barnes, in his *A History of Historical Writing*, had a chapter titled "The Rise of Social and Cultural History: The Era of Discovery and the Growth of Rationalism. The exploration and discovery is generally considered 1450-1750, so there is considerable overlapping of the contents of my chapters. The historical writings are now shifting from the ancient, Christian, and multi-religious into more about the common people, geography, and the social and cultural interactions of people, not just churches and governments. I have adopted his chapter title because I do not know enough to think of a better title.

Pietro Martine d' Anghiera, February 2, 1457-October 1526, was an Italian-born historian of Spain and the discoveries of her representatives during the Age of Exploration. Martine was born in Arona, near Anghiers, on Lake Maggiore about 35 miles northwest of Milan. He wrote the first accounts of explorations in Central and South America in a series of letters and reports, grouped in the original Latin publications of 1511-1530 into sets often chapters called "decades." His decades are thus of great value in the history of geography and discovery. His *De Orbo Novo* (published 1530; "On the New World") describes the first contacts of Europeans and Native Americans and contains, for example, the first European reference to India rubber.[1] There were many historians, particularly Spanish, who wrote about the New World. Martine will be representative of those folks.

William Bradford, March 19, 1590-May 9, 1657, was a leader of the separatist settlers of the Plymouth Colony in Massachusetts. He was born near Doncaster, about 150 miles north of London. He was the primary architect of the Mayflower Compact in Provincetown Harbor on November 11, 1620. This compact stated they would submit to the will of the majority, and thus laid the foundation for a new form of government— democracy. Bradford's hand-written journal (1620-1647) was published as *Of Plymouth Plantation*. He is credited as the first to proclaim what popular American culture now views as the first Thanksgiving. Bradford was a Separatist, those English who believed that they should separate from the Church of England, and who went to Holland before they left for the New World. The Puritans, typified by John Winthrop, below, believed in purifying the Church of England by cleansing it of the Catholic rituals.[2]

John Winthrop, January 12, 1587/8-March 26, 1649, led a group of English Puritans to the New World and joined the Massachusetts Bay Colony in 1629 and was its governor numerous times. He was born in Edwardstone, England, which is about 60 northeast of London. Winthrop's *History of New England* was a "dignified narrative in the annalistic form and described the history of the Massachusetts Bay Colony to the year 1648. It was not a history of New England as a whole, the title of the book being altered by a London publisher to enhance interest and sales. It was the best of the Puritan historical compositions in the New World."[4]

Cotton Mather, February 12, 1663-February 13, 1728, was a Bostonian and

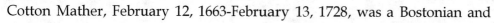

politically influential Puritan minister, prolific author and pamphleteer. He wrote *The Ecclesiastical History of New England.* "It was a comprehensive affair running from the alleged biblical prophecies of the settlement of New England to the history of higher education in Massachusetts. It included the lives of administrators, educators, ministers and other prominent personages, the history of Harvard College, the Indian wars, and the evidences of God's Providence in the course of the history of New England. In the latter respect, Mather applied the same theories that Bossuet adapted, only to a smaller area."[5]

Cotton Mather

Miguel Venegas, 1680-1764, was a Mexican Jesuit administrator and historian born in Puebla, which is about 50 miles east southeast of Mexico City. His major work was a 600-page manuscript, *Empresas Apostolicas*, completed in 1739 and was an account of Baja California. He never visited the area, but had access to missionaries' reports and correspondence, and exchanged letters with them for additional information. It was sent to Spain, but not published until 1757 after extensive revision by another Jesuit historian. This makes one wonder about the veracity of the final document.[6]

Charles de Secondat, baron de Montesquieu, before January 18, 1689-February 10, 1744, was a French social commentator and political thinker. He was born in Bordeaux, which is about 300 miles south southwest of Paris. His principal historical work was *Considerations on the Causes of the Grandeur and Decadence of the Romans*, in 1734. His analytical methodologies toward political analysis provided a basis for other historians and political theorists and had many disciples. Barnes credits Montesquieu with a "school" of methodology. Montesquieu was not a critical writer of history, but his ideas about the decline of the Romans influenced Gibbon.[7]

Montesquieu

I found 16 citations on Montesquieu. The majority of the citations were the usual suspects parading through the paragraphs and lumped with like-others without explanation of the significance. Collingwood is helpful,

> "Montesquieu had the merit of seizing upon the differences between different nations and different cultures, but he misunderstood the essential character of these differences. Instead of explaining their history by reference to human reason, he thought of it as due to differences in climate and geography...As a historian, Montesquieu was uncritical in the extreme; but his insistence on the relation of man to his environment (even though he misconceived the character of that relation) and on the economic factors which in his view underlay political institutions was important not only in itself but for the future development of historical thought."[8]

Voltaire (Francois-Marie Arouet), November 21, 1694-May 30, 1778, was a French Enlightenment writer, essayist, deist and philosopher known for his wit, philosophical sport, and defense of civil liberties, including freedom of religion and the right to a fair trial. He was born in Paris. Among many other fields of writing, he wrote historical essays, but they are not always noted for their accuracy. Voltaire's historical works include: *History of Charles XII, King of Sweden, The Age of Louis XIV, The Age of Louis XV; Annals of the Empire - Charlemagne, A.D. 742 — Henry VII 1313; Annals of the Empire Louis of Bavaria, 1315 to Ferdinand II 1631; and History of the Russian Empire Under Peter the Great.*[9]

Voltaire was popular with historians, as I found 31 citations. E.H. Carr credits Voltaire with the term *philosophy of history*.[10] Collingwood explains further that Voltaire meant it as "critical or scientific history, a type of historical thinking in which the historian made up his mind for himself instead of repeating whatever stories he found in old books."[11] Ranke cites Voltaire as one of several who have written history as a species of literature and is valued for his artistry.[12] Voltaire remarked that, "history is only a pack of tricks we play on the dead."[13]

Voltaire

Burckhardt wrote about Voltaire, "the impudently ignorant mocker."[14]

"In Voltaire's *Age of Louis XIV* we have the most famous of all French men of letters writing the history of the most famous of all French kings. The result is a brilliant work, describing vividly, though sententiously [excessive moralizing], the splendor of what was, in spite of all its tawdriness, a truly great epoch. We have a gorgeous tableau spread before our eyes, with Louis himself as the centre figure, and revolving about him a glittering galaxy of warriors, statesmen, and poets who had contrived to render his reign illustrious."[15]

"The Renaissance concept was decisively advanced toward maturity during the Enlightenment by Voltaire's elaboration of the principles of the history of culture. He sought to define the distinctive traits of each great historical epoch."[16]

". . . Voltaire enlarged the scope of hitherto monarchical history by showing in his *Essay on the Manners and Customs of Nations* that aspects of civilized life other than battles and kings have importance and can interest the general public."[17]

"In the definition of history contained in the *Philosophical Dictionary*, Voltaire offers the following characteristic observation: 'History is the recital of facts given as true, in contradiction to the fable, which is the recital of facts given as false.' Indeed, the whole 'history of opinions' — what we today would call intellectual history — seemed an especially arid waste to the Frenchman. He was, in a sense, the first modern social and cultural historian who emphasized the growth of technology as perhaps the most important area of historical investigation. History was most useful and instructive when it joins to the knowledge of the invention and the progress of the arts the description of their mechanism."[18]

Paris-Notre Dame

M. Taine writes about Voltaire, "As a simplifier and populariser, he had no rival."[19] Many authors cite Voltaire in conjunction with Rationalism, and use him as a breaking point in the type of history written, sometimes before him and sometimes after him.

David Hume, April 26, 1711-August 25, 1776, was a Scottish philosopher, economist and historian. He is considered one of the most important figures in the history of Western philosophy and the Scottish Enlightenment. He was born in Edinburgh. It was as a historian that he first gained recognition and respect. His *The History of England* was the standard work on English history for sixty or seventy years until Macaulay's. Hume's effort would take fifteen years, ran to over a million words and covered the period from the invasion of Julius Caesar to the Glorious Revolution of 1688. It was published in six volumes in the period 1754 to 1762, and has gone through over one hundred editions.[20]

David Hume

I found seventeen citations for Hume. Similarly to Voltaire, most citations were just in name-dropping or as a philosopher. Barnes points out that Hume wrote his history backwards. In 1750 he covered the period 1603-88, which was about the Stuarts. It caused considerable controversy, so in 1759 he published about the Tudors to defend his earlier volumes. Then in 1762 he composed the history from Julius Caesar to Henry VII. Hume was primarily a philosopher, so his histories were dominated by the idea that history is preeminently a record of intellectual and moral ideas of mankind. He unearthed little new material.[21] Peardon, writing about another historian, makes this observation, "Nor are there any supplementary sections, that sign of literary desperation with which we can have full sympathy, like those into which Hume threw so many facts he wished to include but could not weave into any design."[22] [That sounds like a good idea for me.]

Edinburgh Castle

Thomas Hutchinson, September 9, 1711-June 3, 1780, was the American colonial governor of Massachusetts from 1771 to 1774 and a prominent Loyalist. He was born in Boston. He wrote *The History of the Province of Massachusetts Bay*, in three volumes, which was under the Rationalist attitude toward history. Rationalism is the reliance on reason as the basis for the establishment of religious truth. His history was reliable and judicious, and especially competent in treating legislative and institutional developments.[23]

Thomas Hutchinson

Johann Joachim Wincklemann, 1717-68, was a German archaeologist and historian born in Stendal, which is about 65 miles west of Berlin. He settled in Saxony near Dresden, which had many art treasures. He obtained a position in the library of a count, and thus was able to visit the libraries and art collections in Dresden. He learned to be an art critic and wrote *Thoughts on the Imitation of Greek Art* (1755), which contained the expression, "Noble simplicity and calm greatness of Greek statutes." In 1754 he became a Catholic and in 1755 moved to Rome where he studied art of many types and became the greatest authority of archaeology. His other notable work was *History of Ancient Art* (1764). He was assassinated at Trieste in 1768. "*...died a devout and sincere Catholic.*"[24] Please note that the paragraph above came from the Catholic Encyclopedia and the italics are mine. And now for the rest of the story.

So far this inquiry has been dry and dull. I am duty-bound to provide a salacious story to reward you for getting this far. What follows are excerpts from Gay History & Literature. "In 1740 Wincklemann was the tutor to Frederick Wilhelm Peter Lamprecht, son of the Dean of the Chapter of Magdeburg Cathedral. Lamprecht went with Wincklemann to Seehausen, where the latter got a job as a teacher, and where they shared the same room (not simply the same apartment) until their highly emotional break-up in 1746. ...bragging how he would be supping with a 'beautiful young eunuch.'

> "I have no worries other than my work, and have found someone with whom I can speak of love: a good-looking, blond young Roman of sixteen, half a head taller than I am;..."

In June 1768, while waiting for a ship from Trieste to Rome, he fell in with an unemployed cook and small-time thief. For several nights Wincklemann showed him medals he had won and the man admired Wincklemann's fine clothing. The robber threw a rope around Wincklemann's neck, there was a struggle, Wincklemann was stabbed in the chest and 'lower down.' In 1868 the Villa Albani was reopened as a private museum and a bust of Wincklemann was donated by the gay Ludwig I of Bavaria."[25] It is probable that Ludwig I was not gay, as he produced nine children. His grandson, "Mad" King Ludwig II, was probably gay, and responsible for Bavaria's three wonderful castles, Neuschwanstein, Linderhof and Herrenchiemsee. The *Catholic Encyclopedia* states that Wincklemann "died a devout and sincere Catholic", as he was a most popular figure of the Rome and Vatican community, yet nothing is very secret in that atmosphere, which includes the personal lives of the notables. The Catholics are against homosexuality, yet throughout its long history it has been riddled with homosexual activity. Thus, everyone writes their history to ignore its bad aspects and highlight its good aspects. I found nine citations on Wincklemann. He is credited with being the first to write about the art itself, rather than about the artists.

William Robertson, September 19, 1721-June 11, 1793, was a Scottish historian born in Borthwiek, about 12 miles southeast of beautiful downtown Edinburgh. His major historical work was the *History of Scotland*, which he started in 1753 and was published in 1759. It was an immediate success and reached its fourteenth edition by the time he died. He was one of the first to see the importance of *general ideas* in history. He saw that the immediate narrative of events needed a background of broad and connected generalizations, referring to the social state of which the detailed history formed a part. He was friends with the other two great historians of the eighteenth century, Hume and Gibbon. Hume and Robertson were both Scottish, so one easily draws the conclusion that Scotland contributed far more than it per capita share of British literature, compared with the bottom half of the island. Perhaps we should not be considering whether Robertson was the equal of the other two, but whether he was superior to both. Justice requires that we should estimate his performance in view of the means at his command, and few critics would hesitate to subscribe to the verdict of Buckle, "that what he effected with his materials was wonderful." His style is singularly clear, harmonious and persuasive.

Robertson also wrote *History of the Reign of the Emperor Charles the Fifth*, which took ten years. He also wrote *History of America and Disquisition concerning the Knowledge which the Ancients had of India.* [26]

I found seven citations for Robertson. David Garrick, the English actor and theatrical manager, said of *History of Scotland*, "Upon my soul, I was never more entertained in my life... I finished the three first books at two sittings."[27] Gibbon, sixteen years younger than Robertson, wrote, "The perfect composition, the nervous language, the well-turned periods of Dr. Robertson inflamed me to the ambitious hope that I might one day tread in his foot-steps."[28]

Let me now present a situation for my readers to ponder about the historian's problem of writing about the present, and the past. Robertson wrote in his preface to *History of America*, "The longer I reflect on the nature of historical composition, the more I am convinced that scrupulous accuracy is necessary. The historian who records the events of his own times, is credited in proportion to the opinion which the public entertains with respect to his means of information, and his veracity. He who delineates the transactions of a remote period, has no title to claim assent, unless he produces evidence in proof of his assertions. Without this, he may write an amusing tale, but he cannot be said to have composed an authentic history."[29] Let us transfer that noble thought to a quotation he wrote earlier in *History of Scotland*, in which he described Mary of Lorraine, the Scottish Regent (1544-49) whom John Knox had maligned, "No princess ever possessed qualities more capable of rendering her administration illustrious or the kingdom happy. Of much discernment, and no less address; of great intrepidity and equal prudence; gentle and humane without weakness; zealous for her religion without bigotry; a lover of justice without rigor. One circumstance, however, and that, too, the excess of virtue, rather than any vice, poisoned all these great qualities, and rendered her government unfortunate and her name odious."[30] I went on the Internet to get a short biography of Mary of Lorraine. Whoa, I wonder if Robertson did any homework before he wrote about her. It seems as if he was writing about his own mother. Mary was French and a staunch Catholic, who eventually was regent to Mary, Queen of Scots. John Knox was the leader of the Scottish church, which was neither Catholic nor English Anglican. One needs to realize that king, queens, and especially regents must be constantly scheming to maintain or to get power, so let's throw in the religion factor, and Scotland was in total turmoil from many perspectives. Robertson's description of Mary fits the perception that he was a Catholic apologist, but apparently was not. His description cannot be accepted by me. I wonder what "evidence" he used to arrive at his conclusions.

Adam Ferguson, June 20, 1723-February 22, 1816, was a Scottish philosopher and historian of the Scottish Enlightenment. He was born near Perth, which is about 30 miles north of Edinburgh. His principal historical work was *Essay on the History of Civil Society* (1767). It was not a description of events, but a conjectural (speculative) history, by trying to explain why things happened.[31] Barnes cites it as the beginnings of historical sociology.[32] Peardon discusses another of Ferguson's efforts, which is about the Romans, but I mention this because Peardon uses the "Ferguson is no longer the historian, content to analyse, but the moralist passing judgment."[33] The analysis of events and people invariably lead to judgments and many historians, by definition, make moral judgments, which are in the eyes of the beholder (writer).

Adam Ferguson

Thomas Warton, January 9, 1728-May 21, 1790, was an English literary historian, critic and poet. He was born in Basingstoke, Hampshire, which is about 50 miles west southwest of the Parliament in beautiful downtown London. He is best known for his three-volume work, *The History of English Poetry* (1774-1781).[34]

August Ludwig von Schloezer, July 5, 1735-September 9, 1809, was a German historian who laid the foundations for the critical study of Russian history. He was born in what is now Kirchberg an der Jagst, which is about 80 miles southeast of Frankfurt. He wrote history on a variety of topics and his *Allgemeine nordische Geschichte* was long considered a reference work on Russian history (1772). Schloezer's *Vorbereitung zur Weitgeschichte fuer Kinder* (1779) provided guidance for education. He tackled three challenges: the scope, the topic and the structure of a global history. He identified five fundamental factors for development: "The life-style determines, climate and nutrition creates, the sovereign forces, the priest teaches, and the example inspires." He developed a structure for a universal history, separating it into six epochs:

-Primeval world — from the Creation to the Flood
-Dark world — from the Flood to Moses and the first written sources
-Preworld — up to the Persian Empire
-Old world — up to the fall of the Roman Empire in 476 A.D.
-Middle Ages — up to the discovery of America by Christopher Columbus in 1492
-The new world — up to the present

August von Schloezer

This classification was not new, except for setting the Middle Ages between 476 and 1492. These time borders for the Middle Ages are still accepted today. Schloezer's most important innovation was his suggestion to count backwards from the birth of Jesus. An incentive for this was the growing disbelief of the biblical Creation and the then generally acknowledged creation date of 3987 B.C. First speculations that the Sun and Earth were perhaps created tens of thousands of years ago emerged in the 18th century. Schloezer's suggestion offered room for further theories about the creation of the Earth. He mentioned he adopted this idea from foreign historians, but did not provide names. This idea is of tremendous importance for it was the fundamental for all ancient history.[35]

I found five citations for Schloezer. Let us try Eric Hobsbawm. On second thought, only try him at the point of a sword. He briefly mentions Schloezer in the context of cliometrics. Gotcha. Cliometrics is the application of methods developed in other fields (in this case economics) to the study of history. Hobsbawm "Who cannot count, cannot write history." Schloezer wrote that statistics are static history, history is statistics in movement. Seems profound to me.[36] Schloezer was of the Goettingen "school" of German historians in the 18th century who took a more scientific approach to history. Goettingen University is in the town of the same name, which is about 160 miles southwest of Berlin. Schloezer has been called "the father of universal history."[37]

Edward Gibbon, April 27, 1737-January 16, 1794, was an English historian primarily known for his *The History of the Decline and Fall of the Roman Empire*, which was published in six volumes between 1776 and 1788. He was born in Putney, about 5 miles southwest of foggy downtown London. He had a strong bias against Christianity. He dismissed the Middle ages as the "triumph of barbarism and Christianity." Because of this latter bias, he was severely attacked by several contemporaries. As a result of these attacks, he published in 1779 his *Vindication of some Passages in the Fifteenth and Sixteenth Chapters of the Decline and Fall of the Roman Empire*. Because of his use of primary sources, he is considered by many to be one of the first modern historians.[38] Gibbon's effort covered 1300 years in some million and a quarter words. He drew most of his information from the works of seventeenth century scholars and almost none from primary-source documents.[39]

Edward Gibbon

I found Gibbon cited in thirty-six books, six of them within the first four pages, so apparently most historians like to include him in their indices to add gravity to their efforts. George Kennan wrote,

"Think of Gibbon's magnificent cadences."[40] I now want to provide a quotation from Hobsbawm, because it has a reference to Gibbon's writing, but also the first two sentences have general messages about the writing of history.

> "Now history has plainly something in common with this second kind of discipline, if only because historians not only write but above all read books, including quite old ones. On the other hand, historians do become obsolete, though probably at a rather slower rate than scientists. We don't read Gibbon as we still read Kant and Rousseau, for their relevance to our own problems. We still read him, though certainly with enormous admiration for his scholarship, not to learn about the Roman Empire but for his literary merits; that is to say most historians don't read him at all, except in their leisure hours."[41]

Lord Acton said, ". . . Gibbon as masterly in the craft of composite construction."[42] Schevill wrote, "Many hold it to be the only work worthy of being associated with the greatest classical authors on account of the dignity of style and the weight of its contents... His style is of unapproachable majesty."[43] Porter described Gibbon's *Decline and Fall*:

> "Gibbon coped with bias by revealing it; by exposing the prejudices of his sources, and presenting, rather than suppressing, the personality of 'the historian of the Roman Empire.' Impartiality arose not out of fetishism of facts but from the operations of the mind, from analysis, imagination, wit and a capacity to hold judgment in suspense. Gibbon's 'great work' reads like a chorus of voices. The contemporaries speak; Gibbon's sources comment on them; Gibbon adds his glosses, often scolding away in the footnotes; and the reader is invited to listen and participate in the intellectual symposium."[44]

Powicke said, "The reputation of Gibbon as one of the two or three greatest historians who have ever lived...."[45] "Most historians regard the study of history as a way for human beings to acquire self-knowledge. Edward Gibbon, the great English historian of the Roman Empire, sadly described the historical record as consisting of 'the crimes, follies, and misfortunes of mankind."[46] Vincent was writing about historians' biases, "A Gibbon who lacked a sadistic bias against Christianity would be insipid."[47] Davies puts Gibbon along with Thucydides and Macaulay as the three greatest historians the world has ever seen, with Gibbon on top.[48]

Gilbert Stuart, 1742-86, was a Scottish historian who was a brilliant but erratic writer.

> "He protested against the unsympathetic attitude towards the Middle Ages which had been taken by Hume and Robertson. In his Historical Dissertation on the English constitution, and his View of European Society he eulogized the alleged democratic political institutions of the primitive Germans and claimed that Anglo- Saxon England was purely Teutonic. He believed that the English constitution really originated in the backwoods of Germany. He was, thus, a forerunner of the Germanicists of the next century in England. He admired the early Middle ages more than the later medieval period. He composed a whole series of works on the history of Scotland, designed to combat the views and interpretations given by Robertson in his *History of Scotland*.[49]

Thomas Somerville, 1741-1830, was a Church of Scotland minister and historian. He had a strong enthusiasm for the English Revolution of 1688 and "those illustrious patriots, who, under Heaven, were the instruments of rescuing their contemporaries and posterity from the yoke of despotism." In his *History of the Political Transactions, and of Parties, from the Restoration of King Charles the Second, to the*

Death of King William (1792) he sought to incorporate the new evidence while giving it an interpretation different from that of the writers mentioned....The *History of Political Transactions* was a solid, scholarly work. Somerville tells us that it was well received,...but complains that the sale was not up to the expectations so aroused." He also wrote *The History of Great Britain during the reign of Queen Anne* (1798).[50]

Ludwig Timotheus Spittler, November 11, 1742-March 14, 1810, was a German historian born in Stuttgart, which is about 110 miles south of Frankfurt. He was a younger colleague of Schloezer (above). Spittler was a rationalist historian for the Christian church and the lesser German states, with his *Survey of the History of the European States* (1793) and *History of the Christian Church* (1782). He idealized the Middle Ages, which led into the Romanticist school later. He adopted the peculiar attitude of judging the Church from the standpoint of an instrument for advancing the cause of Rationalism.[51] Now, apparently contrary to the previous sentence, Acton wrote that Spittler had no knowledge of religion and hated the church.[52]

Johann Gottfried Herder, August 25, 1744-December 18, 1803, was a German philosopher, poet and literary critic born in Mohrungen, East Prussia, which is now Morag, Poland, and is about 150 miles north northwest of Warsaw. His first important work was *Treatise on the Origin of Language* (1772).[53]

Johann Herder

"Herder believed that people thought as they spoke. It followed that people of one tongue thought and behaved differently from those of another. He therefore divided people into linguistic units, which he defined with the word Volk. A Volk was not based on racial grounds. It was a partnership linking a group of contemporaries living in a given place into a great cultural dialogue with their forebears and, by implication, with later generations. As a result, every existing nation was a unique compound of blood, soil, environment, experience and destiny. Central to this vision was the sense that every Volk was engaged on some great trek toward self-realization. This led him to view history itself as a continuous process in which nations struggled to achieve self-fulfillment."[54]

I found twelve citations about Herder. His "*Ideas toward a Philosophy of History* (1774-four volumes) described human life as closely related to nature and portrayed history as an evolutionary process."[55] The quotation about Herder's thought, by Adam Zamoyski above, makes eminent sense to me, based on visiting about ninety countries and observing the cultures of each. I wish that thought had come to my attention about forty years ago, as it would have provided the basis for a deeper understanding of the different locations and cultures. The next chapter will contain more German philosophers, but of a different ilk.

Gottlieb Jakob Planck, November 15, 1751 -August 31, 1833, was a German Protestant divine and historian born at Nurtingen, which is about 110 miles south of Frankfurt. In 1781 he published anonymously the first volume of his *History of the Protestant Teaching/Learning*, which was eventually completed in six volumes in 1800.[56] Planck followed with *History of the Christian Constitution of Society*, which studied the political organization of the medieval Church to assert its ascendancy over the state. Planck believed in the accidental theory of history. Therefore, he believed the Reformation was accidental, which proved that Providence must have been in favor of the outcome.[57] How one can believe that the purposeful Martin Luther was an accident is beyond me.

Johannes von Mueller, January 3, 1752-May 29, 1809, was a Swiss historian and public official born in Schaffhausen, where the Rhine River has a significant falls on the border with Germany. He was once considered as the ablest Germanic historian of his era. He regarded himself as a second Tacitus. Apparently he suffered no ego problems. His most famous work was the *History of the Swiss Confederation*. Mueller praised the virtues of a fictitious Middle ages and

Rhine Falls near Schaffhausen

advocated a return to its ideals and institutions.[58] Mueller believed in the meaningfulness of a divine plan for world history. A young Ranke was so influenced by Mueller that he wrote, "Johann Mueller says somewhere that there must also be an archive of God's above in heaven."[59] Acton considered Mueller as the first universal historian.[60] Acton maintained his admiration for Mueller long after he had been discredited by critics.[61] Mueller was a Goettingen student of Schloezer, above.

William Roscoe, March 8, 1753-June 30, 1831, was an English historian and miscellaneous writer born in Liverpool, about 190 miles northwest of London on the island's west coast. His major historical works were the *Life of Lorenzo de 'Medici* (1796) and *The Life and Pontificate of Leo the Tenth* (1805). *Lorenzo* gained Roscoe a reputation and it was often reprinted and also translated into French, German and other languages.[62] Lord Acton, writing about the importance of Ranke, said,

William Roscoe

> "Before Ranke appeared, modern history was in the hands of Robertson and Roscoe, Coxe and Sismondi, good easy men whose merit consisted chiefly in making things more accessible which were quite well known already."[63]

Is this a high compliment, or a back-handed one, "quite well known" to historians, or to the general public?

Barnes believes that Roscoe was trying to fill a gap between Gibbon and Robertson, and despite the specific titles, states that Roscoe's efforts "were in reality surveys of the history and culture of the age. Roscoe contrasted the glories of this period with what he regarded as the gloom and fanaticism of both medieval Catholicism and Reformation Protestantism."[64]

Roscoe wrote two books about Italians of almost three centuries earlier. Peardon gives credit to Roscoe for procuring copies of manuscripts for his books, but points out that Roscoe did not visit Italy. His representative, William Clarke, was not trained in the selection and use of historical materials. This leads top the conclusion that the materials' usage was twice biased. From my limited efforts in research, I quickly discovered the opportunities for new areas to research and directions within the main themes. Only the primary writer can sense the implication for his effort, not a researcher who must also arrange for copies (before the era of the copy machine).[65]

Mason Locke Weems, October 11, 1756-May 23, 1825, known as Pastor Weems, was an American printer and author born in Anne Arundel County, Maryland. He is famous, or infamous, for being the author of *The Life of Washington* (1800), in which he fabricated the story of George Washington chopping down a cherry tree as a boy.[66]

Johann Christoph Friedrich von Schiller, November 10, 1759-May 9, 1805, was a German poet, philosopher, historian and dramatist. He was born in Marbach am Necker, which is just north of Stuttgart and about 100 miles south of Frankfurt. He wrote three histories: *The Revolt of the Netherlands; A History of the Thirty Years War;* and *On the Barbarian Invasions, Crusaders and Middle Ages.* He was far more famous for his other talents and his later-in-life friendship with Johann Wolfgang Goethe. Schiller wrote the words to Ode to Joy, which Beethoven set to music in the final movement of his famous Ninth Symphony, which is included in the national anthems of nine nations.[67]

Friedrich Schiller

I found nine citations for Schiller. Acton wrote in the mid-19th century about the relatively few German historians to that time. He

Schiller's House-Weimar

cited Schiller for first teaching the Germans the value of form and elegance in historical writing.[68] Barnes stated that Schiller's poetic and dramatist skills overcame the historical-writing skills as Schiller crafted his words.[69] Ranke wrote Schiller, ". . . had no vocation as a writer of history..."[70] Collingwood cites Schilling's famous aphorism, *The World History is the World Judgment.*[71] Since you've gotten this far in inquiry, you should take a moment to ponder the truth of Schiller's statement before we move to the next personality.

Arnold Hermann Ludwig Heeren, October 25, 1769-March 6, 1842, was a German historian born in Arbergen, which is in the vicinity of Bremen, in the northwest corner of Germany. He was a professor of history are the University of Goettingen, previously identified with Schloezer above. His chief merit as a historian was that he looked at the ancient world from a fresh point of view. Instead of merely narrating their political events, he examined their economies, their constitutions and their financial systems, and thus was able to throw new light on the development of the old world. He possessed vast and varied learning, perfect calmness and impartiality, and great power of historical insight, and is now looked back to as the pioneer in the movement for the economic interpretation of history.[72] I found seven citations for Heeren. His great work was entitled *Reflections Concerning the Politics, Intercourse and Commerce of the Leading Nations of Antiquity.*[73]

Jean Charles Leonard de Sismonde, May 19, 1773-June 25, 1842, was a Swiss writer of French and Italian history, and his economic ideas. He was born in Geneva, which is the southwest corner of the country and almost on the French border. His most important historical work was *The History of the Italian Republics in the Middle Ages,* in sixteen volumes between 1807 and 1818. Also well known are *Political Economy* (1815) and *History of France* (1821-1844). Notice the date as it was published after his death. This is most common throughout history as the writers left many papers, to be completed and published later. His custom for many years was never to work less than eight hours per day.[74]

Sismondi wrote, "There is for the historian a holier mission than of working to extend the renown of a great people, and that is to judge every event by the great touchstone of the laws of morality."[75]

> "Sismondi breaks out in especially great lamentations over the general practice of married women having a lover. This practice had emanated from the court and come into being as a contrast to Spanish jealousy; it was a reaction to it. In the end, no one knew in any respected Italian family whose son, father, or brother he was. At the same time, it was an excellent remedy for the general depression of spirits."[76] [No comment.]

Sismondi was a careful scholar for his time and, if he did not rival Gibbon as a literary artist, he wrote in a clear and dignified manner.[77]

Friedrich Christoph Schlosser, November 17, 1776-September 23, 1861, was a German historian born in Jever, East Friesland, which in the northwest corner of the country. The scientific history era was emerging, but Schlosser wrote histories for the common people and thus was the most popular German historian for a quarter of a century. Much of his success was because he was bold and stern with his judgments about men and events, which met with popular approval. In 1812 his *History of the Iconoclastic Emperors of the East* was published and he contradicted several points in Edward Gibbons' work.[78]

Marcks commented that Schlosser approached the discipline of history with preconceived ideas.[79] Let us ponder that supposition. Suppose you were going to write a history about a certain era or person. Could you really start with a blank slate? You have to have some starting knowledge about you intended target. By that knowledge you already have a bias of some kind, otherwise you would not have picked that subject. We each start out with a proposed theme of the work, which may change as your research continues. Probably your bias changed also. So Marcks was completely correct, but he should not have singled Schlosser out, because I believe that applies to all historians (and other writers).

Barnes writes that Schlosser's most important work, A *History of the Eighteenth and Nineteenth Centuries*, anticipated Lord Acton's position

> "that history should judge men sharply according to high moral standards. He (Schlosser) passed judgment on historical events and public figures according to the principles of the Kantian precepts of individual morality. He was not a critical scholar, his treatment of political history was superficial, and he ignored social and economic history. His chief significance as a historian lies in the fact that he was one of the first notable writers to lay great emphasis upon the political importance and influence of a national literature. Schlosser's outlook had its greatest value years afterwards when scholars used it to correct the notions of Burckhardt and Symonds as to the uniqueness of the Renaissance and its separation from medieval culture."[80]

Barnes later linked Schlosser with Acton and Tacitus as passing such moral judgments described immediately above.[81]

Henry Hallam, July 9, 1777-January 21, 1859, was an English historian probably born in Windsor, which is about 22 miles west of the Westminster Abbey in London. Heathrow Airport is about 6 miles toward London from Windsor. I really need to tell you the

Windsor Castle

story about the American tourist visiting the Queen's Windsor Castle, a popular tourist attraction. The planes coming and going from Heathrow produce constant noise over the castle. An American asked why they built the castle so close to the airport. There now, I feel better.

Hallam produced three great works: *The View of the State of Europe during the Middle Ages* (1818); *Constitutional History of England* (1827); and *Introduction to the Literature of Europe in the 15th, 16th and 17th Centuries* (1838-39)[82] I found six citations for Hallam. Davies writes that Hallam's Middle Ages was so dull that it was harder to read his three volumes than nine volumes by Milman on the same material. (How, Davies, 110) Barnes states that Hallam really belonged to the tradition of Gibbon and the Rationalists, believing that history should teach a lesson to the present. He also resembled Gibbon and Robertson in his scholarly attributes. He was more widely read in historical materials than Gibbon or Robertson and rather more faithful to his sources.[83] "Macaulay declared Hallam's *Constitutional History of England* to be the most impartial book he had ever read.[84] "Hallam's *Constitutional History* marked an epoch both in party history and in historical writing in general. Its superior learning, its depth of observation, its measured and dignified style, and its honest, balanced tone raised the level of English history to a new height."[85] "Hallam's *View of the State* is one of the outstanding monuments of English literature, the first great history after Gibbon."[86]

Francis Palgrave, born Francis Ephraim Cohen, 1788-July 6, 1861, was an English historian born in London. In 1822 he suggested publishing the national records, which was approved, and from 1827 to 1837 he edited a series of volumes. His works include *A History of the Anglo-Saxons* (1831), *The Rise and Progress of the English Commonwealth* (1832), *An Essay on the Original Authority of the King's Council* (1834), *Truths and Fictions of the Middle Ages: the Merchant and the Friar* (1837) and the *History of Normandy and England* (1851-64, four volumes). The last two volumes were published after his death. He was appointed Deputy Keeper of His Majesty's Public Records in 1838 and apparently held that position until his death. He should be remembered as the founder of the English Public Record Office.[87] Later you will encounter numerous historians on both sides of the Atlantic who depended heavily on that office. I would like to add here that in 1538, during the reign of King Henry VIII, a law was passed that ordered parish registers to be started and record baptisms, marriages and burials. It was not uniformly followed, but it was the beginning of establishing national information about the country, and has certainly provided a wealth of data over the centuries. The Royal Historical Society was started in 1868 as the Historical Society for Great Britain.

William H. Prescott

William Hickling Prescott, May 4, 1796-January 29, 1859, was an American historian born in Salem, Massachusetts. He suffered from failing eyesight after a thrown crust of bread was temporarily lodged in his eye. It was a problem that would haunt him for the rest of his life, losing eyesight in one eye completely and in the other significantly, with the remaining eye suffering ups and downs, sometimes being inactive altogether for periods of time. This occurred while he was attending Harvard University, where he graduated in 1814. After ten years of study, in 1837 he published his *History of Ferdinand and Isabella*, which at once gained for him a high place among historians. It was followed by *History of the Conquest of Mexico* (1843) and *Conquest of Peru* (1847). In all his works he displayed great research, impartiality and an admirable narrative power. The disadvantage at which, owing to his very imperfect vision, he worked, makes the first of these qualities especially remarkable, for his authorities in a foreign tongue were read to him, while he had to write on a frame for the blind. [So you think you have good reasons why you do not write history.] The town of Prescott, Arizona was named after him for his *The*

Conquest of Mexico.[88] His Mexico and Peru were literary masterpieces, but need modification in the light of subsequent archeological work.[89] Nothing is perfect forever, so what was significant about Barnes last clause?

Remembering Prescott's disabilities cited above, it has been said that the loss of one of our five senses increases the acuteness of the others. Prescott never visited the scenery of Mexico, so he used his imagination to enhance his narrative. So far you have been exposed to my basic simple language for several reasons. First, I was an Army officer and we do not write in flowery phrases, only the simple *facts*. Second, I still cannot, and do not want to, write flowery because it seems so phony and fictitious. I will now provide a *lengthy excerpt from Prescott*, which Black uses to compare with Robertson. I will not quote Robertson, but just want to show you what *narrative art* is in the eye of one historian so you can gain an appreciation of that skill.

> "They has not advanced far, when, turning an angle of the sierra, they suddenly came on a view which more than compensated the toils of the preceding day. It was that of the valley of Mexico, or Tenochtitlan, as more commonly called by the natives, which, *with its picturesque assemblage of water, woodland, and cultivated plains, its shining cities and shadowy hills*, was spread out like some gay and gorgeous panorama before them. *In the highly rarified atmosphere of these upper regions, even remote objects have a brilliancy of colouring and a distinctness of outline which seem to annihilate distance.* Stretching far away at their feet were seen noble forests of oak, sycamore, and cedar, and beyond, yellow fields of maize and the towering maguey, intermingled with orchards and blooming gardens: *for flowers, in such demand for their religious festivals, were more abundant in this populous valley than in other parts of Anahuac.* In the centre of the great basin were beheld the lakes, occupying then a much larger portion of its surface that at present; their borders thickly studded with towers and hamlets, and, in the midst — *like some Indian Empress with her coronal of pearls* — the fair city of Mexico, with her white towers and pyramidal temples — *the far-famed "Venice of the Aztecs."*…It was like the spectacle which greeted the eyes of Moses from the summit of Pisgah, and in the warm glow of their feelings, they cried out, "It is the Promised Land."[90]

Black writes, "Prescott's art is undoubted. He could decorate a blank panel in the vast void of the past with the hand of a master; and no one would imagine, from the intimacy of the description, that he had never visited the scenery he portrays. Compared with the plain homespun of Robertson, his diction and imagery are impressive to the last degree. Yet, of the two accounts, Robertson's is the more valuable, historically, because it practically reproduces a first-hand document, and gives all the features which the eye of the Spaniard actually took in. Prescott's is, by contrast, essentially a subjective effusion (unrestrained expression of words). Excise the italicized passages, which are really importations and have no basis in contemporary documents, and the superiority of Robertson will become clear at a glance."[91]

Alexis de Tocqueville

Alexis de Tocqueville, July 29, 1805-April 16, 1859, was a French political thinker and historian born in Normandy (somewhere). He is best known for his two-volume *Democracy in America* (1835 and 1840), which is today considered an early work of sociology, not history. He also wrote *The Old Regime and the Revolution* (1856). In both these works, he explored the effects of rising equality of social conditions on the individual and the state in western societies. He was also deeply involved in French politics.[92] I found thirteen citations on Tocqueville.

John Dawson Gilmary Shea, July 22, 1824-February 22, 1892, was an American historian born in New York. He learned fluent Spanish as a boy, became a Jesuit and later left the Society to become a historian. His first note-worthy publication was the *Discovery and Exploration of the Mississippi Valley with the original narratives of Marquette, Allouez, Membré, Hennepin and Anastase Douay* (1852). In 1854 he published the *History of the Catholic Missions among the Indian Tribes of the United States 1529-1854*. In the *Cramoisy Series* of twenty-six small volumes, he initiated in 1857 the republication of rare and valuable pamphlets touching on the voyages of early explorers to America. The articles on the Indians in the *Encyclopedia Britannica* and the *Encyclopedia Americana* are all from his pen, and he was looked upon as the best informed man in America on everything pertaining to the aborigines. His list of publications is lengthy.[93]

Samuel Rawson Gardiner, March 4, 1829-February 24, 1902, was an English historian. Regarded into the 21st century as the foremost historian of the Puritan revolution, he wrote its history in a series of volumes, originally published under different titles. The series is *History of England from the Accession of James I to the Outbreak of the Civil War, 1602-1642* (10 volumes, 1883-4); *History of the Great Civil War, 1642-1649* (5 volumes, 1893); and *History of the Commonwealth and Protectorate, 1649-1660* (4 volumes, 1903). Gardiner's treatment of the subject is exhaustive and philosophical, taking in political and constitutional history, the changes in religion, thought and sentiment, their causes and their tendencies.[94]

Justin Winsor, January 2, 1831-October 22, 1897, was a prominent American writer, librarian and historian born in Boston. He published his first book, *A History of the Town of Duxbury*, during his first year at Harvard. He edited some of the most important historical works of the 19th century. Among them; *Reader's Handbook of American History* (1879), *The Memorial History of Boston* (4 volumes, 1880-81), and the *Narrative and Critical History of America* (8 volumes, 1884-89). The latter was the standard history reference for most of the next century. He was a founding member of the American Historical Association and served as the president during the 1886-1887 term.[95]

Winsor had a significant history as a librarian, which is undoubtedly far more important than his work as an historian. I now digress from historians to some history about libraries and Winsor. In 2005 I finished writing *From Carnegie to Fort Book, The History of the Huntsville* (AL) *Madison County Public Library*, ISBN 0-7414-2488-6. Since Huntsville's first library was founded in 1818, a year before Alabama became a state, my research necessarily included a short history of public libraries in the United States. Enter Winsor, stage right. Although several New England towns claim credit for the first public library, Boston is given credit for the tax-supported public library in 1854. Winsor was one of the creators of the librarian profession, a strong proponent of the ability to uplift, and a leader in the effort to make libraries the center of universities. He started his library career as a Trustee (1867-68), then Superintendent (1868-77) of the Boston Public Library. In an effort to increase book use, he worked for the establishment of branch libraries, extended hours, and relaxed restrictions on use. In 1877, following a struggle with Alderman Hugh O'Brien over the professionalism of library management, Winsor left the Boston Public Library to become Librarian of Harvard University, where he served until his death. Winsor was also a founder of the American Library Association (ALA) (1876) and the Library Journal. He was president of the ALA from 1876 through 1885. In this position, he emphasized the need for trained professionals and provided a rationale for the need for libraries in combating attacks on American morals and social standards.[96] The librarians and libraries of the United States have done far more good for our country than all our historians combined.

Hastings Rashdall, 1858-1924, was an English historian and philosopher. His major historical work was the *Universities of Europe in the Middle Ages* (1894, three volumes). It has about 1,500 pages and includes more than you ever wanted to know about the development of Europe's universities. Each page has footnotes in two columns, but many of them are in Latin. It is laborious reading, which I have done in order to gain an appreciation of the universities. It is in my library.

Lessons Learned:

-Bradford kept a journal of the Plymouth Colony.

-Voltaire is credited with the term *Philosophy of History*.

-Hume wrote a history of England of over one million words.

-Wincklemann wrote about art, and was killed as a homosexual.

-Robertson was one of the first to see the importance of *general ideas* in history.

-Warton is best known for his three-volume work, *The History of English Poetry*.

-Schloezer divided history into six epochs.

-Gibbon's *The History of the Decline and Fall of the Roman Empire* and its magnificent cadences.

-Herder analyzed history on the basis of languages.

-Weems fabricated stories about George Washington, which we still believe.

-Heeren was a pioneer in economic history.

-Palgrave was instrumental in establishing the British Public Record Office.

-Prescott wrote histories while essentially blind.

-Tocqueville's two-volume *Democracy in America*.

-Winsor was a creator of public libraries and the American Historical Association.

- Rashdall wrote the *Universities of Europe in the Middle Ages*.

Chapter 8

Romanticism and Philosophy of History

Once again my paragraphing source, Harry Barnes, has started a new chapter with the title above. The theme has to do with writings associated to the sentimental past. I would like to write that it is easy to get involved in the topic of the philosophy of history, but I shied away. Au contraire, it was easy as pie to avoid getting mixed up with a bunch of philosophers and historians who philosophized but don't actually write history. I gave those folks a quick look and went the other way. Our players in this chapter are ordered by birth date.

Justus Möser, December 14, 1720-January 8, 1794, was a German jurist and social theorist born in Osnabrück, about 75 miles west of Hannover in northwest Germany.[1] His *History of Osnabrück* is "regarded by many as the first real constitutional history, in that it revealed the manner in which political institutions develop out of the deeper social and economic forces in the life of a state."[2]

Justus Moeser

"Möser was personally convinced that his age was especially favorable to liberty and he wrote the history of his country as a good German patriot. The idea of freedom plays a large part in it. Möser hoped to bring about a change in the interpretation of German history by showing that ordinary landowners were the true components of the nation and were therefore to be regarded as the proper subject of investigation....Möser may today be regarded as one of the founders of German economic history."[3]

Immanuel Kant

Immanuel Kant, April 22, 1724-February 12, 1804, was a German philosopher born in Königsberg, then in East Prussia, but now Russian territory (Kaliningrad) sandwiched between Poland and Lithuania. He wrote *Idea of a Universal History from a Cosmopolitan Viewpoint*, which became one of the leading elements of the philosophy of history. Other philosopher/historians soon jumped into this emerging discipline. I found 16 citations on Kant. Kant wrote, "The mind is the law giver of nature." Carl Becker, therefore, offered the conclusion that the historian cannot see the historical reality but only images called up in his own mind.[4] At this point I will let go of something I never grasped, philosophy. Kant was not a historian, but the heavyweight thinkers included him in their books, and so have I. So there!

James Macpherson, October 27, 1736-February 17, 1796, was a Scottish poet, known as the "translator" of the Ossian cycle of poems. He was born at Ruthven, which is about 75 miles north northwest of Edinburgh. Repeat after me, "Macpherson + Ossian = Fake" Get it firmly in your mind, then repeat it to yourself. Macpherson got into translating Scottish Gaelic verses from the highlands and islands. Apparently most of these were authentic. In 1761 he announced the discovery of an epic on the subject of Fingal (related to the Irish mythological character Fionn mac Cumhaill/Finn McCool) written by Ossian (based on Fionn's son Oisín), and in December he published *Fingal, an Ancient Epic Poem in Six Books, together with Several Other Poems composed by Ossian, the Son of Fingal, translated from the Gaelic Language*, written in the musical measured prose of which he had made use of in his earlier volume. The authenticity of these so-called translations from the works of a 3rd century bard was immediately challenged in England. Dr. Samuel Johnson, after some local investigation, asserted (in *A Journey to the Western Islands of Scotland*, 1775) that Macpherson had found fragments of ancient poems and stories, which he had woven into a romance of his own composition. Macpherson immediately challenged Johnson, but Macpherson never produced his originals, which he refused to publish on the grounds of expense. Despite the fakery, he is considered one of the greatest Scottish writers because he actually wrote the disputed works-not Ossian.[5]

James Macpherson

Johann Gottlieb Fichte

Johann Gottlieb Fichte, May 19, 1762-January 27, 1814, was a German philosopher born in Rammenau, which is about 15 miles northeast of Dresden. He is credited with being the philosophical link between Kant and Hegel, based on the perception of the greatness of the German people and therefore the nation. I mention him because there were 12 citations on Fichte. In so many words, I researched him, only to discover that he was a philosopher, not a historian. If I'd known that, I would have saved my time by ignoring him![6]

Friedrich Wilhelm Joseph von Schelling, January 27, 1775-August 20, 1854, was another one of those German philosophers popping up like rabid rabbits during this period. They studied earlier philosophers, then later disagreed with them as each found his way to make himself a player in that world by attacking others. My comments on Fichte above apply, except I only found nine citations. He was born in Leonberg, about 4 miles west of Stuttgart.[7]

Friedrich von Schelling

By now I'd discovered some of the philosophers of history; Kant, Fichte and von Schelling. More will come later, as I try to order folks by birth date as much as possible. The popularity of philosophy of history is that the heavy thinkers, and especially writers, are not bound by ugly, thorny things, such as facts. They enjoy expressing their opinions without have to back them up or footnote sources. Yes, they get criticized, but they can respond with more words from their point of view, and the beautiful thing is, there is no endpoint to their arguments! They just keep writing and talking, to themselves if necessary. The eighteen and nineteenth centuries were a wonderful time for such activities because there were revolutions, scientific discoveries and nation-states being hatched. Knowledge and opinions were flowing freely across Europe, much more so than in earlier centuries when the pace was slower.

Anne Louise Germaine de Staël, April 22, 1766-July 14, 1817, was born in Paris. Although not really a historian, her most important book, *Literature in Its Relation to the Moral and Political Condition of Nations* (1800), used the history of literature to confirm her thesis that literary styles and models are a direct product of the social environment which, in turn, is deeply influenced by the geographical setting, especially by climate. This latter notion she obtained in part from Montesquieu. She maintained that democracy as a new social system required a new type of literary tradition.[8]

Paris-Dom d'Invalis

Madame de Stael

François-Rene de Chateaubriand, September 4, 1768-July 4, 1848, was French writer, politician and diplomat. He was born in Saint-Malo, which is about 180 miles west of Paris and about 30 miles west of Mont St. Michel, the well-known monastery on the coast which is inaccessible to walkers at high tide in the olden days. There is now a causeway for those folks who do not like to get wet feet. His first work examined the causes of the French Revolution, *Essay on the Revolution* (1797). In 1802 he gained fame with *The Genius of Christianity*, an apology for the Christian faith which contributed to the post-revolutionary religious revival in France. He is considered the founder of Romanticism in French literature.[9]

François-Rene de Chateaubriand

Sharon Turner, September 24, 1768-February 13, 1847, was an English historian born in Pentonville, a community in northern London. He settled in Red Lion Square, which is less than 600 yards from the British Museum in London. The British Museum was also the British Library until the early 1990s. Utilizing his access to rare material, he was the first serious scholar to examine the migrations of the Anglo-Saxon peoples. The results of his researches were published in his *History of the Anglo-Saxons* (1799-1805). Thereafter he continued the narrative in *History of England* (1814-29), concluding with the end of the reign of Elizabeth in 1603. Against the emergence of the French Consulate, he promoted the notion of Anglo-Saxon liberty as opposed the Norman tyranny (strong since the 17th century). His books sold well in part because he made the British reason to feel self-confident: he wrote that his nation was "inferior to none in every moral and intellectual merit, [and] superior to every other in the love and

British Museum

Georg Hegel

possession of useful liberty." The British were said to cultivate with equal success "the elegancies of art, the ingenious labours of industry, the researches of science and the richest productions of genius."[10] Wow, who wouldn't buy and read such a wonderful book?

Georg Wilhelm Friedrich Hegel, August 27, 1770-November 14, 1831, was a German philosopher born in Stuttgart. Here comes one of the most famous philosophers, and there he goes, as I shall not write much. He was with Fichte, above, and Schlegel, below, pushing German idealism and bringing the blessing of freedom to mankind. He is not a historian, but twenty of my historians put his name in their books. Remember, name-dropping is important to those historians who do not actually write history, but just philosophize about it. Hegel did write his *Philosophy of History*, which many of those twenty citations mentioned, agreed with, or disagreed with. That is far beyond the scope of this inquiry, but it was a superb learning experience: Avoid Hegel! If you see him, cross the street.

Friedrich Nietzsche

Friedrich Nietzsche, October 15, 1844-August 25, 1900, was a German philosopher born in Röcken bei Lützen, which is about 12 miles southwest of Leipzig. I found fourteen citations from my research, so naturally I need to include him in my index. Wonderful. He definitely was not a historian, but he did write an essay, *The Use and Abuse of History*.[11] As with Hegel, avoid Nietzsche! Make sure you quickly cross the street.

August von Schlegel

Karl Wilhelm Friedrich von Schlegel, March 10, 1772-January 12, 1829, was a German poet, critic and scholar born in Hanover, which is about 150 miles west of Berlin. His major historical work was *Philosophy of History* (1829). He and his older brother August Wilhelm von Schlegel, September 8, 1767-May 12, 1845, were the critical leaders of the Romantic school, which influenced historians but also other writing fields.[12] Karl Schlegel's *Philosophy of History* was a narrow one based on Christianity. "The major task of history is to trace the restoration of the image of God to mankind through the successive stages of human history."[13]

Friedrich von Savigny

Friedrich Carl von Savigny, February 21, 1779-October 25, 1861, was a German jurist born in Frankfurt. He is most famous for his *The Law of Property* (1803), which remains a prominent landmark in the history of jurisprudence. During the period 1815-1831 he wrote multi-volumes of *History of the Roman Law in the Middle Ages*. His treatment of the subject was not merely that of a bibliographer; it was philosophical. It revealed the history of Roman law, from the breaking up of the empire until the beginning of the 12th century, and showed how, though considered dead, the Roman law lived on in local customs, in towns, in ecclesiastical doctrines and school teachings, until it blossomed out once more in full splendor in Bologna and other Italian cities.[14]

"Savigny tried to show that laws are the exact reflection of the life of a people, that they have never been imposed by legislators, but that they have arisen from the nation itself....Condemning in politics all *a priori* notions, all abstract principles in the name of which reforms might be introduced, they held that no innovation could be introduced save first in the mind of the nation, and that the peoples themselves show us their true needs in their history."[15]

Karl Friedrich Eichhorn, November 20, 1781-July 4, 1854, was a German jurist born in Jena, which is about 140 miles northeast of Frankfurt. He is regarded as one of the principal authorities on German constitutional law. His chief work is the *History of German Law and Institutions*.[16]

"Eichhorn was himself an intense patriot by reason of his experiences in the Napoleonic period and his chagrin over Jens-Auerstaedt in 1806 (two victories by Napoleon). He proceeded to apply this nationalistic idea in a long work on the origins of Germanic law. He dealt with German law as a whole, showed its antecedents, and indicated the influence of all aspects of national culture upon its development. He particularly stressed the evolutionary character of law. His work was almost as stimulating to German nationalism as to German studies.[17]

Amable Guillaume Prosper Brugière, baron de Barante, June 10, 1782-November 22, 1866, was a French statesman and historian born in Riom, which is about 200 miles south of Paris. His major historical work was the *History of the Dukes of Burgandy*. Its narrative qualities, and purity of style, won high praise from the romantic school, but it exhibits a lack of the critical sense and of scientific scholarship.[18] Oh well, we all can't be perfect.

Karl August Varnhagen von Ense, February 21, 1785-1858, was a German biographer born in Düsseldorf. Although he developed a reputation as an imaginative and critical writer, he is famous chiefly as a biographer. He possessed a remarkable power of grouping facts so as to bring out their essential significance, and his style is distinguished for its strength, grace and purity. His biographies are of General von Seydlitz (1834), Field-Marshal Gebbard Leberecht von Blucher (1837), Field-Marshal Schwerin (1841), Field-Marshal Keith (1844), and General Bulow von Dennewitz (1853). Varnhaghen's wife, Rahel, was an accomplished writer. (Wikipedia) Leopold von Ranke, as a young historian, was attracted into the lively and liberal discussions hosted by Varnhagen and his wife.[19]

Karl Varnhagen von Ense

Jacques Nicolas Augustin Thierry, May 10, 1795-May 22, 1856, was a French historian born in Blois, which is about 125 miles south southwest of Paris. His major works were *History of the Conquest of England by the Normans* and *Narratives of the Merovingian Period*. His style was both precise and picturesque and was dominated by an idea, at once generous and false, that of Anglo-Saxon liberty resisting the invasions of northern barbarians, and reviving, in spite of defeat, in the parliamentary monarchy. Thierry is also given credit for initiating the critical study of medieval communes.[20]

Thomas Carlyle, December 4, 1795-February 5, 1881, was a Scottish essayist, satirist and historian born in Ecclefechan, which is about 10 miles northeast of the English-Scottish border on the west coast. His first major historical effort was the three-volume work *The French Revolution* (1837). He is well known for *On Heroes, Hero-Worship, and the Heroic in History*, which emphasizes the importance of heroic leadership. This is currently known as The Great Man Theory or in Carlyle's own words, "history is the biography of great men." Carlyle's last major historical work was the life of Frederick the Great.[21] Carlyle had to rewrite the entire manuscript of *The French Revolution* (1837) after a friend's maid accidentally burned it.[22] I found 21 citations for Carlyle. Davies comments on the *History of the French Revolution*,

Thomas Carlyle

"This is a magnificent prose poem rather than a history in the strictest sense of the word. But it is written in Carlyle's early manner, before his worship of the superman had entirely subverted his judgment. It abounds in descriptive passages which, for vividness, have not been surpassed; and it contains a galley of portraits so graphically painted that one has to go back to Tacitus to find anything worthy of comparison with them."[23]

"Turning to Carlyle, (A. J. P.) Taylor is devastating. Nothing could be more damning than to say, 'the hero he worshipped was his own opposite.' Taylor analyzed Carlyle as a man who had supreme sympathy for the masses but deserted them during the Chartist agitation and spent the rest of his life paying for his betrayal. According to Taylor, Carlyle was compelled to lay about him in every direction in order to avoid the necessity of accounting to himself for his social treason."[24]

Acton was only twenty four when he wrote the following about Carlyle.

"…There is no English historian who has the right to be judged by a higher or severer test, for no one has spoken more deeply and truly on the character and dignity of history….Of this conception of history *Past and Present* and *The French Revolution* were not entirely unworthy. The disgust which Mr. Carlyle feels for the men and things of his own time seemed to give him a clearer eye for the past than most of those possess whose vision is distorted by the prejudices of their age. He showed an intelligence of things which no other English historian has understood….But he…failed even to maintain himself on the high ground he had reached….It [*Frederick the Great*] is a history made up of eccentricities….In such a book it seems hardly fair to take note of errors in matters of fact…."[25]

"The least attractive personality of the group, and the least worthy as a historian was the English author, Thomas Carlyle (1797-1881). In radical contrast to Michelet (below), he was possessed of a sour contempt for the masses and an equally exaggerated interest in the picturesque figures in history. He thought that 'the common herd must be drilled, led and punished by their superiors.'…Carlyle was as responsible as any other historian for the conventional disdain of the modern historian for those commonplace things of daily life which have often had incomparably greater influence upon social development than the dramatic personalities. His biographical interpretations, brilliant as they were in a literary sense, were more concerned with a subjective interpretation of the character of the personalities considered than with an intelligent appraisal of their public acts."[26]

Jules Michelet

Jules Michelet, August 21, 1798-February 9, 1874, was a French historian born in Paris. He was a man of letters and an inquirer into history. His first major historical work was *Introduction to Universal History*, 1831. The *Encyclopedia Britannica* "the peculiar visionary qualities which made Michelet the most stimulating, but the most untrustworthy (not in facts, which he never consciously falsifies, but in suggestion) of all historians." This next sentence should only be read at home with a dictionary at your side. "…but they contain in miniature almost the whole of his curious ethicopolitico-theological creed—a mixture of sentimentalism, communism, and anti-sacerdotalism, supported by the most eccentric arguments, but urged with a great deal of eloquence." In the middle of the 1830s Michelet started on his monumental work, *History of France*. It occupied him for 30 years and the usual edition comes in 19 volumes. I have used the word "occupied" loosely, because Michelet was busy during the time writing many smaller books and pamphlets. Michelet was perhaps the first historian to devote himself to anything like a picturesque history of the Middle Ages, and his account is still the most vivid that exists. His inquiry into manuscript and printed authorities was most laborious, but his lively imagination and his strong religious and political prejudices, made him regard all things from a singularly personal point of view.[27]

I found 19 citations on Michelet. "Did he use the 'sources'? Yes, he did. But since he distorted them to make them yield to his message, the use of sources loses its meaning. Michelet is the perfect romantic."[28] Frederic Harrison described Michelet's *History of France*:

> "Michelet has some of the moral passion and insight of Tacitus, no little of the picturesque colour of Carlyle, and more than the patriotic glow of Livy. Alas! Had he only something of the patient reserve of Thucydides, the simplicity and precision of Caesar, the learning and harmonious completeness of Gibbon! He is a poet, a moralist, a preacher, rather than a historian in the modern sense of the word. Yet with all his shortcomings (and his later work has but flashes of his old force) Michelet's picture of mediæval France will long remain an indispensable book."[29]

The above paragraph represents a bargain, a six-for-one sale on quick thumbnail descriptions of notable historians. Zamoyski describes Michelet's French history as secular and patriotic religion of his great country embodied in the idea that all will be saved by all. History is not just the king or the aristocracy, but all elements of society, whether up or down the strata of individuals or across the varied professions. Michelet also wove liberty and freedom into the fabric of society as he saw it.[30] Evans cites Michelet as among the few historians who can be read for literary pleasure.[31] Imagine that, reading a history book just for the literary pleasure. Have you ever done that? Don't answer.

Heinrich Leo, March 17, 1799-April 24, 1878, was a Prussian historian born in Rudolstadt, which is about 170 miles northwest of Frankfurt. His doctoral thesis was on the free Lombard cities (modern northern Italy) and his extensive research efforts laid the basis for his first major historical work in five volumes of the Italian states (1829-1832). His *History of the Netherlands* (2 volumes, 1832-1835) was a glorification of the counter-Reformation. Leo also wrote *Universal History* in 6 volumes (1835-1844).[32] Leo became embroiled in a controversy with Ranke as there were two schools of thought, which are beyond the scope of this effort.[33] I have five citations for Leo.

Georg Gottfried Gervinus, May 20, 1805-March 18, 1871, was a German literary and political historian born in Darmstadt, which is about 25 miles south of Frankfurt. His first major work was the five-volume *History of the German Poetry* (1835-1842). This was the first comprehensive history of German literature written with both scholarly erudition and literary skill. His second most important work was *History of the Nineteenth Century*.[34] I have seven citations for Gervinus.

François Laurent, July 8, 1810-February 11, 1887, was a Luxembourgian historian and juriconsult. His major historical work was the eighteen-volume *Studies on the History of Humanity* (1855-1870).

"This work was an elaborate history. Hence, Laurent knew more actual history [historical facts] than any other man who had written on the philosophy of history down to his time. But he failed to make very intelligent use of his extensive knowledge in his philosophy of history, which was a culmination and a sort of *reductio ad absurdum* of the theistic attitude—the attempt to put God into history on a grand scale....The most interesting and important aspect of his history of philosophy related to his emphasis on the development of the principle of nationality and its contributions to the intellectual and moral evolution of the human race. He concluded with a rather noble plea for the unity and coöperation of the nations of the contemporary world."[35]

John Lothrop Motley, April 15, 1814-May 29, 1877, was an American historian born in Dorchester, now a southern neighborhood of Boston. Motley studied at Göttingen University in Germany, where he became a friend of Otto von Bismarck, later the Iron Chancellor of Germany. About 1846 Motley begun to plan a history of The Netherlands, in particular the period of the United Provinces, and he had already done a large amount of work this subject when, finding the materials at his disposal in the United States inadequate, he went to Europe in 1851. The next five years were spent at Dresden, Brussels and The Hague in investigation of the archives, which resulted in 1856 in the publication of *The Rise of the Dutch Republic*, which became very popular. It speedily passed through many editions, was translated into French, and also into Dutch, German and Russian. In 1860 Motley published the first two

John Motley

volumes of its continuation, *The United Netherlands*. This work was on a larger scale, embodied the results of a still greater volume of original research. Motley's merits as an historian are undeniably great. He told the story of a stirring period in the history of the world with full attention to the character of the actors and strict fidelity to the vivid details of the action, but his writing is best where most unvarnished, and probably no writer of his caliber has owed less to the mere sparkle of a highly polished literary style.[36] Davies cites Motley's *Rise* as "one of the greatest historical works ever written, and one which is likely to endure as long as the English language itself."[37] Barnes, in his preface, cites Motley along with Thucydides, Tacitus, Hume, Gibbon, Parkman and Macaulay as "The great historians have always possessed a glamour and romance for cultivated readers of the world's literature."[38]

James Anthony Froude

James Anthony Froude, April 23, 1818-October 20, 1894, was an English historian born in Dartington, which is about 180 miles southeast of London. Froude's first major work was *History of England from the Fall of Wolsey to the Defeat of the Spanish Armada* (twelve volumes) (1856-1870). Froude came under the influence of Carlyle, which led him to write as though tyranny and brutality were excusable and he admired strong rulers and strong government. Although exposed to many original manuscripts, he used his materials carelessly and seemed to investigate with his mind made up. His *Life of Caesar* (1879), a glorification of imperialism, betrays little acquaintance with Roman politics and the life of Cicero. A travel book about the West Indies shows he made little effort to master his subject, simply assuming that his racist prejudgments were true. Froude had great literary style and was a master of English prose.[39]

In 1864 Froude made a notorious remark which was vigorously attacked, "It often seems to me as if history is like a child's box of letters, with which we can spell any word we please. We have only to pick out such letters as we want, arrange them as we like, and say nothing about those which do not suit our purpose."[40]

> "Nationalism suffused the whole cast of his mind, it was part of the essence of his thinking, almost the *fons et origo* [source and origin] from which his interpretations of history, his religious adherence. His whole intellectual life took their rise."[41]

Barnes disputes the item from Wikipedia above that Froude predetermined facts. He said today the best and impartial critics disagree with the attacks on Froude.[42] Davies said that Froude's *Caesar* was the most brilliant biography of him[43] and he could make even the dullest affairs interesting.[44]

Henry Thomas Buckle, November 24, 1821-May 29, 1862, was an English historian born in Lee, Kent. Kent is the shire to the southeast of London, which includes Dover and Hastings, but I could not find Lee. He had delicate health, and so in his early adulthood he decided to devote all his energies to the preparation of some great historical work. For the next seventeen years, he is said to have spent ten hours a day on it. Buckle's fame rests solely on his *History of Civilization in England*. It is a gigantic unfinished introduction, of which the plan was, first to state the general principles of the author's method and the general laws which govern the course of human progress; and secondly, to exemplify these principles and laws through the histories of certain nations characterized by prominent and peculiar features—Spain and Scotland, the United States and Germany.[45]

I found seventeen citations for Buckle. He saw certain naturalist laws of historical development: physical, moral and intellectual.[46]

> "And the enquiry as to "moral progress" we may leave to Buckle, who was so naïvely astonished that there is none to be found, forgetting that it is relevant to the life of the individual and not to whole epochs. If, even in bygone times, men gave their lives for each other, we have not progressed since."[47]

Buckle was in the vanguard of the "scientific" historians and wrote, "Statement of the resources for investigating history, and the proofs of the regularity of human actions. These actions are governed by mental and physical laws: therefore both sets of laws must be studied, and there can be no history without the natural sciences."[48] Buckle wrote, "There will always be a connection between the way in which men contemplate the past and the way in which they contemplate the present."[49]

Walter Bagehot, February 3, 1826-March 24, 1877, was a British businessman, essayist and journalist born in Langport, which is about 120 miles west southwest of London. For seventeen years he edited the *Economist* newspaper, which was founded by his father-in-law. Taking over in 1860, he expanded the *Economist's* reporting on the United States and on politics, and is considered to have increased its influence among policymakers. The last column of the section *Britain* in the paper still bears his surname as a title.[50] The *Economist*, adhering to the English age-old custom that not much changes, still calls it a newspaper, but it looks like, feels like and is written like a weekly magazine. Its coverage of the world is far superior to the combination of any ten magazines and newspapers.

Bagehot's major historical work is *The English Constitution* (1867), which explored the constitution of the United Kingdom, specifically the functioning of Parliament and the British monarchy and the contrasts between British and American government.[51] His work that closely pertains to the philosophy of history is *Physics and Politics*. A discussion of this may be best understood by Hobsbawm's explanation.

Walter Bagehot

"Paradoxically, the past remains the most useful analytical tool for coping with constant change, but in a novel form. It turns into the discovery of history as a process of directional change, of development or evolution. Change thus becomes its own legitimation, but it is thereby anchored to a transformed 'sense of the past'. Bagehot's *Physics and Politics* (1872) is a good nineteenth-century example of this; current concepts of 'modernization' illustrate more simple-minded versions of the same approach. In brief, what legitimates the present and explains it is not now the past as a set of reference points (for example Magna Carta), or even as duration (for example the age of parliamentary institutions) but the past as a process of becoming the present. Faced with the overriding reality of change, even conservative thought becomes historicist. Perhaps, because hindsight is the most persuasive form of the historian's wisdom, it suits them better than most."[52]

Joseph Barber (J.B.) Lightfoot, April 13, 1828-December 21, 1889, was an English theologian and Bishop of Durham born in Liverpool. From 1854 to 1859 he edited the *Journal of Classical and Sacred Philology*. He did little outside the usual religious apologetics and commentaries.[53] If you can remember back to the Classical chapter, several folks tried to define time or chronology in their histories. Lightfoot should be remembered for the ultimate chronology basis. Please allow me provide a long quotation from Barnes to roll-up the long history of *Christian* chronology.

"All computations in Christendom were still based upon biblical statements of Creation, and human history was supposed to begin with Adam. An accepted Jewish computation reckoned Creation as having taken place in the year 3761 B.C. The Christian chronologers varied this to conform with their symmetrical scheme of history. This was based upon the idea that there would be seven symbolic ages of man—a cosmic week—each enduring a thousand years. Creation was placed at 4000 B.C., and it was believed that the Christian era would last for two thousand years more, after which the final millennium would come. Luther sanctified this scheme, placing Noah at 2000 B.C. The great scholar and student of chronology, Scaliger, estimated the Creation took place in 3947 and that Christ was born in 4B.C. He held that Adam was created on April 23. Johannes Kepler, relying on astronomy as well as the Bible, put Creation in 3992 B.C. and the birth of Christ in 5 B.C. Most influential of all these chronological reconstructions was that of Bishop James Usher, who reached great exactness in his *Annals of the Old and New Testament* (1650-53). He held that the week of Creation began on Sunday, October 23, 4004 B.C., and that Adam was created on Friday, October 28, 4004 B.C., while Christ was born in 4 B.C. This was made more precise a little later by *Lightfoot*, who dated Creation to the hour by contending that Adam was created on Friday, October 28, 4004 B.C., at 9 A.M. But contemporaneously with this most precise of all the pious chronologers, the early geologists were bringing forth ideas and information which made the whole scheme appear infantile and preposterous."[54]

Andrew Dickson White, November 7, 1832-November 4, 1918, was a U.S. diplomat, author, and educator, best known as the co-founder of Cornell University. He was born in Homer, New York, which is about 30 miles northeast of Ithaca, the location of Cornell. Western Union tycoon Ezra Cornell, with White, founded Cornell and White became the first president. He was also a professor of history. For thirty years he refined his analysis about the battlefields between religion and science. In 1896 he published his two-volume *History of the Warfare of Science with Theology in Christendom*. He was also U.S. Ambassador to Germany, 1879-1881 and 1897-1902, and Ambassador to Russia, 1892-1894.[55] *Warfare*, "...was, in, reality, a historical justification of his own life work in the cause of intellectual freedom and toleration. It was probably the most impressive of all "free-thought" historical enterprises and one of the most thrilling and absorbing historical books ever written."[56]

Andrew Dickson White

William Lecky

William Edward Hartpole Lecky, March 26, 1838-October 22, 1903, was an Irish historian and publicist born near Dublin. He published his first work in 1861, *Leaders of Public Opinion in Ireland*, a brief sketch of the lives and work of Jonathon Swift, Henry Flood, Henry Grattan and Daniel O'Connell. His major work was *A History of England during the Eighteenth Century*, with volumes 1 & 2 in 1878 and completed with volumes 7 & 8 in 1890.[57] "Lecky's political views, again, shine through the pages of his Irish history, albeit he did more than most to preserve the impartiality of the judge."[58]

Lecky wrote in his *Value of History*, "The men of each age must be judged by the ideal of their own age and country,"[59] This obvious axiom apparently does not apply to historians, because much of their professional work is based on commenting on people of an earlier era.

Robert Flint, 1838-1910, was a Scottish theologian and philosopher born in Dumfries, which is about 75 miles south of Edinburgh. He was important chiefly for his historical studies of the development of the philosophy of history in modern times. His *The Philosophy of History in Europe: France and Germany* (1874) was partially expanded into a whole volume, *The Philosophy of History in France* (1893).[60] Flint's work was limited to a collection and discussion of others' works, and he "never properly thought out his own point of view, and consequently his criticism of others is superficial and unsympathetic."[61]

> "Not even the above-mentioned [not cited here] Flint carried it out, for he lost himself in preliminaries of historical documentation and never proceeded to the promised construction."[62]

I provided a short commentary earlier in this chapter about historian-philosophers. Let me add to that. This *philosophy of history* seems to boil down to the development of conceptual frameworks about the progression of humankind, and each philosopher takes his own approach to the concept. I really do not want to grasp my arms around the philosophy because if I squeeze too hard I might discover it was all smoke and mirrors. In the end I desire something of more substance. But I feel bound to allow my other readers to make their own decisions in this matter.

Herder, who we met previously, wrote, "Every civilization buds, flowers and fades according to the natural laws of growth." Flint summarized Herder's main propositions in his (Flint's) philosophy of history.

"I. The end of human nature is humanity; and that they may realize that end, God had put into the hands of men their own fates.

II. All the destructive powers in nature must not only yield in time to the preservative powers, but must ultimately be subservient to the perfection of the whole.

III. The human race is destined to proceed through various degrees of civilization, in various revolutions, but its abiding welfare rests solely and essentially on reason and justice.

IV. From the vary nature of the human mind, reason and justice must gain more footing among men in the course of time. And promote the extension of humanity.

V. The wise goodness disposes the fate of mankind, and therefore there is no nobler merit, no purer or more abiding happiness, than to coöperate in its designs."[63]

You didn't ask, but you have received. Who among you will develop a one-hour class to explain the above?

Karl Lamprecht

Karl Gottfried Lamprecht, February 25, 1856-May 10, 1915, was a German historian born in Jessen, which is about 50 miles south southwest of Berlin on the Elbe River. He studied German and European social and economic history, particularly of the Middle Ages. He aroused considerable controversy with his interdisciplinary methods and focus on broad social, environmental and even psychological questions in history. His ambitious *German History* (12 volumes + 2 incomplete, 1891-1909) on the whole trajectory of German history sparked a famous methodological dispute within Germany's academic history establishment. Lamprecht came under criticism from more traditionally-minded scholars like Friedrich Meinecke and Georg von Below for his lack of methodological rigor, and inattention to important political trends and ideologies. As a result, Lamprecht and his students were marginalized by the German academy and interdisciplinary social history remained something of a taboo among German historians for much of the twentieth century.[64] I found thirteen citations on Lamprecht. "In the last analysis, his merit rests perhaps less with his writings as such than with their challenging force."[65]

"The intensity of the reaction in Germany to Karl Lamprecht's *German History* is in some ways surprising because Lamprecht's work was so steeped in romantic notions of morphology, national psyche, and cycles of development not entirely alien to the German tradition of historical writing."[66]

Paul Barth, August 1, 1858-September 30, 1922, was a German historian and sociologist born in Baruth, Silesia, Prussia, which is about 30 miles south of Berlin. "His large and important work, *The Philosophy of History as Sociology* (1897, 1922), is both an important survey of the philosophy of history and an argument in support of his contention that the philosophy of history is sociology, a claim which most conventional historians have been only too glad to concede."[67]

Benedetto Croce, February 25, 1866-November 20, 1952, was an Italian critic, philosopher, politician and historian born in Pescasseroli, which is about 70 miles east southeast of Rome. "History, to Croce, is a manifestation of reality in the present, which contains within itself the impressions from the past and the germs of insight into the future."[68] Okay, readers, it is time for you to prepare a one-hour class on the above sentence.

I found eighteen citations on Croce and I'm citing him from two books, so I am duty bound to include him.

> "Croce argued that historians were guided in their judgment as to what documents and events were important in the past, and what were unimportant, by their present concerns. All history was thus written, consciously or unconsciously, from the perspective of the present; 'all history,' in Croce's famous phrase, 'is contemporary history.'"[69]

Oswald Spengler, May 29, 1880-May 8, 1936, was a German historian and philosopher born in Blankenburg, which is about 110 miles southwest of Berlin. He is best known for his book *The Decline of the West* in which he puts forth a cyclical theory of the rise and decline of civilizations (1918). This work was written before 1914, the beginning of World War I, but was not published and read until after the War. Spengler's influence ranged far and wide. German National Socialism (Nazis) both adopted and condemned him. Wikipedia has a full page of people who have been influenced by him. Spengler lived as a cloistered scholar, supported by his modest inheritance. He lived on a very limited means and was marked by loneliness. He owned no books. In his final years he was able to buy thousands of books.[70] I wonder what and how he might have written if he had the pleasure of his own library all those many years of loneliness.

I found seventeen citations for Spengler. "Spengler, in endowing civilizations with an organic development, forced them into a fixed life span thus leading to his prediction of the imminent and inevitable decline of the West."[71] Barnes writes, "While the general philosophy of the work (*Decline*) is dubious and its conclusions highly debatable, one must admit it throws off thousands of interesting suggestions."[72] "Spengler's book, however, became a Bible, and a source of inspiration for tens of thousands of educated middle-class Germans during a period of bewilderment."[73] (post-WW I)

Lessons Learned:

-Möser may have written the first constitutional history.

-Macpherson + Ossian = Fake.

-Savigny wrote about Roman law.

-Eichhorn wrote on German constitutional law.

-Carlyle and his Great Man Theory.

-Motley wrote about Dutch history.

-Bagehot wrote about the English constitution.

-Lightfoot calculated that Adam was created on Friday, October 28, 4004 B.C., at 9 A.M.

Chapter 9

Nationalism and Historical Writing

The feudal monarchies of the Middle Ages gradually gained economic power which allowed them to increase capital and hire officialdom and military forces to further crush smaller opposition and bring into being the nation-states. The patriotic pride of these states led to the production of historical narratives to glorify their past and establish the legitimacy of their states. These forces were concurrent with the eras of the writings of our last several chapters. The folks building their respective countries by glowing words are ordered by country and by birth date.

These nationalist writings will be covered by country, starting with Germany because that country used the historians, and vice versa, to establish its new-found unitary country. Germany had a much more fragmented national history than did France and England.

Friedrich Wilken, May 23, 1777- December 24, 1840, was a German librarian, historian and orientalist born in Ratzeburg, which is about 60 miles east of Hamburg. He wrote numerous histories about Berlin, but should be noted as the first Western historian to write about the Crusades utilizing Islamic texts, but with emphasis on the German participation.[1]

Friedrich Wilken

Heinrich Luden, April 10, 1778-May 23, 1847, was a German historian born in Loxstedt, which is about five miles south of Bremerhaven, Germany's well-known port for refugees going to America in the 1800s and for American soldiers arriving or departing during the Cold War. He produced a long *History of the German People* (to 1235), in which he aimed to arouse national enthusiasm for the magnificence of medieval Germany.[2]

Friedrich von Raumer

Friedrich Ludwig Georg von Raumer, May 14, 1781-June 14, 1873, was a German historian born in Wörlitz, which is about 70 miles southwest of Berlin. He wrote about the long lineage of the Hohenstaufens, thus popularizing the heroes of medieval Germany.[3]

Johannes Voight, August 27, 1786-September 23, 1863, was a German historian born in Bettenhausen, which is about 80 miles east of Frankfurt. He was a student of Luden (above). He is remembered for his large number of writings concerning the history of Prussia. However, his best known work was a book about Pope Gregory VII, *Hildebrand as Pope Gregory VII and his Times.* It is considered an important work because it is an impartial writing by a Protestant who depicts Gregory as a reformer.[4]

Georg Heinrich Pertz, March 28, 1795-October 7, 1876, was a German historian born in Hanover, which is about 140 miles west of Berlin. Pertz's greatest work was as an archivist for Heinrich

Friedrich Karl, Baron vom Stein. Vom Stein was a leading German statesman who wanted to stimulate interest in German history. He raised private funds to found the Historical Society of Germany (1819). In 1823 vom Stein charged Pertz with the publication of *Momumenta Germaniae Historica,* which was a collection and compilation of the texts of all the more important historical writers on German affairs down to the year 1500, as well as laws, imperial and regal archives, and other valuable documents, such as letters, falling within this period. Pertz complied 24 volumes by the time he resigned in 1874 and this effort was not finished until 1925 which resulted in 120 volumes. This work for the first time made possible the existence of the modern school of scientific historians of medieval Germany.[5]

Georg Pertz

Johann Gustav Droysen, July 6, 1808-June 10, 1884, was a German historian born in Treptow, Pomerania, now northwest Poland and about 140 miles northeast of Berlin. His first major work was the *History of Alexander the Great* (1833). A significant political history was *The Policy of Denmark towards the Duchies of Schlesweig-Holstein* (1850). This work formed German public opinion on the rights of the duchies in their struggle with Denmark. Another of Droysen's works was *History of Prussian Policy,* in seven volumes. It forms a complete history of the growth of the Prussian monarchy to the year 1756. This, like all Droysen's work, shows a strongly marked individuality, and a great power of tracing the manner in which important dynamic forces worked themselves out in history. It was his characteristic quality of comprehensiveness that also gave him so much influence as a teacher.[6]

Johann Droysen

Droysen was the founder of the "Prussian School" of historians..."[7] but others generally credit Treitschke and Sybel along with Droysen as the three founders.

I found sixteen citations for Droysen. In 2007 an author wrote a book about the Greeks and the period of Alexander the Great. The book reviewer started his review by citing the importance of Droysen's book on Alexander's period because so little was known of that era until Droysen's book in 1833.[8]

"Droysen in his lectures on the nature of history and historical method, delivered in the mid-nineteenth century, provided a basis and theory for a broad and social and cultural approach to history, which he, however, did not pursue in his own historical writings."[9]

"Droysen has at once the heavy style of the philologist who desires to express everything and the elusive style, bristling with abstractions, of the metaphysician. Those who wish to see what point of abstruseness German prose can reach, I can advise to read a little work by Droysen, *"The Science of History,* a veritable Chinese head-racker written in German gibberish."[10]

"Droysen is the writer who has most clearly perceived and resolutely affirmed that historiography consists of the '*frage* [question],' of putting the historical question. This is a fertile concept which he sets forth in the definition that the aim of historiography is 'to understand the inquiry' (*forschend zu verstehen*), though he did not elaborate it with sufficient emphasis or depth or application."[11]

"Droysen's is surely the most sustained and systematic defense of the autonomy of historical thought ever set forth—including the attempts of Croce and Collingwood in this century."[12]

Maximilian Wolfgang Duncker, October 15, 1811-July 21, 1886, was a German politician and historian born in Berlin. Among his notable works were: *History of Antiquity*; *The History of the German Reich Assembly in Frankfurt*; and *History of Attempts at Unity since Frederick the Great: Treatises on Prussian History*.[13]

Maximilian Duncker

Wilhelm von Giesebrecht, March 5, 1814-December 17, 1832, was a German historian born in Berlin. In 1841 he published a reconstruction of a lost old annale, a medieval source of which fragments only were known to be extant and these were obscured in other chronicles. The brilliance of this performance was shown in 1867, when a copy of the original chronicle was found, and it was seen that Giesebrecht's text was substantially correct. The first volume of his great work, *History of the German Imperial Period*, was published in 1855, and his fifth volume in 1888. This work was the first in which the results of the scientific methods of research were thrown open to the world at large. Largeness of style and brilliance of portrayal were joined to an absolute mastery of the sources in a way hitherto unachieved by any German historian.[14]

Berlin-Brandenburg Gate

Heinrich Rudolf Hermann Friedrich von Gneist, August 13, 1816-July 22, 1895, was a German jurist and politician born in Berlin. His major work was *History of the English Constitution* (1882, English, 1886), which placed the author at once on the level of such writers on English constitutional history as Hallam and Stubbs, and supplied English jurisprudence with a text-book almost unrivaled in its historical research. He also wrote *The English Parliament* (1886), *To the Legal Reform in Prussia* (1880) and *The State Law* (1872).[15]

Berlin-Charlottenburg Castle

Heinrich von Sybel

Heinrich Karl Ludolf von Sybel, December 2, 1817-August 1, 1895, was a German historian born in Düsseldorf, which is a major city (little town for Sybel) on the lower Rhine River. His first major work was the *History of the First Crusade* (1841). The cause of German nationalism was enhanced by Sybel's *The Origins of German Kingship* (1844). His *History of the French Revolution, 1789-1800* was a polemic against the French influence on Germany. He was appointed director of the Prussian archives and was able to research secret government papers to write *The Foundation of the German Empire by William I*, which was a defense of Bismarck's politics and diplomacy. In 1859 Sybel founded the bi-monthly *Historical Magazine*, which featured historical science and methodology, and is still the leading German historical magazine in 2007.[16] I found fourteen citations on Sybel.

> "Historical science in its results ended for him in the same conclusions as his political and religious views."[17] "In Sybel we shall find a historian who subordinates everything to his own ideas and for whom every circumstance of the past serves as a pretext to prove the excellence of the Hohenzollern institutions and the truth of the principles of National Liberal politics."[18] "But to Sybel history was not scientific through the exactitude of researches alone, but also through the number of moral, social, and political truths it could establish."[19]

Ludwig Hausser, 1818-1867, was a German historian born at Kleeburg, in Alsace, which is now a northeast province of France bordering the upper Rhine River. His greatest achievement, and the one on which his fame rests, was the *German History from the Death of Friedrich the Great to the Beginning of the German Union* (Treaties of 1815). This was the first work covering that period based on a scientific study of the archival sources. He wrote numerous other books about German history.[20]

Dresden-Opera House

Heinrich Gotthard von Treitschke, September 15, 1834-April 28, 1896, was a nationalist historian and anti-Semitic writer born in Dresden. His great achievement was the *History of Germany in the Nineteenth Century*. The first volume appeared in 1879, and during the next sixteen years four more volumes appeared, but was only up to 1847. The work shows extreme diligence and scrupulous care in the use of authorities. It was discursive and badly arranged, and partisan, but stylish and vigorous. He also wrote nationalistic and anti-Semitic essays and journal articles. One of his themes was the dominance of Prussia among the German states and also to swallow up smaller countries.[21]

I found eighteen citations for von Treitschke. Zamoyski cites Treitschke as writing that Prussian dominance as a natural and wholesome condition.[22] "Treitschke's first volume has never been surpassed in vigour and brilliancy."[23]

...France – The French started their nationalistic writing after the Germans.

François Guizot

François Pierre Guillaume Guizot, October 4, 1787-September 12, 1874, was a French historian, orator and statesman born in Nimes, which is near the southern coast about 65 miles northwest of Marseille. Guizot was the leader in organizing the movement for systematic scientific work in collecting and organizing the sources of French history. But he was also a historical scholar who wrote numerous valuable books. In 1833 he organized the *Society for the History of France*. He wrote the *History of the Origin of the Representative Government, 1821-22*, two volumes. He also wrote the *Memoirs of the History of England* in 26 volumes and the *Memoirs of the History of France* in 31 volumes.[24]

I found fourteen citations for Guizot. His Society "brought out dozens of volumes of hitherto hidden sources. Old châteaux were ransacked, government bureaus became research centers, and private papers emerged from cellars and attics to be classified and published with zealous care. Universities everywhere started or multiplied courses in history, and with national interest in mind. This often took the form of demonstrating the antiquity and continuity of the national culture."[25]

"One of the earliest avowed histories of civilization was the *General History of European Civilization* by the French historian and publicist, François Guizot, which appeared in 1828. It surveyed European development from the Roman Empire to the eighteenth century, laying special stress upon the rise of *bourgeois* ideas and the growth of representative government. It well reflected the conservative middle-class ideals of the first half of the nineteenth century in France."[26]

Francois Auguste Alexis Mignet, May 8, 1796-March 24, 1884, was a French historian born in Aix-en-Provence, which is about 20 miles north of Marseille on the southern coast. His *History of the French Revolution* (1824) was an enlarged sketch done in four months, in which more stress was laid on fundamental theories than on facts. Remember, in this section we are talking about nationalistic history, and Mignet's effort was in support of the Liberal cause at the time of turmoil.[27] It represented "the French Revolution as the necessary and inevitable outgrowth of the tendencies of the age and as the dawn of a new and better era in the history of the world."[28]

Louis-Adolphe Thiers, April 16, 1797-September3, 1877, was a French politician and historian born in Marseille. His major historical work was the *History of the French Revolution*, which was in ten volumes between 1823 and 1827. It was immensely popular. He also wrote *The History of the Consulate and the Empire*, which was about the Napoleonic era. The well-known sentence of Scottish historian Thomas Carlyle, that is "as far as possible from meriting its high reputation", is in strictness justified, for all Thiers' historical work is

Adolphe Thiers

marked by extreme inaccuracy, by prejudice which passes the limits of accidental unfairness, and by an almost complete indifference to the merits as compared with the successes of his heroes. But Carlyle himself admits that Thiers is "a brisk man in his way, and will tell you much if you know nothing." Karl Marx described Thiers in his *The Civil War in France*, "before he became a statesman, he had already proved his lying powers as an historian."[29] I found ten citations on Thiers. [Apparently Marx was a good judge of historians and politicians.]

Marseille Church

Henri Martin, February 20, 1810-December 14, 1883, was a French historian born in Saint Quentin, which is about 75 miles north northeast of Paris. His major work was the *History of France*, in nineteen volumes, with the first volume in 1833. This work is in parts defective; Martin's descriptions of the Gauls are based rather on romance than on history, and in this respect he was too much under the influence of Jean Raymond and his cosmogonic philosophy. However he gave a great emphasis to Celtic and anthropological studies. His knowledge of the Middle Ages is inadequate and his criticisms are not discriminating. As a free-thinking republican, his prejudices often biased his judgment on the political and religious history of the *ancien régime*.[30] I found five citations on Martin. "For a half century it remained the popular national history of France on account of its logical arrangement, lucid presentation, urbane *bourgeois* liberalism, and its central theme of the steady growth of French national unity.[31]

Count Joseph Arthur de Gobineau, July 14, 1816-October 13, 1882, was a French aristocrat, novelist and a man of letters, but not an historian. His book, *An Essay on the Inequality of the Human Races* (1853-1855), became famous for developing the racialist theory of the Aryan master race. This theme was picked up by those countries which wanted to enhance their own histories, at the expense of others. The Nazis were one such group, although they had to selectively pick which ideas fit their goals. Gobineau was later utterly discredited, but bad and wrong ideas survive a long time, sometimes forever.[32]

Numa Maua

Paris-Sacre Ceour

Numa Denis Fustel de Coulanges, March 18, 1830-September 12, 1889, was a French historian born in Paris. He took his doctor's degree with two theses about the Greeks and Romans. His minute knowledge of the language of the Greek and Roman institutions, coupled with his low estimate of the conclusions of contemporary scholars, led him to go direct to the original texts, which he read without political or religious bias. When, however, he had succeeded in extracting from the sources a general idea that seemed to him clear and simple, he attached himself to it as if to the truth itself, employing dialectic of the most penetrating, subtle and even paradoxical character in his deduction of the logical consequences.

...In 1864 he published his remarkable volume, *The Old City*, in which he showed forcibly the part played by religion in the political and social revolution of Greece and Rome. The book was so consistent throughout, so full of ingenious ideas, and written in so striking a style that it ranks as one of the masterpieces of the French language in the 19th century. The work is now largely superseded.

Fustel de Coulanges was the most conscientious of men, the most systematic and uncompromising of historians. In 1874 the first volume of his *History of the Political Institutions of Ancient France* was published. His thesis about the Germanic invasions of (Roman) Gaul were not marked by the violent and destructive character usually attributed to them; that the penetration of the German barbarians was a slow process; that the Germans submitted to the imperial administration; that the political institutions of Merovingians had their origins in the Roman laws at least as much as, if not more than, in German usages; and, consequently, that there was no conquest of Gaul by the Germans. His thesis was keenly attacked in Germany as well as France. He reexamined and recast his work, but in general did not change his thesis as he demonstrated a total disregard for the results of such historic disciplines as diplomatics. The results showed that he lacked all sense of historical proportion. He always claimed to ascertain the truth, and in France they tended to believe him.[33]

I found seventeen citations for Fustel. He said in a lecture, "Do not imagine you are listening to me; it is history itself that speaks."[34] Fustel stated, "History is not the accumulation of events of all kinds which occurred in the past. It is the science of human societies."[35]

Albert Auguste Gabriel Hanotaux, November 19, 1853-April 11, 1944, was a French statesman and historian born in Beaurevoir, which is somewhere in Brittany. In 1848 he published his *Origins of the Institution of the Provincial Administrators*, which was an authoritative study.[36] In 1904 his *The History of Contemporary France* is one of the finest products of nationalistic historiography in which he described and defended the establishment and policies of the Third Republic.[37] "The most ambitious work (on the First World War) by a single author is that by Gabriel Hanotoux, but it is pretty well shot through with French patriotic pride and the defense of the stupidities of the French high command at the beginning of the war."[38]

England

Sylvester O'Halloran, 1728-1807, was an Irish surgeon and historian born in Limerick, which is about 100 miles southwest of Dublin. In 1772 he wrote *An Introduction to the Study of the History and Antiquities of Ireland*. When Thomas Leland produced his conservative *History of Ireland* (1773), O'Halloran replied with *Ierne Defended* (1774), asserting the value of Irish manuscripts. His *General History of Ireland* (1778) defended the civilization of pre-Norman Ireland.[39]

John Pinkerton, February 1758-March 10, 1826, was a British antiquarian, author, forger, numismatist, pseudo-historian and early advocate of Germanic racial supremacy theory. [What a resume.] Pinkerton very much wished to purge his country's history of all Celtic elements. In this aim, through two works, the *Dissertation on the Origins and Progress of the Scythians or Goths* (1787) and the *Enquiry into the History of Scotland preceding the reign of Malcolm* III (1789), he developed the theory that the Picts were in fact of the race of ancient Goths, that the Scots language was a pure descendant of the Picto-Gothic language; and, moreover, that the Gaels, or Highlanders, were a degenerate imposter race. He did some other things not deserving of recording. His personal correspondence with fellow academics is characterized by insecurity, slandering, bullying and extreme malevolence. Hugh Trevor-Roper, one modern historian inclined to sympathize with at least the spirit of his views, called him "eccentric." Other historians have hinted at mild insanity.[40]

Edward Gibbon in the 1790s pointed out the shortfall of systematic collection of English historical documents. A serious effort did not start until the 1850s. Gibbon actually proposed that the erratic Pinkerton, above, be the editor of an effort to collect national documents.

Thomas Babington Macaulay, October 25, 1800-December 28, 1859, was an English historian, politician, poet, essayist and reviewer born in Leicestershire, which is about 120 miles north northwest of London. His major historical work was *The History of England from the Accession of James the Second* (1848-61).[41]

Thomas Babington Macaulay

I found 30 citations for Macaulay. "...there is a vulgarity, a narrowness, in Macaulay which causes him to irritate even at his most brilliant."[42] "...is comparably the greatest of the Whig historians."[43] Ranke expressed admiration for Macaulay, especially for "the way in which he explains the present through the past."[44] "...Macaulay, although a brilliant writer, was blinded by Whig prejudice."[45] "Macaulay insisted that all his histories be readable."[46] "Macaulay generally indulges in exaggeration,..."[47]

"...Macaulay also favored romance. As a prose stylist he had few equals. High-blown and self-consciously magisterial in the approved fashion of the nineteenth century, Macaulay's *History of England* obtained a wide audience and established history as a branch of great literature. It also articulated an uncompromising version of the Whig interpretation of England's past by treating the nation's story as synonymous with the emergence of liberty."[48]

"We can always remember, for example, that it is better for our pupils to have read Macaulay and Stubbs and Freeman and Froude before they learn all about the things in which these famous historians have said to err."[49]

"No one ever surpassed Macaulay in the power of making the past live. His knowledge was boundless; and he knew how to employ is all to illustrate by themes. But the proportion is always perfect. There is no ostentatious parade of learning, for Macaulay was always the master, and not the slave, of his own erudition."[50]

"A formidable array of essayists and historians—Thomas Carlyle and Walter Bagehot, Matthew Arnold and Lord Morley, Sir Leslie Stephen and Sir Charles Firth—condemned it as verbose, artificial, overemphatic: a virtuoso's instrument played not to interpret the music but to glorify the performer. Macaulay's most discriminating readers found his style wearisome and ultimately profoundly irritating, ..."[51] Acton wrote, "Macaulay on the contrary invents details and imagines scenes out of very slender materials, and distorts the truth by what he adds."[52]

John Mitchell Kemble, 1807-57, was an English historian. His major work was *The Saxons in England* (1849) "The historiography of nationalism was hardly less forceful in England than in Germany or France. Its most conspicuous feature was a variant of the Aryan and Nordic myths. This dogma stressed the political superiority of the Anglo-Saxon peoples, and became very popular in the nineteenth century. It rested primarily on the assumption that the Teutonic invaders of England has made a clean sweep of the early Roman and Celtic inhabitants and had created an England purely Germanic in culture and almost purely Germanic in race. Kemble's book not only taught this Anglo-Saxon doctrine to the English, but was widely read in Germany and served to furnish the German nationalists with further confirmation of their convictions regarding the 'Germanic' mission. Kemble believed that the English institutions of the nineteenth century were directly derived from Germanic sources."[53]

Charles Kingsley, June 12, 1819-January 23, 1875, was an English novelist (poet-historian) born in Holne, which is about 180 miles west southwest of London. He apparently wrote many historical novels, some of which were for children. His work, *The Roman and the Teuton*, was notorious for its Germanist interpretation. "Highly entertaining but almost wholly unscientific and non-historical, it did more to pervert the interpretation of early medieval history than any other book of its time. ...It is a sufficient commentary upon the accuracy of his work to note that the labors of scholarly medievalists for the last generation have discredited every one of his main theses. The book, however, gained a great popular vogue and no Englishman could well read it without desiring to trace his ancestry back to Arminius [Germanic leader who defeated Roman legions in 9 A.D.] and Alaric [king of Visegoths who conquered Rome in 410 A.D.]."[54] In 1860, four

Charles Kingsley

years before *The Roman*, he was appointed the Regius (Royal) Professor of Modern History at the University of Cambridge. There appears to be a huge disconnect between his very prestigious position and his writings, none of which seem to be really serious history efforts.

Edward Augustus Freeman, August 2, 1823-March 16, 1892, was an English historian born in Harborne, a suburb of Birmingham, which is about 120 miles northwest of London. His major work was the *History of the Norman Conquest of England*, which had fifteen large volumes. His work were large because he did not like to leave out details, so only serious students read his books and not the public at large which was his intended audience. He advanced the study of history in England in two special directions: by insistence on the unity of history, and by teaching the importance and right use of primary sources.[55]

I found 12 references on Freeman. "Freeman wrote under the influence of his favorite doctrine that the essence of history is continuity, and the essence of continuity, politics; and deliberately ignored the social, economic, and ideological aspects of the subjects he treated."[56] Several authors cited one of Freeman's sentences, "History is past politics." "Although admitting the biases, rigidity, and narrowness of Edward Augustus Freeman, H.A. Cronne has rightfully underlined Freeman's role as a stimulator of medieval studies and concluded that 'Freeman was the Erasmus of the nineteenth-century reformation in English historiography.'"[57] "...that arrogant nineteenth-century historian, Edward A. Freemam, whose work on William Rufus was first discredited by an earlier critic, appears conclusively as no historian at all, but a prejudiced man pushing a thesis in the teeth of the evidence."[58]

William Stubbs, June 21, 1825-April 22, 1901, was an English historian and Bishop of Oxford born in Knaresborough, Yorkshire, which is about 180 miles north of London. His most notable work is the *Constitutional History of England*, which traces the development of the English constitution from the Teutonic invasions of Britain until 1485. Although he wrote other material, his efforts as an author are usually judged on the basis of his *Constitutional History*. He belongs to the front rank of historical scholars both as an author and as a critic. He stands out as a master of every department of the historian's work, from the discovery of materials to the elaboration of well founded theories and literary production. He was a good paleographer [you remember what that is?], and excelled in textual criticism, in examination of authorship, and in other such matters, while his vast erudition and retentive memory made him second to none in interpretation and exposition.[59]

I found eighteen citations on Stubbs. He is cited as making a remark that the devoted student of history may be a wiser man, but will be a sadder one.[60] "The fact that Bishop Stubbs believed in the German historical myth of his day did not invalidate the whole, or even a very large part, of the *Constitutional History of England*." (Man, Butt, 190) "Finally, let us take the two historians who approached the opinion of most critics, most nearly to the ideal of pure objectivity, viz. Ranke and Stubbs."[61] "...the greatest of English medievalists before Maitland..."[62] "...did more than anyone to found history as a mainstream university subject."[63]

John Robert Seeley, 1834-January 13, 1895, was an English historian born in London. His major works were *Expansion of the England* and *Growth of British Policy*. He was a nationalist and an imperialist, and along with Freeman, was chiefly responsible for holding English historiography in the narrow and limited channels of political history.[64] "History is past politics and politics is present history." is a frequently quoted passage from Seeley, as well as, "History without politics descends to mere literature." Acton had a longer version of the preceding two statements by Seeley, "Politics are vulgar when they are not liberalized by history, and history fades into mere literature when it loses sight of its relation to practical politics."[65] Seeley sure had a narrow focus.

I found eleven citations for Seeley. Prothro wrote, "In dealing with history he always kept a definite end in view—the solution of some problem, the establishment of some principle, which would arrest the attention of the student, and might be of use to the statesman."[66]

John Richard Green

John Richard Green, December 12, 1837-march 7, 1883, was an English historian born in Oxford, which is about 65 miles northwest of London. His major work was *Short History of the English People* (1874). It combined a discreet appropriation of the German doctrines with primary interest in the development of English civilization as a mass culture.[67] The work may be said to have begun a new epoch in the writing of history, making the social, industrial, and moral progress of the people its main theme. To infinite care in the gathering and sifting

Oxford University

of his material Green added a style of wonderful charm, and an historical imagination which has hardly been equaled.[68] It was expected to sell a few thousand copies, but it sold 32,000 copies in its first year, and a half million copies thereafter. Green was critical figure in the transition from the writing of history of the elites to a broader history of social and cultural change.[69] He expanded his *Short History* into *A History of the English People* in four volumes and was writing *Making of England* in only one volume when he died.[70]

I found ten citations on Green. "The reader will be well advised to read every book by J.R. Green."[71]

...Italian

Ludovico Antonio Muratori, October 21, 1672-January 23, 1750, was an Italian historian born in Vignola, which is about 50 miles north of Florence. He spent much of his career as archivist and librarian at the ducal library in Modena, which is only twelve miles from his hometown. What a great career to be an archivist, librarian and historian, all wrapped up at the same place! He discovered the Muratorian fragment, which is a copy of perhaps the oldest known list of books of the New Testament. The fragment lacks its beginning and ending, and is a 7th century manuscript, which internal cues [of course, you remember technical philology] identify it as a translation from a Greek origin of about 170. He discovered it in the Ambrosian Library in Milan, which about 95 miles northwest of Modena.

Lodovico Muratori

I discovered eight citations on Muratori. He edited the *Rerum Italicarum scriptore* (28 vol., 1723-1751) and *Antiqiquitates Italicae medii aevii* (6 vol., 1738-1742), both important collections of sources, and wrote a history of Italy (1744-1749 in 12 volumes). [72] The importance of the work of archivists needs to be restated, since it is of immense value to later historians in their researches. "...Muratori, who did not restrict himself to testing the genuineness of tradition, but initiated criticism of the tendencies of individual witnesses, of the interests and passions which colour and give their shape to narratives."[73]

Vincenzo Cuoco, October 1, 1770-December 14, 1823, was an Italian writer born in Civitacampomarano, which is about 105 miles east of Rome. His principal work was the *History of the Neapolitan Revolution of 1799*.[74] "Here he recited the reason for its failure and maintained that Italian unity could only be achieved by the Italians themselves. It would be necessary to create a national consciousness in Italy and a mental atmosphere favorable to revolution."[75]

Carlo Troya, 1784-1858, was an Italian politician and historian. His *Italy in the Middle Ages* surveyed the history of medieval Italy for evidence to support his idea for papal leadership in creating Italian unity. It eulogized Dante, the Church and the popes. This was a common theme for that era.[76]

Cesare Cantù, December 5, 1804-March 15, 1895, was an Italian historian born at Brivio, which is near Milan. He produced the first complete national history in 72 volumes over six years, which popularized the reading of national history.[77] His views are colored by strong religious and political prejudice, and by a moralizing tendency, and his historical work has little critical value and is for the most part pure book-making, although he collected a vast amount of material which has been of use to other writers. He was arrested in 1833. While in prison writing materials were denied him, but he managed to write on rags with a tooth-pick and candle smoke, and thus composed the novel *Margherita Pusterla* (1838)[78] You are challenged to write your novel the way he did, but you can work at home.

Pasquale Villari, 1826-1917, was an Italian historian and politician born in Naples. "He devoted his historical writings primarily to medieval and Renaissance Florence and her heroes, such as Savonarola and Machiavelli, using their memory to inspire the movement for Italian unity. Villari did much to popularize medieval Italian history. His work on the history of Florence was a masterpiece."[79] "Villari is one of the greatest of all modern Italian historians, a man of immense learning, and of considerable literary gifts."[80] "While sharply critical of the grandiose old philosophy of history, Villari held that the task of the historian is not complete until he has arranged his facts in a logical and orderly synthesis.[81]

…Other national historians.

Warsaw Palace

Joachim Lelewel, March 22, 1786-May 29, 1861, was a Polish historian and politician born in Warsaw. His major work was *History of Poland* in twenty volumes. One of his most important publications was *The Geography of the Middle Age* (5 volumes, 1852-1857), with an atlas (1849) of fifty plates entirely engraved by himself, for he attached such importance to the accuracy of his maps that he would not allow them to be executed by anyone else. The characteristics of Lelewel as an historian are great research and power

Joachim Lelewel

to draw inferences from his facts; his style is too often careless, and his narrative is not picturesque, but his expressions are frequently terse and incisive.[82] He wrote according to the Romanticist notion of the national soul and the collective genius of the people.[83]

Adam Bernard Mickiewicz, December 24, 1798-November 26, 1855, was a Polish poet, but we will call him a poet-historian. He was born in Zaosien near Nowogródek, which I believe is about 75 miles southwest of Minsk, Belarus. In his days that area was in the Russian Empire, and later the Grand Duchy of Lithuania, which included current Poland. It is also near the current Polish border. Mickiewicz traveled around the area, usually under exile or other stressful situations. He called Lithuania his Fatherland. When my wife and I visited Lithuania in September 2001, our guide mentioned him frequently, as his works are considered the greatest interpreter of the people's hopes and ideals. When we went to Poland in September

Adam Mickiewicz

2002, Mickiewicz was widely lauded as the great voice of Poland appealing to other nations in her agony. Poland did not exist as a separate country, but the strong Polish culture continued to exist. He has over ten statue-monuments of him in several countries.[84] In two countries Mickiewicz was their nationalist voice!

Valerian Kalinka, 1826-1886, was a Polish historian born near Cracow, which is about 180 miles south of Warsaw. He wrote *Galicia and Cracoio*, a historical and social picture of Poland from 1772 to 1850. He published two volumes as *The Last Years of Stanislaus Augustus (1787-95)*. This placed him at once in the first rank of Polish writers. It pointed out errors of the past and showed how they might have been avoided. He later wrote *The Four Years Diet*. It exhibits all the weaknesses in the leading men in Poland, and all their political blunders. To many fierce reproaches it called forth Kalinka replied, "History calls first for truth; nor can truth harm patriotism."[85]

Joseph Szujski, 1835-1883, was a Polish historian born in Tarnow, which is about 50 miles east of Cracow. He wrote *History of Poland* (1862-66), which was of great literary merit which especially extolled the ancient Polish republic. Barnes labeled it the ablest of all the nationalistic histories of

Cracow-Wilanov Castle

Poland.[86] As historians of Poland, Szujski and Kalinka rank equally at the top. He united the most ardent patriotism with a supreme love for truth and a remarkable comprehension of political situations and the characters of those who played their parts in them; consequently no one could explain so well as he the sequence of events and the causes which, for good or evil, influenced the nation.[87]

Vyacheslav Lipinsky, 1882-1931, was the foremost Ukrainian nationalistic historian. "He gave special attention to the historical role of the Ukrainian nobility. He interpreted Ukrainian history as a perpetual struggle to reestablish Ukrainian independence, stressing the leadership of the Ukrainian nobility in this process."[88]

Nicholas Mikhailovich Karamzin, December 1, 1766-June 3, 1826, was a Russian historian born in Mikhailovka, Orenburg, which is about 1,500 miles southeast of Moscow. He is best remembered for his *History of the Russian State*, a 12-volume national history modeled after the works of Gibbon. He secluded himself for two years to write this effort. He is well regarded as a historian. Until his work, little had been done in this direction in Russia. Karamzin was most industrious in accumulating materials, and the notes to his volumes are mines of interesting information. Perhaps Karamzin may justly be criticized for the false gloss and romantic air thrown over the early Russian annals.[89] "He brought the story down to 1611, when the Romanovs appeared on the scene. It was conceived in Romanticist terms, stressing the national genius of the Russian people. Russian national culture was regarded as superior to that of the West because of its oriental heritage, its devoted church, and its aristocratic political institutions.[90] Of course, in Russia in the olden times as well as modern, folks who criticize the government tend to have a shorter life mortality.

Nikolay Karamzin

Michael Shcherbotov, 1733-90, was Russian historian who wrote the first scholarly and comprehensive history of Russia, *Russia History from the Most Ancient Times*. It painted Russian national development in glowing terms and stressed the primary significance of the outstanding leaders in this achievement.[91]

Sergius Soloviev, 1820-79, was a Russian historian who "was of the 'western school" of nationalism. His *History of Russia from the Most Ancient Times* (21 volumes) dealt in great detail with Russian history down to 1774. It was far more scholarly than any preceding work of its kind and was cordial to the westernization of Russia. Hence, it eulogized the achievements of Peter the Great. The most voluminous history of Russia ever written, Soloviev's work was too long to become a popular masterpiece.[92]

Vasiliev Kluchevsky, 1841-1911, was a Russian historian "whose *Course of Russian History* traced the evolution of Russian folk-life, institutions and nationality. It is the Russian version of John Richard Green's English work discussed previously. It was a scholarly work and one of the masterpieces of modern historiography. Kluchevsky especially stressed the importance of Russian colonization and expansion, though he was not a professional pan-Slavist."[93]

Jerónimo Zurita y Castro, 1512-November 3, 1580, was a Spanish historian who founded the modern tradition of historical scholarship in Spain. His style is somewhat crabbed and dry, but his authority is unquestionable, he displayed a new conception of an historian's duties, and, not content with the ample material stored in the archives of Aragon, continued his researches in the libraries of Rome, Naples and Sicily.[94]

Alexandru Dimitrie Xenopol, March 23, 1847-February 27, 1920, was a Romanian scholar, economist, historian, professor, sociologist and author. He was born at Iaşi, which is about 75 miles north northeast of Bucharest, east of the Carpathian Mountains and about 5 miles from Moldava. He is credited with being the Romanian historian credited with authoring the first major synthesis of the history of the Romanian people.[95]

Adolfo Francisco Varnhagen, February 17, 1816-June 29, 1878, was a German born in Brazil who became a volunteer soldier in the Portuguese Revolution, a naturalized Brazilian diplomat and an historian, noted for his *General History of Brazil* in two volumes (1854-57).[96]

Barnes moved rapidly through a series of names of historians from the Benelux and Scandinavia, but none seemed to sufficiently important enough to pursue, especially on sketchy information.

Joseph M. White, May 10, 1781-October 19, 1839, was an American who was the Delegate to the U.S. House of Representatives from the Florida Territory. His major historical work was a *New Collection of Laws, Charters, etc., of Great Britain, France, and Spain Relating to Cessions of Lands with the Laws of Mexico*, in two volumes published in 1839.[97]

Jared Sparks, May 10, 1789-March 14, 1866, was an American historian, educator and Unitarian minister. He was born in Connecticut and was president of Harvard University, 1849-1853. After extensive researches at home and (1828-29) in London and Paris, he published the *Life and Writings of George Washington* (12 volumes, 1834-1837; redated 1842), his most important work; and in 1839 he published separately the *Life of George Washington* (abridged, 2 volumes, 1842). He also wrote *The Diplomatic Correspondence of the American Revolution* (12 volumes, 1829-30; redated 1854). During his research on this effort, he discovered in the French archives the red-line map, which in 1842, came into international prominence in connection with the dispute over the north-eastern boundary of the United States. Sparks was one of the intellectuals who received Alexis de Tocqueville during his 1831-32 visit to the United States.[98]

> "One of the first and most learned exploiters of the nascent attitudes was Jared Sparks, whose biographies of the Founding fathers created some indelible portraits that the passage of time has not significantly altered."[99] On the day that I word processed Jacque Barzun's quotation, 1 December 2007, he was 100 years and 1 day old, as the Wall Street Journal had a story on him in its December 1, 2007 issue. I heartily recommend his *From Dawn to Decadence*, which he wrote at the age of 93."

Sparks was apparently the first American to have access to French public archives. Sparks had been encouraged in his historical projects by General Lafayette, who had offered the use of his own papers.[100]

Francis Parkman, September 16, 1823-November 8, 1893, was an American historian born in Boston. He is best known as the author of *The Oregon Trail: Sketches of Prairie and Rocky-Mountain Life* (1847) and his monumental seven-volume *France and England in North America*. These works are still valued as history and especially as literature, although the biases of his work have met with criticism. Parkman suffered from a debilitating neurological illness, which plagued him his entire life, and which was never properly diagnosed. He was often unable to walk, and for long periods he was effectively blind, being unable to stand but the slightest amount of light. Much of his research involved having people read documents to him, and much of his writing was written in the dark, or dictated to others.

Parkman has been hailed as one of America's first great historians and as a master of narrative history. The Society of American Historians annually award the Francis Parkman Prize to the best nonfiction book on an American theme published the previous year. Parkman's biases, particularly his attitudes about nationality, race, and especially Native Americans, has generated criticism. As C. Vann Woodward wrote in 1984, "Too often Parkman could ignore evidence that was not in accord with his views, permit his bias to control his judgment, or sketch characterizations that are little better than hostile caricatures."

The English-born and Sorbonne-educated Canadian historian W.J. Eccles harshly criticized what he perceived as Parkman's bias against France and Roman Catholic policies, as well as what he considered Parkman's misuse of French language sources. Parkman's most severe critic was the American historian Francis Jennings, an outspoken controversial critic of the European colonization of North America. In 1988 Jennings wrote:

"Parkman's work is fiction rather than history....Parkman was a liar. He fabricated documents, misquoted others, pretended to use his great collection of sources when he really relied almost entirely on a small set of nastily biased secondary works, and did it all in order to support an ideology of divisiveness and hate based on racism, bigotry, misogyny, authoritarianism, chauvinism, and upper-class arrogance."[101] [Jennings did not leave much out.]

"...one of the greatest, if not the greatest, of American historical writers, Francis Parkman. Parkman combined in a rare degree the qualities of a scholar and the man of letters. He was faithful and thorough, and his brilliant powers of analysis, characterization and description have been rarely excelled by any writer who has used the English language."[102]

Alfred Thayer Mahan, September 27, 1840-December 1, 1914, was an American Navy officer, geostrategist and educator born at West Point. His most important work was *The Influence of Seapower Upon History, 1660-1783* (1890). This book was intensively studied in the United States, Britain and Germany in the years before World War I. Between the world wars it also heavily influenced the Imperial Japanese Navy, and many other countries.[103]

Herbert Levi Osgood, 1855-1918, was an American historian of colonial American history born in Maine. He received his doctorate at Columbia University and then went to London to study documents relating to colonial America in the archives of the British Museum and the Public Records Office. He remained a professor at Columbia for the rest of his life. He wrote extensively on colonial American history, his major effort was the seven-volume, *History of the English Colonies in America*. Osgood's work is characterized by frequent and detailed analysis of primary sources. His work is descriptive, aimed as a careful analysis of the source material for the consumption of other historians, with little narrative running through it. He was an admirer of von Ranke, and his style is sometimes compared with von Ranke's.[104] "Unlike Osgood, (and, in fact, most professional historians), who begrudged time spent on improving the form of what they had to say,..."[105] Let us note two teaching points. First, the two locations in London were virtually the only place primary, or secondary, documents were available for information about the American colonies until into the 19th century. Second, note the differentiation of target audiences. University professors write to be recognized within their limited community in order to gain prestige and better jobs. This is different from the last half of the 20th century when the audience was the common people and the publishers were the driving factor to sell popular books with good profit margins.

Lessons Learned:

-Wilken wrote about the Crusades utilizing Islamic texts.

-Raumer wrote a long lineage of the Hohenstaufens.

-Pertz collected and compiled documentation about Germany's past.

-Droysen was the founder of the "Prussian School" of historians.

-Gneist wrote about English jurisprudence.

-Sybel was an archivist and wrote about Bismarck's politics.

-Thiers' historical work is marked by extreme inaccuracy, by prejudice and indifference.

-Coulanges was the most conscientious of men, the most systematic and uncompromising of historians.

-Pinkerton was an antiquarian, forger, and pseudo-historian.

-Macaulay has been both praised and criticized for his English history.

-Stubbs was a bishop, medievalist and paleographer.

-Muratori was an archivist, librarian and historian, all at the same place. Lucky fellow.

-Lelewel wrote about Polish history.

-Mickiewicz was the voice of both Poland and Lithuania.

-Parkman has been hailed as one of America's first great historians and as a master of narrative history. Parkman History Award named after him.

-Mahan's *Influence of Seapower* studied worldwide.

Chapter 10

Critical Historical Scholarship

Until now I have been following Harry Elmer Barnes' chapter scheme by titling mine after his. This chapter will be the last under that approach. Shortly after his discussion of Leopold von Ranke, as I will do, he rapidly degenerates into naming as many historians on one page as possible, and then competing against himself on the next page. He provides 20-40 names on a page, and tries to out do himself on the next. Too, too many.

There were far more academic historians in the world of the 19th century, and they are all trying to make their way in the now-expanding profession of historians. As cited in the last chapter, archivists and similar folks are now expanding the availability of documents and archives not readily available in the earlier centuries. For lack of any obvious themes, I will explore our new friends chronologically.

Jean Mabillon, November 23, 1632-December 27, 1707, was a French Benedictine monk and scholar born in Saint-Pierremont, which is somewhere in the Champagne area east of Paris. In 1681 he published *De re diplomatica libri sex,* which investigated the different types of medieval scripts and manuscripts and is now seen as the foundation work of palaeography (the study of ancient handwriting) and diplomatics (the study of the provenance of ancient documents).[1] Mabillon should probably receive credit for being the father of scientific history.[2]

Jean Mabillon

Let us now take a short excursion from the personalities to understand the importance of the above two terms in the research and writing of history. Palaeography is in many ways a prerequisite for philology (the study of language as used in literature), and it tackles two main difficulties: first, since the style of a single alphabet has evolved constantly (Carolingian minuscule, Gothic, etc.), it is necessary to know how to decipher the individual characters. Second, scribes often used many abbreviations, usually so that they could write the text more quickly, and sometimes to save space, so the palaeographer must know how to interpret them. Knowledge about individual letter-forms, ligatures, punctuation, and abbreviations, enables the palaeographer to read the text as the scribe intended it to read. The fundamental work of the palaeographer is to decipher the writings of the past and to assign them a date and a place of origin. This is why the palaeographer must take into account the style and formation of the manuscript or text. The first time the term "palaeography" was used was perhaps in 1703 by Bernard of Montfaucon, a Benedictine monk.[3]

Diplomatics is forensic palaeography. Specifically it is a branch of study that seeks clues as to the provenance of written documents, especially handwritten documents. It seeks to validate or disconfirm the alleged origin and authenticity of written documents by studying:
- The materials on which they are written;
- The penmanship and alphabets or other scripts used in them;
- The language and style of language they were written in, including their vocabulary, usage, and literary.

The term diplomatics was first coined by Mabillon in 1681, cited above. The study of diplomatics is important to history, to determine whether alleged documents are in fact true or forgeries. For the same reason, diplomatics occasionally comes into play in law. Some famous cases involving diplomatics issues include;

- Lorenzo Valla's proof of the forgery of the Donation of Constantine;
- The Hitler diaries hoax.

Another case for diplomatics was back in the Classical chapter, under Justus of Tiberius, where words about the existence of Jesus were added into an earlier document that had not mentioned him before.

Pierre Bayle, November 18, 1647-December 28, 1706, was a French philosopher and writer born near Pamiers in the south about 35 miles north of Andorra and the Spanish border. His major work was the *Historical and Critical Dictionary* (1695-97). It actually constituted one of the first encyclopedias (before the term came into wide circulation) of ideas and their originators. It was noted for its objective discussions of controversial figures before objectivity became a standard criterion of scholarship in the modern world. Thomas Jefferson named the English translation as one of the one hundred foundational texts that formed the first collection of the Library of Congress.[4]

Pierre Bayle

"...summed up the results of the scholarly attitude that had been at work in Europe for two centuries: the word 'critical' was a triumphant declaration of independence for research."[5]

Bayle's first significant work was a criticism of Louis Maimbourg's history of Calvinism.

"Bayle took special delight in pointing out the grave discrepancies between the views and opinions of authorities contemporary with the events described and he did not hesitate to extend his methods to the examination of 'sacred' history. Indeed, Bayle demolished the idea of sacred history."[6]

Jean Baptiste Dubos, December, 1670-March 23, 1742, was a French author born in Beauvais, which is about 50 miles north of Paris. His *Critical Study of the Establishment of the French Monarchy in Gaul* (1734, three volumes) was a work to prove that the Franks had entered Gaul, not as conquerors, but at the request of the nation, which, according to him, had called them in to govern it. This approach was later victoriously refuted by Montesquieu.[7]

Friedrich August Wolf, February 15, 1759-August 8, 1824, was a German philologist and critic born in Hainrode, which is about 70 miles southeast of Hannover. In nearby Nordhausen Wolf went to

Jean-Baptiste Dubos

grammar school where he soon acquired all the Latin and Greek that the masters could teach him, besides learning French, Italian, Spanish and music. [What did you learn in grammar school?] At age eighteen he went to the University of Göttingen. There is a legend that his first act there was a prophecy: he chose a "faculty" which did not yet exist, that of philology; this omen was accepted, and he was enrolled as he desired. In Halle he was able to carry out his long-cherished ideas and found the science of philology. Wolf defined philology broadly as "knowledge of human nature as exhibited in antiquity." The matter of such a science, he held, must be sought in the history and education of some highly cultivated nation, to be studied in written remains, works of art, and whatever else bears the stamp of national thought or skill. It has therefore to do with both history and language, but primarily as a science of interpretation, in which historical and linguistic facts take their place in an organic whole. Such was the ideal which Wolf had in his mind when he established the philological *seminarium* at Halle. His writings were few, and were always subordinate to his teaching.[8]

Friedrich August Wolf

"A model for the use of what came to be called the critical-philological method of the scientific school was contained in F.A. Wolf's famous *Prologomena to Homer* (1795) in which he sought to establish the authorship of the Homeric poems. Wolf proceeded from the assumption that a source can never be understood in terms of linguistic analysis alone but must be viewed as an historical document reflecting the spirit of the nation (*Volksgeist*), which alone is the key to the understanding of the source.[9]

"We know what this method comprises: the point is to gather together all the evidence one can about the history of a people, to subject this evidence to the most exacting criticism, and to retain only what has the character of strict authenticity."[10]

Louis de Beaufort, ?-1795, a French historian of whose life little is known. In 1738 he publish a *Dissertation on the Uncertainties of the Earlier Centuries of Roman History*, in which he showed what untrustworthy guides even the historians of highest repute, such as Livy and Dionysius of Halicarnassus, were for that period, and pointed out by what methods and by the aid of what documents truly scientific bases might be given to its history. Although not a scholar of the first rank, Beaufort has at least the merit of having been a pioneer in raising the question, afterwards elaborated by Niebuhr, as to the credibility of early Roman history.[11]

Barthold Georg Niebuhr, August 27, 1776-January 2, 1831, was a German statesman and historian born in Copenhagen. His major work was *Roman History* (1827-28), which was a follow-on to Beaufort's work. He brought in inference to supply the place of discredited tradition by popularizing that conception of it which lays stress on institutions, tendencies and social traits to the neglect of individuals.[12] I found 17 citations for Niebuhr. Ranke admitted that Niebuhr was his mentor and first influence on history. ..."hailed by German philological and anti-philosophical historians as their master and guide..."[13]

Barthold Niebuhr

"...wielded source criticism to penetrate the veil of legend behind which history of the early Roman Republic moved in barely recognizable form. Ranke, who greatly admired Niebuhr, generalized these practices into a principle."[14]

"His manner of investigation was that of the exact sciences: it consisted in the first place in determining the truth of the historical facts, then in grouping them, and then in drawing no conclusion which could not be deduced strictly from these facts alone."[15]

Niebuhr wrote his history of Rome with the intention to provide political lesson which would lead to the rise of Prussia after its defeats by Napoleon. "Niebuhr's contemporaries regarded is as one of those classical works which cannot be superseded even if it were refuted in every detail"[16]

Copenhagen-Royal Palace Square

"But there is one good quality lacking in Niebuhr: the gift of form. His *Roman History* is not pleasant to read: it is badly composed, diffuse, confused, involved, and unsystematic: it bristles with technical discussions, and is interrupted by parentheses which bar the way and interfere with the progress of the narrative.[17]

"Macaulay was right in saying of Niebuhr: 'A man who would have been the first writer of his time if his talent for communicating truths had borne any proportion to his talent for investigating them.'"[18]

Leopold von Ranke, December 21, 1795-May 23, 1886, was a German historian born in Weihe, which is about 20 miles north of Weimar and about 20 miles south of Eisleben, Martin Luther's birth and death place. He is considered one the greatest German historians of the 19th century, and is frequently considered one of the founders of modern source-based history. Ranke set the tone for much of later historical writing, introducing such ideas as reliance on primary

Leopold von Ranke

sources, and emphasis on narrative history and especially international politics. He is well known for, and frequently quoted, *"wie es eigentlich gewesen"* ("how it actually was"). While a student at Leipzig University he became an expert in philology and the translation of the ancient authors into German.

Eisleben-Luther Memorial

At age twelve his home of Weihe was close to the towns of Auerstadt (6 miles) and Jena (20 miles) where the Prussians were severely beaten by Napoleon in two battles on October 14, 1806. The Prussians suffered 25,000 killed and wounded and 25,000 captured. Napoleon wrote that the Prussians were finished, but in the following years the Prussians princes recovered great strength and the nationalistic historians of the mid-19th century glorified Prussia, which led to the self-fulfilling rise of the Prussian and German state of the late-19th century and the early to mid-20th century.

Beginning with his first book in 1824, *History of the Latin and Teutonic Nations from 1494 to 1514*, Ranke used an unusually wide variety of sources for a historian of that age, including " …memoirs, diaries, personal and formal missives, government documents, diplomatic dispatches and first-hand accounts of eye-witnesses." In this sense he leaned on the traditions of philology but emphasized mundane documents instead of old and exotic literature. Ranke became a professor at the University of Berlin. He became the first historian to utilize the forty-seven volumes that comprised the diplomatic archives of Venice from the 16th and 17th centuries. Ranke came to prefer dealing with primary sources during this time.

During 1834-1836 Ranke produced the multi-volume *History of the Popes, their Church and State*. Since he was a Protestant, Ranke was barred from viewing the Vatican archives in Rome, but on the basis of private papers in Rome and Venice, he was able to explain the history of the Papacy in the 16th century. In the book, Ranke coined the term Counter-Reformation and offered colorful portrayals of Pope Paul IV, Ignatius of Loyola, and Pope Pius V. The Papacy denounced Ranke's book as anti-Catholic while many Protestants denounced Ranke's book as too neutral. In particular, the British Catholic historian Lord Acton defended Ranke's book as the most fair-minded, balanced and objective study ever written on the 16th century Papacy. Ranke's next book was the multi-volume *History of the Reformation in Germany* (1845-47), for which he utilized the ninety-six volumes from ambassadors at the Imperial Diet in Frankfurt to explain the Reformation in Germany as the result of both politics and religion.

In 1841 Ranke was appointed Royal Historiographer to the Prussian court. In 1849 he published *Memoirs of the House of Brandenburg and History of Prussia, during the Seventeenth and Eighteenth Centuries*, where he examined the fortunes of the Hohenzollern family and state from the Middle ages to the reign of Frederick the Great. Many Prussian nationalists were offended by Ranke's portrayal of Prussia as a typical German medium-sized state rather than as a Great Power.

At the core of his method, Ranke did not believe that general theories could cut across time and space. The historian had to understand a period on its own terms, and seek to find only the general ideas which animated every period of history.[19]

I found 39 citations on Ranke. Ranke identified history with political history and ignored the history of art, religion, science, etc.[20] "…the greatest of all historians of this school (Positivism)…"[21] "…it is not always treated with the intelligence, the balance, and the finesse of a Leopold Ranke."[22] "More than anyone, he transformed history into a modern academic discipline, university-based, archive-bound, and professional in that the leading proponents underwent extensive postgraduate training.[23] "All were agreed that Ranke was by no means a true historian, that he lacked originality and was dull."[24]

> "His unfortunate phrase—*wie es eigentlich gewesen*—was actually very far from what Ranke in fact considered to be the essential task of the historian, but it was seized on with remarkable avidity by successive generations of historians, who took it to mean much more than Ranke has ever intended."[25]

> "Ranke is the representative of the age which instituted the modern study of history. He taught it to be critical, to be colourless, and to be new. We meet him at every step, and he has done more for us than any other man." Lord Acton.[26]

Georg Waitz, October 9, 1813-May 24, 1886, was a German historian and politician born in Flensburg, in the duchy of Schleswig. He was the foremost pupil of von Ranke and developed an early interest in German medieval history which was to be his life's work. He eventually became a professor at the great historical school at the University of Göttingen. His major works included *German Constitutional History* (8 volumes, 1844-1878); *Schleswig-Holstein History* (1851-1854); *Lubeck under Jurgen Wullenwever and the European Politics* (1855-1856); and *Basis for Politics* (1862). He, like many others of that era, became a delegate to the Frankfurt Parliament of 1849.[27]

I found seven citations on Waitz. "But the extraordinary merit of Waitz, in my opinion, lies elsewhere, in the fact that by the most careful analysis of his sources he set limits to their application, and as far as possible avoided the use of late documents."[28]

George Waitz

Theodor Mommsen

Theodor Mommsen, November 30, 1817-November 1, 1903, was a German classical scholar, historian, jurist, politician, archaeologist and writer born in Garding, Schleswig, which is about 75 miles northwest of Hamburg. [Who among us can take credit for so many skills?] He published over 1,500 works, and effectively established a new framework for the systematic study of Roman history. He pioneered epigraphy. Are you going to look that up in the dictionary, or should I tell you? Epigraphy is the study of inscriptions in material artifacts. Mommsen's most famous work was *History of Rome*, which appeared in four volumes between 1854 and 1856. He is also well known for his *Corpus Inscriptionum Latinarum*, which would consist of sixteen volumes. He wrote five of them himself. He won the Nobel Prize in Literature in 1902 for his *History of Rome*, the only historian other than Churchill to win the literature award.[29]

I found 25 citations on Mommsen. When researching him take care not to include his historian grandsons, Hans and Wolfgang. A number of my references state that *Corpus* has more lasting value than *Rome*. "...historical profession knows Mommsen preeminently as a meticulous inquirer and inventive entrepreneur, who inspired younger men with his enthusiasm for the sources."[30]

> "It has been said that all history is contemporary history in fancy dress. As we all know, there is something in this. The great Theodor Mommsen was writing about the Roman Empire as a German liberal of the '48 vintage [revolutions over all of Europe] reflecting also on the new German Empire."[31]

> "...Mommsen, who declared in 1874 that it was a 'dangerous and harmful illusion for the professor of history to believe that historians can be trained at the University in the same way as philologists or mathematicians most assuredly can be.' The true historian, he said, was 'not trained but born.' Modern historians frequently agree with this point."[32]

Jacob Burckhardt, May 25, 1818-August 8, 1897, was a Swiss historian of art and culture, and an influential figure in the historiography of each field. He was born in Basel, Switzerland. His best known work was *The Civilization of the Renaissance in Italy* (1860). In 1867 he also published *The History of the Renaissance in Italy*. There seems to be considerable overlap between the two efforts, which I will not attempt to discern. Burckhardt was well known and respected, but turned down two professional chairs in Germany, which included Ranke's chair at the University of Berlin. He remained cool to German nationalism and to German claims of cultural and intellectual superiority.[33] Burckhardt did not first use the term renaissance, but he is generally credited with first use of it to describe a whole historical period.

I really like to read Burckhardt's *Judgments on History and Historians*, with emphasis on judgments. In 2-3 pages each, he discusses subjects in simplified and understandable terms that allow the reader to grasp the main points. When I read such books, I make vertical pencil marks in the margins on key points that I would like to review in the future. I marked about ninety percent of *Judgments*.

I found twenty-four citations on Burckhardt.

"Ranke's pupil Jacob Burckhardt once defined history as what one age finds worthy of note in another." Meinecke noted that the critical spirit of Burckhardt, who deplored the excesses of state power and forecast the evils of demagogic mass industrial society, was more relevant to the twentieth century."[34]

"One of Burckhardt's most effective practical contributions to historical writing was his emphasis on the 'style' of a particular period. Instead of making a routine inventory of institutions, political developments, diplomacy, and so on, of each of the successive eras, Burckhardt sought the 'peculiar equilibrium' which gave a certain epoch its 'hierarchy of values'" the relationship of church and state, the quality of the cultural life, the curious 'mix' that constitutes the distinctive character of a nation or an era."[35]

Burckhardt, along with Ranke and Acton, "have provoked more discussion and research than any other people, not because of actual discoveries which they made from manuscript sources, but because of their historical ideas, their principles of interpretation and their comments on the process of things in time."[36]

"Burckhardt sought to cultivate in Basel's citizens a traditionalist sensibility of a kind that would prepare them to live in a world of the unexpectedly emergent and to adapt with cosmopolitan cultural flexibility to the forces of change. The essay [later in reference book] sketches Burckhardt's particular contributions to twenty-century historical consciousness: a richly associative synchronicity in structure that is at the same time processual and undeterministic in its recognition of a diachronic trajectory."[36] [Do not try to explain that sentence to your spouse.]

Wilhelm Wattenbach, September 22, 1819-September 20, 1897, was a German historian born in Ranzau, Holstein, which is about 45 miles northeast of Hamburg, Germany. He studied philology at the universities of Bonn, Göttingen and Berlin. [Beware of those folks who studied philology.] His major effort was *The Sources of Germany History in the Middle Ages*. He was

Wilhelm Wattenbach

distinguished by his thorough knowledge of the chronicles and other original documents of the Middle ages.[37]

Ernest Renan, February 28, 1823-October 12, 1892, was a French philosopher and writer born at Tréguier, Brittany, which is about 55 miles northeast of Brest. One of his significant works was *History of Israel* (1887-1891 and two volumes posthumously). He also wrote *Life of Jesus*, which was controversial because he asserted that the life of Jesus should be written like the life of any other man, and that the Bible could be subject to the same critical scrutiny as any other historical documents, sparked a flurry of debate, and enraged the Roman Catholic Church.[39] I found 16 citations on Renan.

Ernest Renan

"For Apostolic Christianity we have a series of brilliant pictures in Renan's *Apostles* and in his *St. Paul*. All the theories propounded in these two books must not be accepted, for they have not been endorsed by subsequent research; nevertheless, their fundamental value has not been impaired. Nowhere are Renan's marvelous intuition, his insight into character, his graphic powers of description, and his style of haunting beauty and grace, to be seen to greater advantage than in the St. Paul."[40]

Léopold Victor Delisle, October 24, 1826-July 21, 1910, was a French bibliophile and historian born in Valognes, which is about 175 miles west of Paris on the Cherbourg Peninsula near the D-Day beaches. He was taken in by an antiquarian to copy manuscripts and was taught paleography. In 1852 he entered the manuscript department of the Bibliothèque Imperiale (National), and in 1874 he became the head of the Bibliothèque. He was already known as a compiler of several valuable inventories of its manuscripts. When the French government decided on printing a general catalogue of the printed books in the Bibliothèque, Delisle became responsible for this great undertaking and took an active part in the work; in the preface to the first volume (1897) he gave a detailed history of the library and its management.

Under his administration the library was enriched with numerous gifts, legacies and acquisitions, notably by the purchase of a part of the Ashburnham manuscripts. Delisle proved that the bulk of the manuscripts of French origin which Lord Ashburnham had bought in France, particularly those bought from the book-seller Barrois, had been purloined by Count Libri, inspector-general of libraries under King Louis-Philippe, and he procured the purchase of the manuscripts for the library, afterwards preparing a catalogue of them entitled *Catalogue des manuscripts des fonds Libri et Barrois* (1888), the preface of which gives the history of the whole transaction. Delisle was undoubtedly the most learned man in Europe with regard to the Middle ages, and his knowledge of diplomatics, palaeography and printing was profound. His wife was for many years his collaborator.[41] Hmmm?

The above paragraph about the Ashburnham collection is a typical example of the way manuscripts have floated around Europe for centuries. Someone made them; later someone bought, stole, or failed to return a loan; an owner's estate was sold or misplaced; another astute collector gained possession some way; the cycle of ownership repeated itself over several centuries; and then ended up in modern times in an institution (who tends to maintain possession) or an individuals estate surfaces the items. As noted by King Louis above, the French kings have been the leading conquerors in Europe for several centuries because they built and maintained a long-term national dynasty which allowed them the luxury of continuing to build their libraries. Their bibliophile minions continued the search for more acquisitions, and as a result, Paris has more fine libraries and holdings than any other city. Napoleon conquered more new lands than the kings, so his folks found new pastures from which to loot and bring back to Paris. This approach was not all bad, because the French had a long-term perspective as a nation and undoubtedly preserved the documents better than most of the earlier holders, be they individuals or smaller institutions with limited resources for the preservation task.

> Delisle "… raised drudgery to the rank of a fine art. However minute the problem might be, however limited its scope, Delisle saw it in relation to the whole field of medieval knowledge. Hence his work was always to the point. There is no waste, so that the distinction between big work and little work ceases to exist; all is informed with a peculiar quality, like the work of a great surgeon, who is neat and unflurried without pettiness."[42]

Theodor von Sickel, December 18, 1826-April 21, 1908, was a German historian born in Aken, which is about 75 miles southwest of Berlin. He, like many others of his era, participated in the 1848 Revolution and became active in Prussian politics. He spent much of his effort on developing and refining new diplomatic methods. He edited more than 1300 documents of the 10th century of Konrad I, Henry I, Otto I, and later, Otto II and Otto III.[43] Lord Acton called Sickel "the prince of critics."[44] "Sickel, while a great scholar, was the first to create popular interest in the medieval past of Austria through his editorial work and his volumes on the Saxon emperors."[45]

Theodor von Sickel

Hippolyte Adolphe Taine, April 21, 1828-March 5, 1893, was a French critic and historian born in Vouziers, which is about 115 miles northeast of Paris. *History of English Literature*, 1864, was one of his major historical works. I found fourteen citations on him. The French historian wrote, "a candidate for a history degree at the Sorbonne would not make a good impression if he quoted Taine as an authority."[46]

Hippolyte Taine

> "That great historian—a moderate without moderation, and a liberal without liberality—will long be remembered for his hair-raising descriptions of insane rationalism of the social contract, for his horror tales of the flashing blade of the guillotine, and for his interpretation of the people of the great beast…."[47]

> "Taine really does not belong to the history of thought, of philosophy, of criticism, or of historiography, but rather to that of tendencies and cultural fashions, a typical representative of the fanatical interest in the natural sciences, and especially in medicine, which, after 1850, filled a good forty years of European life, accompanied by inane efforts to remodel the whole of culture on a similar basis."[48]

John Emerich Edward Dalberg-Acton, 1st Baron Acton, commonly known as Lord Acton, January 10, 1834-June 19, 1902, was an English historian born in Naples, Italy. Contrary to the other persons in this inquiry, Acton wrote no history books. His fame rests primarily on his vast knowledge of history, his editorship of papers and journals, and his leadership of the *Cambridge Modern History*. He was eventually appointed to the Regius (Royal) Professorship of Modern History at Cambridge

University. Acton is famous for his frequently quoted statement, "Power tends to corrupt, and absolute power corrupts absolutely." This statement appears in his letter dated April, 1887, to Professor (later Bishop) Mandell Creighton. In the history of all humankind, there may be no truer statement. He also stated in the same context, "Great men are almost always bad men." He was a Roman Catholic, yet his power statement refers to Papal power in the aftermath of the Pope's infallibility decree of 1870.[49]

Lord Acton

There were twenty-four citations on Acton. "Than Lord Acton there was probably never a historian who grasped more firmly, or more trenchantly expressed, the conviction that history is a great moral teacher."[50] Acton picked the contributors to write the chapters in the *Cambridge Modern History* with the dictum to write without revealing the country, the religion or the party to which they belonged.[51] Much of Acton's fame came from his lectures as Regius Professor. The two editors of some of his lectures wrote, "Of all the previous occupants of the chair none is to be named with Acton for a career unique in interest, variety, and pathos.[52] "Acton, by his birth, his career, and his studies, and above all, his detachment, was driven to regard history from a standpoint neither English nor German, but universal."[53]

"Acton's great precept, 'Study problems, not periods.'...Scientific historians study problems: they ask questions, and if they are good historians they ask questions which they see their way to answering."[54] "By all these criteria, Lord Acton was an amateur, and so he was, a prince of amateurs."[55] "Historians such as Lord Acton who accept human responsibility and freedom often feel the need to judge the past figures they describe."[56] "Lord Acton's 'duty to the sacred, inviolable past' has a Victorian ring: the past is raped by every historian, even those with the most honorable intentions."[57]

> "Lord Acton had the reputation of being the greatest man of learning in England in the closing decades of the nineteenth century. He was the type of historian who is primarily the omnivorous reader, at home in many centuries, and familiar with the older literature as well as the new. He reflected much on this knowledge, perpetually turning it this way and that, and constantly working on it to a higher state of organization."[58]

Gustav von Schmoller, June 24, 1838-June 27, 1917, was the leader of the "younger" German school of economics and probably the most distinguished Continental (European) economist of the time around 1900. He was born in Heilbronn, which is about 75 miles south southeast of Frankfurt. Schmoller's influence on academic policy, economic and fiscal reform, and economics as an academic discipline for the time between 1875 and 1910 can hardly be overrated. Most of his works deal with *industrial history*. One of the reasons of Schmoller's being-forgotten is that his myriad of books was not translated into English, because at his time, *Anglo-American economists generally read German.* [59] I found six citations for Schmoller.

> "Schmoller, a man of endless energy and inventiveness whose interests were so wide-ranging that they embraced all of the social sciences, exerted enormous influence during the emergence of the historical school of national economics in Germany,...The task of placing the mercantilist policies of the seventeenth and eighteenth centuries in a historical setting was

successfully performed by Schmoller in another fundamental contribution;…he did succeed in making economics more historical, just as he succeeded in making history more economic."[60]

"In embarking on researches in the service of Strassburg, Schmoller performed an important service to historical effort. He opened local archives and placed his seminarists at work in them. He secured the co-operation of local officials and, in time, grants of city money for the work of publication of documents. He demonstrated how such detailed local history could be used as a test case for the study of wider economic changes."[61]

Mandell Creighton, July 5, 1843-January 14, 1901, was an English historian and ecclesiastic born in Carlisle, which is about 270 miles north northwest of London and about 22 miles south of the Scottish border. His chief works was the *History of the Papacy during the Period of the Reformation* (five volumes, 1882-1897) and *The History of the Papacy from the Great Schism to the Sack of Rome* (six volumes, 1897). He also wrote *The Early Renaissance in England* (1895); *Cardinal Wolsey* (1895); and *Life of Simon Montfort* (1876).[62] Lord Acton was so exercised about the content of Creighton's first work that Acton got into a dispute with Creighton and wrote the letter containing the famous statement about *power corrupting*.[63] See Acton above.

Mandell Creighton

Henry Preserved Smith, October 23, 1847-February 16, 1926, was an American Biblical scholar born in Ohio. He studied theology and rose to be a professor of theology. In 1892 he was tried for heresy by the Presbytery of Cincinnati, was found guilty of teaching (in a pamphlet entitled *Biblical Scholarship and Inspiration*, 1891) that there were "errors of historic fact, "suppressions of "historic truths," etc., in the Books of Chronicles, and that the "inspiration of the Holy Scriptures is consistent with the "unprofitableness of portions of the sacred writings,"—in other words, that inspiration does not imply inerrancy, and he was suspended from the ministry. In *Inspiration and Inerrancy* (1893), he reprinted the papers on which the heresy charge was made, and outlined the case. He also wrote *The Heretic's Defense: A Footnote to History* (1926)[64]

Frederic William Maitland, May 28, 1850-December 19, 1906, was an English jurist and historian. Though he suffered poor health, his intellectual grasp and wide knowledge and research gradually made him famous as a jurist and historian. Some of his works include: *Gloucester Pleas* (1884); *Justice and Police* (1885); *Domesday Book and Beyond* (1897); *Township and Borough* (1898); *Canon Law in England* (1898); and *English Law and the Renaissance* (1901). His written style was lively, and as a historian he used original sources; he was no pendant.[65] I found seventeen citations on Maitland. "Maitland's *History of English Law*, the greatest of all books on medieval England,…"[66] "Maitland is one of the immortals. He transcends all boundaries."[67] "Maitland was the greatest master of descriptive analysis that we have ever had in England."[68]

"…a medievalist's medievalist, a visibly clever man, and for most of the twentieth century the only historian to be a cult figure among his own kind."[69]

"Only Maitland was free from this censure, and what made him exceptional was his manifest willingness to tackle the most recondite and technical problems without any concession to the reader's supposed inability to grasp them, yet in language so splendidly lucid that he invariably did grasp them."[70]

Herbert Baxter Adams, April 16, 1850-July 30, 1901, was an American educator and historian born in Shutesbury, Massachusetts, which is about 24 miles north of Springfield. He spent most of his professional life at Johns Hopkins University in Baltimore, Maryland. In 1880 he began his famous seminar in history, where a large proportion of the next generations of American historians trained. Adams founded the "Johns Hopkins Studies in Historical and Political Science," the first of such series, and brought about the organization in 1884 of the American Historical Association. He was the first secretary of the AHA and remained in that position for sixteen years. If you notice his death date above, he was apparently the secretary until his health forced retirement. Adams studied at Göttingen and Berlin, and received his Ph.D. at Heidelberg, Germany, so he was well imbued with the Germanic "scientific history."[71] Gay called him the father of American graduate training.[72] In one of his seminars Baxter showed that the American lineage of liberty and democracy came from remote German villages. It was later soundly refuted by several historians, as that lineage really came from England.[73]

Herbert Baxter Adams

Paul Vinogradoff, November 18 (30), 1854-December 19, 1925, was a Russian historian born in Kostroma, which is about 200 miles northeast of Moscow. He became a professor of history at the University of Moscow, but his zeal for the spread of education brought him into conflict with the authorities, and consequently he was obliged to leave Russia. [Russian culture and authoritarianism never, never changes.] Having settled in England (December 1901), Vinogradoff brought a powerful and original mind to bear upon the social and economic conditions of early England, a subject which he had already begun to study in Moscow. Do you know why there is a "30" in Vinogradoff's birthdate? See end of next paragraph.

His *Villainage in England* (1892) is perhaps the most important book written on the peasantry of the feudal age and the village community in England; it can only be compared for value with F.W. Maitland's *Domesday Book and Beyond*. In masterly fashion Vinogradoff here shows that the villain of Norman times was the direct descendant of the Anglo-Saxon freeman, and that the typical Anglo-Saxon settlement was a free community, not a manor, the position of the freeman having steadily deteriorated in the centuries just around the Norman Conquest. The status of the villain and the conditions of the manor in the 12th and 13th centuries are set forth with a legal precision and a wealth of detail which shows its author, not only as a very capable historian, but also as a brilliant and learned jurist.[74] His original birth date was the 18th, but they gained thirteen days when Russia Europeanized its calendar in 1918, so his new date was the 30th. Russia also had several other calendar changes.

Charles Seignobos, 1854-1942, was a French historian born in Lamastre, which is about 120 miles north of Marseille. He was the author on numerous books of political history enforcing the German historical method. He had excellent linguistic skills for reading German and English. Perhaps his best known book is one he wrote with Charles-Victor Langlois, *Introduction to Historical Studies* (1897).[75]

Eduard Meyer, January 25, 1855-August 31, 1930, was a German historian born in Hamburg. His principal work was *History of Antiquity* (1884-1902) "...was the first history of the ancient world written from the sources and with the mentality commensurate with the task. He will probably rank as the foremost scholar that historical writing has produced down to our day."[76]

"We have selected a man whom we believe to be the greatest living historian. To take Meyer's contradictions and mistakes in his serious historical works is hardly warranted. His contradictions and inadequacies are due to his approach, to his historical attitude that gave his thinking inevitably a form which his deepened intellectual insight could not well accept and which only contradictions could modify."[77]

Friedrich Meinecke, October 30, 1862-February 6, 1954, was a German historian born in Salzwedel, which is about 95 miles west northwest of Berlin. He was probably the most famous German historian of his generation. He was the editor of the *Historical Periodical* (*Historische Zeitschrift*) during 1896-1935. Meinecke was best known for his work on 18th-19th century German intellectual and cultural history. The book that made his reputation was his 1908 work *Weltbürgertum und Nationalstaat* (Cosmopolitanism and the National State), which traced the development of national feelings in the 19th century.[78] I found seventeen citations on Meinecke, but used none of them.

Edward Meyer

Charles-Victor Langlois, May 26, 1863-June 25, 1929, was a French historian and paleographer who specialized in the study of the Middle ages. His 1897 work, *Introduction to the Study of History*, written with Charles Seignobos, is considered one of the first comprehensive manuals discussing the use of scientific techniques in historical research.[79] I found nine citations for Langlois.

Lewis Bernstein Namier, June 27, 1888-August 19, 1960, was an English historian, but he was really Ludwiok Niemirowski, born in Wola Okrzejska in what was then Austro-Hungary and is now Poland. It is about 55 miles southeast of Warsaw. His best known works were *The Structure of Politics at the Accession of George III*, *England in the Age* of *the American Revolution* and the *History of Parliament*. His methods of collecting personal data about members of Parliament to develop statistics about voting patterns drew considerable criticism. He made the case that the politicians cast their votes based on individual and local interests, and not just on party lines. Since he lived through the World War II era, he condemned appeasement, but did not seek to explain the reasons for it. Namier was born a Jew and held right-wing views, and was called the most reactionary British historian of his generation. His principal protégé was the left-wing historian A.J.P. Taylor, whom we shall meet later.[80] I found sixteen citations on Namier.

"E.H. Carr described him as a 'towering outsider.' Arnold Toynbee remembered him as 'a big man with a big mind.' For A.J.P. Taylor, Namier was 'a historian of genius'; and for Isaiah Berlin, 'one of the most distinguished historians of our time.' If any further confirmation of his status were needed, the compilers of the *Oxford English Dictionary* seemed to provide it. In 1976 they formally acknowledged that the verb 'to namerize,' the adjective 'namierian' and the noun 'namierization' had become integral parts of the English language."[81]

"Namierization, or the need to understand the total detail of patronage, influence, and kinship, in order to understand its superstructure of ideas, government, culture and events."[82] Namier wrote, "Men no more dreamt of a seat in the House of Commons in order to benefit humanity than a child dreamt of a birthday cake in order that others might eat in."[83]

Lessons Learned:

-Mabillon might be the father of scientific history.

-Ranke is frequently quoted, *"wie es eigentlich gewesen"* ("how it actually was").

-Mommsen pioneered epigraphy, the study of inscriptions in material artifacts.

-Burckhardt is fun to read.

-Renan said Bible should be scrutinized like other historical documents.

-Delisle was a bibliophile and compiler of books and manuscripts. Lucky fellow.

-Sickel defined and developed new diplomatic methods.

-Acton, "Power tends to corrupt, and absolute power corrupts absolutely."

-Schmoller was a leader in industrial history.

-Creighton received the letter from Acton which contained the *Power* quote.

-Maitland was a medievalist and expert on medieval law.

-Vinogradoff was an expert on feudal England.

-Namier gave his name to "Namierization, or the need to understand the total detail of patronage, influence, and kinship, in order to understand its superstructure of ideas, government, culture and events."

Chapter 11

First-Half, 20ᵗʰ Century

The authors described in this chapter were the ones whose principal productive years were in the first half of the 20ᵗʰ century. They are generally listed by birth year. At the end of this chapter are several pages which describe one of my early encounters with a history book being rewritten by someone almost ninety years later. It still sticks in my craw.

Henry Brooks Adams, February 16, 1838-March 27, 1918, was an American historian, novelist, journalist and academic born in Boston. He is best known for his autobiographical book, *The Education of Henry Adams* (1907), which I will discuss later. He was the great grandson of John Adams, the second President of the United States and the grandson of John Quincy Adams, the sixth president of the United States. Adams was his father's private secretary when Charles Francis Adams was ambassador to England, 1861-1868. While in England he read the works of John Stuart Mill, which showed the necessity of an enlightened, moral and intelligent elite to provide leadership to a government elected by the masses and subject to demagoguery, ignorance and corruption. When Adams worked as a journalist in Washington, DC, he saw

Henry Brooks Adams

himself as exposing political corruption in his writings. In 1872 he married and he and his wife were in the middle of the Washington social life. She committed suicide in 1885, apparently despondent over her father's death, and he became a changed man.

Adams was elected president of the American Historical Association for 1894, but his address, entitled "The Tendency of History" was delivered in absentia. The essay predicted the development of a scientific approach to history, but was ambiguous as to what this achievement might mean. His major work was *The History of the United States of America, 1801-1817*, (nine volumes, 1889-1891). This period covered the presidencies of Jefferson and Madison and has been praised by several historians.[1]

Now let us go to his most famous effort, *The Education of Henry Adams*. It is autobiographical, but he refers to himself in the third person. He published it in a small private edition in 1907. Only after he died was it published publicly by the Massachusetts Historical Society in 1918. It was awarded the Pulitzer Prize in 1919. It ranked first on the Modern Library's 1998 list of 100 Best Nonfiction Books and was named the best book of the twentieth century by the Intercollegiate Studies Institute, a conservative organization that promotes classical education. It was on the basis of the above awards that I read the book about five years before this current effort. The work concerned the birth of forces Adams saw as replacing Christianity. For Adams, The Virgin Mary had shaped the old world, and the dynamo represented modernity (dynamo refers to the huge electric machines he observed at the Chicago World's Fair in 1893). He covers a lot of history in the book beyond himself, and the title seems to be inappropriate. It does not cover the years 1872-1891, or his marriage. He is mightily afraid of the future and sees everything through dark glasses. He spews names around indiscriminately, apparently to impress himself and fellow intellectuals. Several examples follow:

"From Zeno to Descartes, hand in hand with Thomas Aquinas, Montaigne, and Pascal, one stumbled as stupidly as though one were still a German student of 1860." (389);

"Neither Galileo nor Kepler, neither Spinoza nor Descartes, neither Leibnitz nor Newton, any more than Constantine the Great—if so much—doubted Unity. (484);

"If Karl Pearson's notions of the universe were sound, men like Galileo, Descartes, Leibnitz, and Newton should have stopped the progress of science before 1700…" (495).

When I read it without any background, I soon decided it was the ramblings of an unsound mind recalling all the elite memories of the past and fearful of the changes to life in the dark future. If he had been living in the 1980s and 1990s, he would have been driven to madness by the rate of change in our lives that we know today. Several years ago I gave a book report on *Education* to my senior citizens learning group. When finished, someone asked for a reading recommendation. The answer was an adamant NO! It is hard to read and follow, rambling, and definitely geared to the highest academic intellectuals living in another world and isolated from reality. I found seventeen citations on Adams. Ferdinand Schevill said he was probably a congenital pessimist.[2]

"A dejected man sixty years old on undertaking the *Education*, Adams regarded himself as not a partial but a total failure and for a single reason: he had been cursed with a defective education. The core of its defect was that, elaborated in the eighteenth century, it was out of tune with the changed conditions of his lifetime."[3]

Adams was just another historian that we have met, or will meet, that searched for laws of human nature in the past so they could predict the future based on those laws. Generally they have little idea where we are going and are usually wrong if they make a forecast of the future. But they are similar to experts throughout history who tried to apply their expertise in fields not their own, but they have big egos that they couldn't possibly be wrong.

Brooks Adams, June 24, 1848-February 13, 1927, was an American historian born in Massachusetts and Henry Adams' brother. He was a critic of capitalism. He believed that commercial civilizations rise and fall in predictable cycles. First, the masses of people draw together in large population centers and engage in commercial activities. As their desire for wealth grows, they discard spiritual and creative values. Their greed leads to distrust and dishonesty, and eventually the society crumbles. In the *Law of Civilization and Decay* (1895), Adams noted that as new population centers emerged in the west, centers of world trade shifted from Constantinople to Venice to Amsterdam to London. He predicted in *America's Economic Supremacy* (1900) that New York would become the world trade center. He also wrote *The Emancipation of Massachusetts* (1887); *The Gold Standard: An Historical Study* (1894); and *The New Empire* (1902).[4] Stevens writes about Adams' *The Law*, "A cyclical theory which is undermined by some incoherent and fallacious generalizations."[5]

Thomas Frederick Tout, 1855-1929, was a British historian born in London. He was one of the two leading figures of the 'Manchester (University) History School.' He is best known for his chapters in the *Administrative History of Medieval England* (6 volumes, 1920-31), *The Political History of England, 1216-1377* (1905), and *The Place of the Reign of Edward II in English History* (1914).[6]

William Archibold Dunning, 1857-1922, was an American historian born in New Jersey. He spent his lifetime at Columbia University. His reputation is twofold: first, his scholarly studies of Reconstruction led the way to a new interpretation of that era of American history; second, his *History of Political Theories* (three volumes, 1902-20) was a brilliant survey of a hitherto unanalyzed field. Dunning not only wrote two superb studies of Reconstruction—*Essays on the Civil War and*

Reconstruction (1898) and *Reconstruction, Political and Economic, 1865-1877* (1907)—but also inspired and directed the long series of books by his students on Reconstruction in the individual states. His theory of Reconstruction, which held that the freedmen proved incapable of self-government and thus made segregation necessary, dominated historical interpretation of the era until the 1960s.[7] Dunning was elected president of the American Historical Association in 1913 and in his first address said his colleagues "recognize frankly that whatever a given age or people believes to be true *is* true for that age and that people."[8] Is that true?

Williston Walker, 1860-1922, was an American church historian born at Portland, Maine. He graduated at Amherst in 1883, Hartford Theological Seminary in 1886 and received his Ph.D. (1888) at Leipzig University in Germany. He was employed at the Hartford Theological Seminary from 1889 to 1901, when he accepted a position at Yale University. Walker's publications include: *On the Increase of Royal Power under Philip Augustus* (1888); *The Creeds and Platforms of Congregationism* (1893); *A History of the Congregational Churches in the United States* (1894); *The Reformation* (1900); *Ten New England Leaders* (1901); *John Calvin* (1906); *Great Men of the Christian Church* (1908); *French Trans-Geneva* (1909); and *A History of the Christian Church* (1918).[9] I wrote about his education and his publications to demonstrate the secular-religious historian and the breadth of his subjects. This is in contrast to most of the earlier religious writings, which tended to have strong religious biases.

Adolphus W. Ward, ?, was an English historian best known for his *A History of English Dramatic Literature to the Death of Queen Anne*. He "dominated the *Cambridge Modern History* after Acton's death and edited the *Cambridge History of British Foreign Policy* in the 1920's, and was one of the most influential men in the profession. Allegedly an interesting talker, he wrote without colour and drained the colour from others, too. On one occasion he explained the difficulties he had with a contributor's chapter by saying that 'it's a bit lively'."[10] Notice how the British have a funny way of spelling *color*. We need to thank Noah Webster for taking out many superfluous letters when he developed the American English.

The discovery of the connection between Ward and Acton in the paragraph above leads me to a digression from the usual string of unconnected historians. In 2001 I was expanding my library by visiting used-book stores to hunt for bargains. Frequently I am tempted to buy books by the pound, that is, a nice thick reference or history book that had little chance of being actually read by me, but it might be interesting sometime in the distant future. But mainly, I would be the proud owner of this *magnificent* volume. On the shelf was the two-inch thick, faded-brown, gold-lettered *Cambridge Modern History, Volume V, The Age of Louis XIV*, for $3.99. I must own it! It was published in 1908 at the University of Cambridge Press and had that musty-book smell that I love. I must own it! It was planned by the late Lord Acton, L.L.D., Regius Professor of Modern History. One of the three editors was A.W. Ward, which meant absolutely nothing to me at the time, but Lord Acton was special to me as he was the writer of, "Power corrupts, and absolute power corrupts absolutely." The book contained 763 pages of text history in reasonably small print, which meant it was chock full of great reading, if I found time. There was more good news, its bibliography contained 162 pages, and the index had 42 pages. I must own it! This volume had additional redeeming features. It was rebound in Nashville, Tennessee in June 1950, and had an embossed stamp, "Martha M. Brown Memorial Library, Tenn A. & I. State College." No current college carried that name, but the librarian at the University of Alabama in Huntsville found Martha Brown at what is now Tennessee State University in Nashville.

Now back to Acton, who was written up in the previous chapter. He was the planner of the *Cambridge Modern History* series. He selected historians to write the separate chapters and coordinated their efforts by circumscribing their subject responsibilities to prevent overlap. My *magnificent* volume has twenty-five chapters and twenty-nine authors. The authors were not all English, as Acton wanted to get the most expertise from all of Europe. Ward wrote three chapters, as well as picking up the editorship from Acton along with two others.

Hutton Webster, ?, was an American professor of sociology and anthropology at the University of Nebraska. In 1908 he wrote, *Primitive Secret Societies*, which called a study in early politics and religion. He "outlined the rudiments of the secret society in most primitive cultures as: almost exclusively male; serving as the religious, social and civil center of tribal life; requiring a series of secret, ritualistic initiations which stepped the initiated through various grades of prestige and privilege; a tendency to terrorize those that were outside of the sphere of the membership;..."[11] "...Professor Hutton Webster has shown in greater detail, it was the deeds of the gods and not of men that the early calendars were originally designed to fix and record. The methods of measuring time grew up about the need for determining the dates of tabooed or holy days and for fixing and recording the occurrence of unusual natural phenomena which were believed to have religious significance."[12] Webster was not an historian in the usual sense, but he was included to add to the understanding of time discussed in Chapter 2, Classic.

John Bagnell (J.B.) Bury, October 16, 1861-June 1, 1927, was an eminent Protestant Irish historian, classical scholar, Byzantinist and philologist born in Clontibret, which is about 65 miles north northwest of Dublin. Bury's writings, on subjects ranging from ancient Greece to the 19th-century papacy, are at once scholarly and accessible to the layman. His two works on the philosophy of history elucidated the Victorian ideals of progress and rationality which under-girded his more specific histories. He also led a revival of Byzantine history, which English-speaking historians, following Edward Gibbon, had largely neglected. Some of his works include: *History of the Later Roman Empire from Arcadius to Irene* (1889); *History of the Roman Empire From its Foundation to the Death of Marcus Aurelius* (1893); *History of Greece to the Death of Alexander the Great* (1900); and *History of the Freedom of Thought* (1914).[13] I found eighteen citations on Bury. One of the most repeated quotes from Bury is one from his inaugural address as Regius Professor of Modern History at Cambridge in 1902, as he described history as "a science, no more and no less."[14]

Frederick Jackson Turner, November 14, 1861-March 14, 1932, is widely regarded, along with Charles Beard, as one of the two most influential American historians of the early 20th century. He was born in Wisconsin. He is best known for his *The Significance of the Frontier in American History* (1893). Another important work is *The Significance of Sections in American History* (1932), which a collection of his essays. In this he argued that different ethno-cultural groups had distinct settlement patterns, and this revealed itself in politics, economics and society.[15]

Frederick Jackson Turner

"Turner's theory of the frontier asserted that a steadily westward-moving line of settlements had left an indelible impress on the American nation, and especially on the growth of American democratic institutions. Turner was wresting our history-writing from New England and resettling it in his native region, the upper Mississippi Valley. From the history of that section he was now building an image for the entire country."[16]

"Turner reputed the view of Herbert Baxter Adams, his teacher, that American institutions had germinated in the Teutonic woods. Turner saw liberty, democracy and individualism as homegrown traits, the products of the frontier experience....The Turner thesis captivated many historians because, in a single stroke, it accounted for American uniqueness and put ordinary white people, the settlers, at the center of things. It had less to offer native peoples and other victims of westward expansion."[17]

Keying off the two quotes above, the Europeans of the late 20th century (Reagan presidency) and the early 21st Century (George W. Bush presidency) do not think of Americans as New England liberals, but as American cowboys with independent action and wide-open spaces.

"The Turner thesis was to America what the Magna Carta was to the British, Charlemagne to the French, and the Teutonic tribes to the historians of the recently unified Germany. It appeared to explain certain aspects of the American story which were otherwise inexplicable. It was, nevertheless, a myth, albeit a useful and appealing one and one which provided a framework for a host of American historians. But the point is that once this law, or principle of interpretation, had been formulated, it closed the eyes of most historians to any facts which did not conform to it. Honest scholars went to the sources and found what in most instances was not there, namely, confirmation of Turner's thesis."[18]

"While the vast majority of American historians have rejected all the major premises on which Frederick Jackson Turner's frontier thesis professed to rest, one element has remained indestructible — that the frontier experience was of transcendent importance in American history. That is Turner's permanent gift; it has enlarged our understanding of our history by drawing our attention in a most dramatic way to one of its essential ingredients."[19]

Thomas Alfred Walker, 1862-1935, was an English jurist and historian. He was a fellow and historian at Peterhouse, Cambridge University. His major work was *A History of the Law of Nations* (1899).[20]

Henri Pirenne, December 23, 1862-October 25, 1935, was a leading Belgian historian born in Veriers, which is about 65 miles east southeast of Brussels. His reputation rests on three contributions to European History. First, what has become known as the *Pirenne Thesis*, concerning when the Middle Ages started, second, a distinctive view of Belgium's medieval history, and finally, a model for the development of the medieval city. The Pirenne thesis was developed while in a prisoner-of-war camp during World War I. He published it in a series of papers from 1922 to 1923 and spent the rest of his life refining it. The most famous exposition appears in his 1937 book *Mohammed and Charlemagne*.

Traditionally, historians have dated the Middle Ages from the fall of the Roman Empire in the 5th century, a theory Edward Gibbon famously put forward in the 18th century. Pirenne challenged the notion that the Germanic barbarians had caused the Roman Empire to fall. He argued that the barbarians essentially tried to continue the Roman way of life. He argued that the real break in Roman history was in the 7th century when the Islamic conquests around the Mediterranean littoral caused an economic break with Europe.

Pirenne's other major idea concerned the nature of medieval Belgium. Belgium as an independent nation state has appeared only a generation before Pirenne's birth; throughout Western history, its fortunes had been tied up with the Low Countries, which now include the Netherlands, Luxembourg and parts of Northeast France. Furthermore, Belgium lies athwart the great linguistic divide between French and Dutch. The unity of the country might appear accidental, something which Pirenne sought to disprove in his History of Belgium (1899-1932). I have gone to a little extra explanation because during the second half of 2007, the Belgians have been unable to form a government because the parties are split by language. People inside and outside Belgium wonder if there really needs to be a country named Belgium. Why not just split it in two based on language and join France and the Netherlands. I have one more insight about Pirenne in the next paragraph.

Germany invaded Belgium on August 3, 1914 during the First World War. Pirenne was arrested by the Germans in August 1916 and held in different camps until the end of the war in November 1918. He was denied books, which is hard on an historian. He learned Russian from Russian prisoners and then read Russian-language histories made available to him by the Russian prisoners. In confinement he started to write *A History of Europe* completely from memory. It presents a big-picture approach to social, political and mercantile trends, rather than a blow-by-blow chronology of wars, dynasties and incidents. After his death, his son discovered the manuscript and edited it by filling in the missing or uncertain dates.[21] Try that one while you are in prison!

Werner Sombart

Werner Sombart, January 19, 1863-May 18, 1941, was a German economist and sociologist, the head of the "Youngest Historical School" and one of the leading Continental social scientists during the first quarter of the 20th century. He was born in Ermsleben, Harz, which is about 100 miles southwest of Berlin. His major historical work is *Modern Capitalism* (1902, six volumes), which is a systematic history of economics and economic development through the centuries and very much a work of the Historical School. Another noteworthy book is *Why is there no Socialism in the United States?* (1906)[22]

James Harvey Robinson, June 29, 1863-February 16, 1936, was an American historian born in Indiana. In 1919 he was one of the founders of the New School for Social Research, of which he was the first director. Through his writings and lectures, in which he stressed the "new history" — the social, scientific and intellectual progress of humanity rather than merely political happenings — he exerted an important influence on the study and teaching of history. An editor (1892-95) of the Annals of the American Academy of Political and Social Science, he was also an associate editor of the American Historical Review and president (1929) of the American Historical Association. The new annual president of the AHA gives a presentation at his first meeting in which each one tries to set the stage for his thoughts on the direction of historical research. In a similar manner the new Regius Professor of Modern History at Oxford and Cambridge (not an annual) gives a presentation to his colleagues.[23] I found eleven citations on Robinson. He wrote *The New History* in 1912, but several historians found little of substance in it at the time or in the following years.

"Robinson's platform can be summarized in the following way. The past ought to be subordinated to the present in historical writing. The emphasis should be on the closer, not on the more distant, past because recent history has much more to say to present life and needs....This approach raised two problems, which Robinson not only did not solve but may not even have noticed. How do scientific regularities come out of relative and changing values, which he also insisted on? To what extent are historians qualified to perform the kind of operations social scientists were already demanding in their own disciplines?"[24]

Harry Elmer Barnes cited Robinson 22 times in his book that I use for my basic guide but there seems to be a lot less than meets the eye in Robinson's *New History*, except for those philosophers of history who like to argue and attack each other over the smallest minutiae (redundancy intended and needed).

Herbert Albert Laurens Fisher, March 21, 1865-April 18, 1940, was an English historian, educator and Liberal politician born in London. His major work was *Considerations on the Origin of the American War* (1934). He also wrote a three-volume *History of Europe* (1935).[25] I found ten citations for Fisher. He is frequently quoted for his succinct, "History is just one damned thing after another." The above quote was preceded by a longer frequently-cited quotation from his preface to *History*,

Herbert Fisher

"Men wiser and more learned than I have discerned in history a plot, a rhythm, a predetermined pattern. These harmonies are concealed from me. I can see only one emergency following upon another as wave upon wave, only one great fact with respect to which, since it is unique, there can be no generalizations, only safe rule for the historian: that he should recognize in the development of human destinies the play of the contingent and the unforeseen…The ground gained by one generation may be lost by the next."[26]

I will make a slight diversion here. One of my sources, *Historians' Fallacies* (1970), by David Hackett Fischer, takes H.A.L. Fisher to task for making generalizations such as his quotes above. In the citation from Fischer below he refers to historians, but if you read the daily newspaper, a magazine, or watch television news, you can observe the same generalizations. Hackett Fischer's point is well-taken, and has become one of my pet peeves while catching news.

"One might note, in Fisher's prefatorial statement, a common confusion in the author's mind between generalizations concerning the whole of history and the generalizations of a limited sort within history. A good many historians, I think, have condemned both of these things together.

The fallacy of the insidious generalization commonly occurs in a form even more insidious than Fisher's errors. Impressionistic historians, who bitterly inveigh against quantification and its dehumanizing tendencies, are quick to use the words 'few,' 'some,' 'most,' 'many,' 'singular,' 'typical,' 'exceptional,' 'common,' 'customary,' 'normal,' 'regular,' 'recurrent,' 'periodic,' 'widespread,' 'often,' and many others. Theses terms imply numbers, and numbers need counting. And yet they are used without quantification, by scholars who believe that quantifying is no part of their job."[27]

The utterances and writings of today are going to be some historian's sources of tomorrow.

George Arnold Wood, June 7, 1865-October 14, 1928, was an English Australian historian born at Salford, which is about 170 miles north northwest of London in metropolitan Manchester. After receiving his complete education in England, in 1891 he went to Australia to become Challis professor of history at the University of Sydney and remained there until his death. His major effort was an early work on Australian history, *The Discovery of Australia* (1922).[28]

Herbert George (H.G.) Wells, September 21, 1866-August 13, 1946, was an English writer of science fiction (*War of the Worlds*) as well as non-fiction. His bestselling nonfiction work (?) was *The Outline of History* (1920), which was in two volumes and began a new era of popularized world history. It was praised by Arnold Toynbee as the best introductory history available, but drew a mixed response from professional historians. I believe he should be remembered most for the following. In 1927, Florence Deeks sued Wells for plagiarism, claiming that he had stolen much of the content of the *The Outline of History* from a work, *The Web*, she had submitted to the Canadian Macmillan Company, but who held onto the manuscript for eight months before rejecting it. Despite numerous similarities in phrasing and factual errors, the court found Wells not guilty.[29] What a shame! Of course, Wells had the publisher on his side since they were equally guilty, so their lawyers managed to win the day. Never forget that Wells was an opportunistic plagiarist.

Alexander Alexandrovich Vasiliev, 1867-1953, was a Russian born and trained historian who immigrated to the United States in 1925. He was considered the foremost authority on Byzantine history and culture in the mid-20th century. His *History of the Byzantine Empire* (volume 1-2, 1928) remains one of a few comprehensive accounts of the entire Byzantine history, on a par with those authored by Edward Gibbon and Fyodor Uspensky. He also prepared and published a highly influential monograph, *Byzantium and the Arabs* (1907).[30]

Albert Pollard, December 16, 1869-August 3, 1948, was a British historian born on the Isle of Wight, which is the large island just off the southern coast near Southampton and Portsmouth. He specialized in the Tudor period and wrote about it from a political viewpoint. Later in his career, he was a major force in establishing history as an academic subject in Britain.[31]

> "Professor Pollard was also a notable scholar. There are not many historical surveys of which, fifty years after their publication, one can say they are still the best things available. But one can say just that of Pollard's volume on the history of England from 1547 to 1603. And of course his biographies of Henry VIII, Cranmer, and Wolsey remain without peer."[32]

> "That very competent scholar, A.F. Pollard, wrote biographics which all could read and many read with pleasure: but when he turned his hand to a learned article, fluency turned to stammer and proper precision to pernickety obscurity. Scholars took pride in writing for other scholars."[33]

Charles Homer Haskins, 1870-1937, was an American historian born in Pennsylvania. He is considered to be America's first medieval historian. He was a prodigy, and was fluent in Latin and Greek while still a young man. He received his Ph.D. in history at age twenty. Haskins was primarily a historian of institutions like medieval universities and governments. His works reflect an optimistic and mostly 20th century liberal view that progressive government, when staffed with the best and brightest a culture has, is the best course for society to take. His histories of the institutions of medieval Europe stress the efficiency and successes of the bureaucratic institutions, which contained implicit

Charles H. Haskins

analogy to modern nation states. That background was responsible for his selection as one of only three advisors that President Woodrow Wilson took to the Paris Peace Conference of 1919.

The word Renaissance is generally accepted as referring to the 15th century Italian Renaissance as popularized by Jacob Burckhardt. Haskins' most famous book was *The Renaissance of the Twelfth Century* (1927) He made the case that many activities contributed to a fresh and vigorous life during that period.[34] I found five citations for Haskins. I now provide a long citation from Barnes as he discusses annals and chronicles and uses a citation from Haskins' *Renaissance*:

> "An almost universal practice arose of indicating on the margin opposite each year, the events which, in the mind of the recorder, seemed to make that year most significant in the history of the locality. Charlemagne ordered the monasteries in his realms to keep regular and systematic annals. Not only were these early annals very scanty in the information they contained, since they mentioned only a few conspicuous events which occurred during the year. They were rendered still less valuable because the medieval annalist frequently considered most important for his record some insignificant miracle or the transfer of the bones of a saint, information of little value to the modern historical investigator, except in so far as it revealed the state of mind of the medieval annalist and illustrated his limited historical perspective. Professor Haskins well illustrates this by his citation of the early entries in the *Annals* of St. Gall:
>
> 709. Hard winter. Duke Gottfried died.
> 710. Hard year and deficient in crops.
> 712. Great flood.
> 714. Pippin, Mayor of Palace, died.
> 718. Charles Martel devastated Saxony with great destruction.
> 720. Charles fought against the Saxons.
> 721. Theudo drove the Saxons out of Acquitaine.
> 722. Great crops.
> 725. The Saracens came for the first time.
> 731. The blessed Bede, the presbiter, died.
> 732. Charles fought against the Saracens at Poitiers on Sunday.
>
> As Professor Haskins observes, there is no further mention in the entry for the year 732 of the battle of Tours, ranked as one of the decisive battles of the world."[35]

The battle probably took place between Poitiers and Tours, and the names are interchangeable as far as this battle, but Tours is the most common usage. Of course, at that time there was no idea that it would be one of the most significant battles in history.

Mikhail Ivanovich Rostovtzeff (Rostovtsev), November 10, 1870-October 20, 1952, was one of the 20th century's foremost authorities on ancient Greek, Iranian and Roman history. He was born in Zhitomir, Ukraine, which is about 80 miles west of Kiev. He was educated at the universities of Kiev and St. Petersburg, and then as a full professor at St. Petersburg University. While working in Russia, he was recognized as the world's preeminent authority on ancient history of South Russia and Ukraine. He immigrated to the United States in 1918 and eventually became a professor at Yale University in 1925. He oversaw all archaeological activities of Yale in general and the excavations of Duro-Europos in particular. Duro-Europos (Fort Europos) was a Hellenistic (Greek) and Roman walled city on an escarpment ninety meters above the right bank of the Euphrates River in modern

Syria. Rostovtzeff is remembered as the first historian to examine the ancient economies in terms of capitalism and revolutions. *Social and History of the Roman Empire* (1926) and *A Social and Economic History of* the *Hellenistic World* (1941) were his pioneering works that transferred the attention of historians from military or political events to global economic or social problems that had been formerly hidden behind their surface.[36]

Johan Huizinga, December 7, 1872-February 1, 1945, was a Dutch historian born in Groningen, which is about 90 miles northeast of Amsterdam. He started as a student of comparative linguistics and gained a good command of Sanskrit. He wrote his doctoral thesis on the role of the jester in Indian drama in 1897. His interest turned to medieval and Renaissance history, as apparently he realized that the book market on Indian jesters was limited. Huizinga had an esthetic approach to history, where art and spectacle played an important part. His most famous work is *The Waning of the Middle Ages* (1919), where he reinterprets the later Middle ages as a period of pessimism and decadence rather than rebirth. He was held in detention by the Nazis from 1942 until his death in 1945.[37]

Gaetano Salvemini, November 8, 1873-September 6, 1957, was an Italian anti-fascist politician, historian and writer born in Molfetta, which is about 130 miles east of Naples on the Adriatic Sea. After being arrested in 1925 for anti-fascist activities, he left Italy and eventually wound up in the United States. From 1930 to 1948 he lectured in History at Harvard University and became a U.S. citizen in 1940. His notable writings include *The Fascist Dictatorship in Italy* (1928), *Under the Axe of Fascism* (1936) and *Prelude to World War II*.[38]

Gaetano Salvemini

Carl Lotus Becker, 1873-1945, was an American historian born in Iowa. He is best known for his *The Heavenly Gate of the Eighteenth-Century Philosophers* (1932), in which his assertion that philosophers in the "Age of Reason" relied far more upon Christian assumptions than they cared to admit has been influential, but has also been much attacked. He also wrote *The Beginnings of the American People* (1915); *The Eve of the Revolution* (1918); *The Declaration of Independence* (1922); *Everyman His Own Historian* (1935); and *Cornell University: Founders and Founding* (1943).[39] "In 1910 the American philosopher, Carl Becker, argued in deliberately provocative language that 'the facts of history do not exist for any historian till he creates them.'"[40] I found 12 citations on Becker. He was more of a philosopher of history than a historian, therefore, I will give him little attention.

George Peabody Gooch, 1873-1968, was a British historian and political journalist born in London. His first work, *English Democratic Ideas in the Seventeenth Century* (1898), is a classic in its field as he viewed even the most fanatical of his historical subjects with liberal toleration. His most lasting achievement was *History and Historians in the Nineteenth Century* (1913) in which he assessed the writings of over 500 historians, tracing the emergence of the scientific method in historical research, portraying the masters of the craft, and analyzing their influence on their times. His other major contribution to historiography was *Recent Revelations of European History* (1927; revised periodically until 1940), in which he discussed authors and surveyed the publication of documents and memoirs concerned with pre-1914 diplomacy.[41] "The historiography of nationalism and the rise of scholarly and critical historical writing are splendidly described and intelligently evaluated in..." Gooch's *History*.[42]

James Thomson Shotwell, 1874-1965, was a Canadian-born American history professor born in Strathroy, Ontario. He is perhaps best remembered for his instrumental role in the creation of the International Labor Organization (ILO) in 1919, as well as for his guiding influence promoting inclusion of a declaration of human rights in the UN Charter. He wrote *The Diplomatic History of the Canadian Boundary, 1749-1763,* with Max Savelle, *At the Paris Peace Conference* (1937), *War as an Instrument of National Policy* (1929), and *The Origins of the International Labor Organization* (1934). Shotwell was also the editor of a series of 150 volumes of the *Social and Economic History of the World War.*[43] "Professor Shotwell had rivaled James Harvey Robinson as a leader of the new history in the United States.[44]

In the Classical chapter, under Justus of Tiberius, I make a slight excursion into the never-ending issue of who wrote the Bible and when it was written. An excerpt from Shotwell's *An Introduction to the History of History* (1922) is provided below to stimulate your thoughts.

"Let us imagine, for instance, that instead of the Jewish scripture we are talking of those of the Greeks. Suppose that the heritage of Hellas has been preserved to us in the form of a Bible. What would be the character of the book? We should begin, perhaps, with a few passages from Hesiod on the birth of the gods, and the dawn of civilization mingled with fragments of the *Iliad* and both set into long excerpts from Herodotus. The dialogues of Plato might be given by Homeric heroes and the text of the great dramatists (instead of prophets) be preserved, interspersed one with another and clogged with the uninspiring comments of Alexandrian savants. Then imagine that the sense of their authority was so much obscured as centuries passed, that philosophers –for philosophers were to Greece what the theologians were to Israel—came to believe that the large part of this composite work of history and philosophy had been written down by Solon as the deliverance of the oracle of Apollo of Delphi. Then, finally, imagine that the text became stereotyped and sacred, even the words taboo, and became the heritage of alien peoples who knew nothing more of Greek history than what this compilation contained. Such, with some little exaggeration, would be a Hellenic Bible, after the fashion of the Bible of the Jews. If the comparison be a little overdrawn there is no danger but that we shall make sufficient mental reservations to prevent us from carrying it too far. Upon the whole, so far as form and structure go, the analogy holds remarkably well."[45]

Georges Lefebvre, August 6, 1874-August 28, 1959, was a French historian born in Lille, which is about 125 miles north of Paris. He was considered in his day to be the leading authority on the French Revolution. A lifelong socialist, he became more and more influenced by Marxism about the time of the Second World War and was influenced by the Marxist idea that history should be concerned with economic structures and class relations. His accounts of the French Revolution published in 1939 to mark the sesquicentennial of the 1789 Revolution were suppressed by the French Vichy government and 8,000 copies of it were ordered burned. *The Coming of the French Revolution* (English translation) (1947) had established it as a clear, yet subtle, classic.[46] Lefebvre was an honorary member of the American Historical Association.[47]

Charles Austin Beard

Charles Austin Beard, November 27, 1874-September 1, 1948, was an American historian. He was widely regarded, along with Frederick Jackson Turner, as one of the two most influential American historians in the early 20th century. He is mostly widely known for his radical re-evaluation of the Founding Fathers of the United States, whom he believed were more motivated by economics than by philosophical principles. As the leader of the "Progressive School" of historiography, he introduced themes of economic self-interest and economic conflict regarding the adoption of the Constitution and the transformations caused by the Civil War. Beard's most influential book was the wide-ranging and bestselling *The Rise of American Civilization* (1927) and its two sequels, *America in Midpassage* (1939) and *The American Spirit* (1943), written with his wife, Mary Ritter Beard.

Beard's economic approach lost favor in the history profession after 1950 as conservative scholars demonstrated the serious flaws in Beard's research, and attention turned away from economic causation. Beard was one of the leading proponents of United States non-intervention in what became World War II. After the war, Beard's last work, *President Roosevelt and the Coming of the War* (1948), blamed Roosevelt for lying to the American people and tricking them into war. It generated angry controversy as internationalists denounced Beard as an apologist for isolation. As a result, Beard's reputation of history collapsed among liberal historians who had admired him. His whole reputation of history came under widespread attack, though a few leading historians such as Beale and Woodward clung to the Beardian interpretation of American history.[48] It must be quite exhilarating to be known as the founder of a "School," especially one with the name "Progressive," after apparently reinterpreting the evidence to find a dollar-sign under every motive. Then, there is the downside when almost everyone deserts you. I found thirteen citations on Beard. "Historians are always led by their present-day concerns; the truth does not simply emerge from an unprejudiced of neutral reading of the sources, even if such a thing were possible..."[49] Beard turned this "methodological radicalism to the explicit political purposes of the Progressive movement, arguing that the history's fundamental task was to clear away the entrusted myths and dogmas which prevented America, in their view, from reforming and adapting to the modern industrial age."[50] Beard always maintained that his work on the Constitution only added a new dimension, and in no way nullified the political, ideological or institutional treatments.[51]

To gain a sense of Beard's perspective on writing history, Carl Schorske, as a student at Columbia University, saw Beard at the American Historical Association's 1935 convention,

> "Beard poured forth his scorn for the pusillanimity and triviality of a historical scholarship that had lost all sense of its critical function in the civic realm. He gave me a formula for a fine scholarly career: 'Choose a commodity, like tin, in some African colony. Write your first seminar paper on it. Write your thesis on it. Broaden it to another country or two and write a book on it. As you sink your mental life into it, your livelihood and esteemed place in the halls of learning will be assured.'"[52]

Carter G. Woodson, December 19, 1875-April 3, 1950, was an African American historian, author, journalist and founder of Black History Month. He was born in Virginia. He is considered the first to conduct a scholarly effort to popularize the value of Black History. He recognized and acted upon the importance of people having an awareness and knowledge of their contributions to humanity and left behind an impressive legacy. In 1912 he received his Ph.D. in history from Harvard University. In 1915 Woodson and Jesse E. Moorland co-founded the Association for the Study of African American Life and History.[53]

George Macaulay Trevelyan, February 16, 1876-July 21, 1962, was an English historian born in Stratford-upon-Avon (of Shakespeare fame), which is about 80 miles northwest of London. He was the great-nephew of Thomas Babington Macaulay, whom we met earlier. His doctoral dissertation was *England in the Age of Wycliffe* (1899). Wycliffe lived in the 14th century and was the first translator of the Vulgate Latin Bible into English, for which his bones were dug up 44 years after his death so they could be burned, as all heretics' bones were, and cast into the waters. The Roman Catholic Church wanted to be sure that heretics' bones were not available as relics because the Church venerated its own relics.

Trevelyan wrote *England Under the Stuarts* (1904), *The Recreations of an Historian* (1919); *Lord Grey of the Reform Bill* (1920); *History of England* (1926), *The English Revolution 1688-1698* (1938); *English Social History: A Survey of Six Centuries* (1944); and a trilogy on Garbaldi (1907, 1909, 1911). Trevelyan's history is engaged and partisan. Of his Garibaldi trilogy, "reeking with bias", he remarked in his essay *Bias in History*, "Without bias, I should never have written them at all. For I was moved to write them by a poetical sympathy with the passions of the Italian patriots of the period, which I retrospectively shared."[54] After our previous chapter about writing objectively, isn't it refreshing to learn about writing with a strong bias, objectivity be damned! About three months before this paragraph, I read a 600-page biography of Garabaldi. What a man, a fighter, and a patriot!

I found sixteen citations on Trevelyan. His *English Social History* "reached a mass audience such as no political history of England has ever reached. To play down battles, in the midst of the greatest battle the world has yet seen, was no mean feat, yet Trevelyan did it to acclaim."[55] His *Wycliffe*, "...brilliant work..." "It possesses all those qualities of style and matter which have won for its author a place with the two or three greatest historical writers of the present century."[56] The Garibaldi trilogy, "are safely established among the world's greatest books of history."[57]

> "Trevelyan was essentially a *nationalist* historian; his major works were histories of England, and his objection to the 'scientific' conception of history was grounded not least on the fact that it was German....The Germanizing tendencies of the period, he thought, were authoritarian and hierarchical, and unsuited to the liberal traditions of his own country."[58]

Eduard Fueter, November 13, 1876-November 20, 1928, was a Swiss historian born in Basel. He was the author of *History of Ancient Italy* (1914), *History of European National Systems, 1492-1559* (1919) and *World History of the Last Hundred Years 1815-1920* (1921).[59] I found nine citations on Fueter. He also wrote *History of the New Historiography* (1911).[60]

Joan Wake, ?-?, was an English woman interested in preserving county records. In 1920 she established the Northamptonshire Record Society. It was an attempt to stem the wholesale loss of local historical records in the aftermath of the First World War. It currently has about one thousand individual and corporate members.[61] Northamptonshire is about 65 miles north northwest of London. Without records historians would be out of business, so we must remember and support the record keepers.

Lucien Febvre, July 22, 1878-September 11, 1956, was a French historian born in Nancy, which is about 200 miles east of Paris. In 1929, he and Marc Bloch founded the journal *Annales d'histoire, économique et sociale*, from which the names of their distinctive style of history was taken.[62]

> "...the historians making up the *Annales* school rebelled against the prevailing forms of academic history. Rejecting the narrow emphasis on politics, war, and diplomacy, What Lebvre disparaged as histoire *événementielle*, or event-oriented history, the *Annales* group strove to grasp more fully the many dimensions of human reality. As historiographer Ernst Breisach explained, these French scholars envisioned a new, more complete history, inclusive of all aspects of human life. To achieve the aim, they developed a larger repertoire of

investigative techniques, many derived from sociology, and called for extensive cooperation with 'comrades and brothers' across all the social and human sciences. As Febvre expressed the goal, 'Down with all barriers and labels! At the frontiers, astride the frontiers, with one foot on each side, that is where the historian has to work, freely, usefully.'...

...Two traits figured conspicuously in their works. First, *Annalistic* scholars typically built their analyses around a conception of collective consciousness. Termed *mentalité*, this phenomenon focused attention on the mental and psychological characteristics of groups of people at specified times and places and thus moved historians beyond constricted and sometimes myopic concerns for individuals. According to this approach, the collectivity counted most in the formulation of explanations leading to total history. Second, in similar fashion, *Annalistic* historians employed a notion of the *longue durée*, that is, the long duration. Actually a conception of time, this term depicted the structural continuities intruding upon the course of historical change. The *longue durée*, among other things, comprised the land, the sea, the climate, and the vegetation. These conditions represented stabilizing influences on the conduct of human affairs and impelled a slower pace or rhythm than the transitory events of politics, war, and diplomacy. They determined, moreover, the manner of life."[63]

I found ten citations on Lebvre. His field was the Renaissance and Reformation in France: his best-known work was *The Problem of Unbelief in the Sixteenth Century*. (Hist, Vin, 162) Lebvre also wrote *Martin Luther, A Destiny; The Coming of the Book: The Impact of Printing 1450-1800*, co-written with H.J. Martin; and *A Geographical Introduction to History*.[64]

Frederick Maurice Powicke, 1879-1963, was an English medieval historian. He was Regius Professor of History at Oxford from 1929. He was a difficult man, small of build and with something of a Napoleon complex. Having failed as a student at Oxford he was determined to reinvigorate history there, although he believed that medieval history was the only sort worth studying. That being said, he unquestionably made Oxford the leading center in the century for historical study.[65] "To him, more than any single historian, we owe the advances which have been made recently in the study of ecclesiastical records, although his own published works in this field have not been quantitatively as great as in some others."[66]

Richard Henry Tawney, 1880-1962, was an English writer economist, historian, social critic and a university professor born in Calcutta, India. His historical works reflected his ethical concerns and preoccupations in economic history. He was profoundly interested in the issue of the enclosure of land in the English countryside in the sixteenth and seventeenth centuries (although this was later shown to have occurred on a larger scale and with more important consequences in the fifteenth century) and in Max Weber's thesis on the connection between the appearance of Protestantism and the rise of capitalism, "Protestant work ethic". Tawney wrote *The Agrarian Problem in the Sixteenth Century* (1912), *Secondary Education for All* (1922), *Land and Labor in China* (1932), and his most influential, *Religion and the Rise of Capitalism* (1926).[67]

Charles Webster, July 25, 1886-1961, was a British historian and diplomat. He wrote his two major books on the foreign policy of Lord Castlereagh, the first (1925) covered the period 1815-1822 and the second (1931) the period 1812-1815. He also wrote *The Congress of Vienna; The Foreign Policy of Palmerston; The Art and Practice of Diplomacy;* and *Britain and the Independence of Latin America*.[68]

Marc Léopold Benjamin Bloch, July 6, 1886-June 16, 1944, was a French historian born in Lyon, which is about 225 miles southeast of Paris. His specialty was the medieval period. In 1929, Bloch founded, with Luciaen Febvre, the important Annales School, which was explained under Febvre above. In 1924 Bloch published one of his most famous works, *The Magic Kings* or *The Royal Touch: Sacred Monarchy and Scrofula in England and France.* Scrofula is swelling of the lymph nodes in the neck. He collected, described and studied the documents pertaining to the ancient tradition that the kings of the Middle ages were able to cure the disease of scrofula simply by touching people suffering from it. This work by Bloch had a great impact on the social history of the Middle ages but also on cultural anthropology. Bloch has had a lasting influence in the field of historiography through his unfinished manuscript, *The Historians Craft*, which he was working on when he was killed by the Nazis. Bloch's book and Edward Carr's *What is History?* are often considered two of the most important historiographical works of the 20th century.[69] I found thirteen citations on Bloch, and his *Craft* is in my library.

Pieter Catharinus Arie Geyl, December 15, 1887, December 31, 1966, was a Dutch historian born in Dordrecht, which is about 15 miles southeast of Rotterdam. He is best known for his studies in early modern Dutch history and in historiography. In October 1940 the SD (Security Service) of the German SS took Geyl hostage in retaliation for what the Germans alleged to be maltreatment of Germans in the Dutch East Indies. Geyl spent thirteen months at the Buchenwald concentration camp. Even after his release from Buchenwald, Geyl continued to be held by the Germans at a Dutch prison until he was released for medical reasons in February 1944. In 1945 Geyl became the chair of history at the University of Utrecht. In his opening address, he called for his students to disprove political and cultural myths that could lead to movements like National Socialism. Geyl was a critic of the *Sonderweg* interpretation of German history that argued that Nazi Germany was the inevitable result of the way German history developed. In particular, Geyl defended the German historian Leopold von Ranke against the charge of being a proto-Nazi.

Geyl is best known as a critic of the British historian Arnold J. Toynbee, who maintained that he had discovered "laws" of history that proved how civilizations rise and fall. Geyl often debated Toynbee both on the radio and in print. He accused Toynbee of selective use of evidence to support pre-conceived notions, and of ignoring evidence that did not support his thesis. In addition, Geyl considered Toynbee's theory to be simplistic, ignoring the full complexity of the past; he regarded Toynbee's theory of "Challenge and Response" to explain historical change as too loose and a catch-all definition. Finally, Geyl was opposed to Toynbee's claim that Western civilization was in terminal decline.

Geyl's most famous book was *Napoleon For and Against* (1946, English, 1948), an account of how French historians of different ages and views have regarded the French Emperor. From Napoleon's time to the present French historians have presented Napoleon as either a Corsican adventurer who brought death and destruction to France or as a patriotic Frenchman who brought glory and prosperity. Geyl used his book to advance his view that all historians are influenced by the present when writing history and thus all historical writing is transitory. In Geyl's view, there never can be a definitive account for all ages because every age has a different view of the past. For Geyl the best that historians could do was to critically examine their beliefs and urge their readers to do likewise. Geyl felt that history was a progress of "argument without end," but did not feel that this meant that an "anything goes" interpretation of history was acceptable.[70] As I process Geyl I am about ninety percent through the initial processing of my historians and starting to understand historiography. Considering all the controversies, arguments, and back-biting over who is "right," I definitely agree with Geyl's opinions in this paragraph. I found ten citations on Geyl.

Gerhard Albert Ritter, April 6, 1888-July 1, 1967, was a German conservative historian born in Bad Sooden-Allendorf, which is about 100 miles north northeast of Frankfurt. In 1935 he wrote a sympathetic biography of Martin Luther, which established his reputation. Later, he wrote biographies of Prussian statesman Karl vom Stein and King Frederick II of Prussia. Ritter was one of the few involved in the July 20 Plot of 1944 who was not liquidated by the Nazis. After World War II he wrote *Europe and the German Question*, which denied that the Third Reich was the inevitable product of German history. This was a common theme among German historians after the war. I shall go no further on that. In 1959, Ritter was elected an honorary member of the American Historical Association in recognition of what the A.H.A. described as Ritter's struggle with totalitarianism and he was the fifth German so honored by the A.H.A.[71]

Walter Prescott Webb, April 3, 1888-March 8, 1963, was born in Texas and noted for his groundbreaking historical work on the Western Hemisphere (Frontier), *The Great Plains* (1931). This work was a comparison of the European culture, society and economics with the new frontier of the American West. He also launched the project that produced the *Handbook of Texas*.[72]

Robin George Collingwood, February 22, 1889-January 9, 1943, was a British philosopher and historian born in Cartmel Fell, which is about 230 miles north northwest of London. Collingwood is most famous for his book *The Idea of History* (1946), which was collated from various sources soon after his death by his pupil, T.M. Knox. The book came to be a major inspiration for philosophy of history in the English-speaking world. It is extensively cited, leading one commentator to ironically remark that Collingwood is coming to be "the best known neglected thinker of our time." He also wrote six other publications after he died. Collingwood also wrote several normal histories about the Romans in Britain.[73] If you study books you will find that death is not a reason to stop publishing your notes. I do not use many citations from Collingwood, but identify many from other historians. I've tried not to get too deep into the philosophy of history. Vincent spent nine pages discussing Collingwood, which are beyond the scope of my work.

R. G. Collingwood

Collingwood wrote, "History is the re-enactment in the historian's mind of the thought whose history he is studying."[74] That definitely describes my efforts, particularly when I'm reading about someone from the days before the printing press (1454).

> "Scissors-and-paste historians study periods; they collect all the extant testimony about a certain limited group of events, and hope in vain that something will come of it. Scientific historians study problems: they ask questions, and if they are good historians they ask questions which they see their way to answering." R.G. Collingwood[75]

Arnold Joseph Toynbee, April 14, 1889-October 22, 1975, was a British historian born in London. His major work was a twelve-volume analysis of the rise and fall of civilizations, *A Study of History*, (1934-1961) Toynbee presented history as the rise and fall of civilizations, rather than the history of nation-states or of ethnic groups. He identified his civilizations according to cultural rather than national criteria. Thus, the "Western Civilization", comprising all the nations that have existed in Western Europe since the collapse of the Roman Empire, was treated as a whole, and distinguished from both the "orthodox" civilization of Russia and the Balkans, and from the Greco-Roman civilization that preceded it. When a civilization responds to challenges, it grows. When it fails to respond to a challenge, it enters its period of decline. Toynbee argued that "Civilizations die from suicide, not by murder." Hugh Trevor-Roper described Toynbee's work as a "Philosophy of Mish-Mash," which was a clear assault on Toynbee's reputation.[76] I found twenty citations on Toynbee. Fischer points out that Toynbee's style was to use many superfluous words to describe things and people. D.C. Somervell managed to shrink Toynbee's twelve volumes to two, largely by striking out the adjectives.[77]

"The work was hailed by the press as "an immortal masterpiece" and "the greatest work of our time." Yet professional historians, foremost among them Pieter Geyl, a thoughtful writer on modern historiography as well as a leading specialist on the history of the Netherlands, were deeply skeptical. Geyl charged that Toynbee simply selected the evidence he wanted and picked out a few arbitrary strands from the tangled skein of historical fact.[78]

"Toynbee's suggested program of comparing the rise and fall of civilizations was ruined by his extreme theological premises which made his work a theodicy rather than a history."[79]

"It was as though Toynbee had broken faith with a cardinal tenet of the profession by abandoning the empirical spirit in which he had begun his work for a tone that bordered on the polemical. Especially significant were the objections to Volume XI, *The Inspirations of Historians.*" A number of critics upbraided Toynbee for interjecting a personal note into his work. They accused him of egotism and vainglory in recounting the steps by which he had become a historian; they declared that such autobiographical elements had no place in a scholarly treatise.[80]

"...denounced by critics as 'filled with conjuring tricks,' intellectual hanky panky,' and 'a terrific perversion of history.'"[81]

Harry Elmer Barnes, June 15, 1889-August 25, 1968, was an American historian. He was associated with Columbia University most of his career. He is considered to have been a pioneer of historical revisionism, meaning the use of historical scholarship to challenge and refute the narratives of history promulgated by the state and the elite, most often in opposition to Whig history or as Barnes himself termed it, "court history." Long regarded as a leader of the progressive intelligentsia, Barnes joined many of its intellectual leaders such as Charles Beard in opposing from the left the New Deal and, at the price of their reputations, American entry into World War II. In the years following the war, he argued that Hitler did not want to go to war and that Roosevelt had deliberately provoked Pearl Harbor. He also questioned many aspects of the Holocaust, but did not attempt to deny or defend it, arguing that all sides were guilty of equally awful atrocities.[82] In 1937 he wrote *A History of Historical Writing.* I have been using his 1963 revised version of that book as my guide for chapters and to help order my chronological writing sequence.

Herbert Butterfield, October 7, 1900-July 20, 1979, was a British historian and philosopher of history born in Oxenhope, which is about 180 miles north northwest of London. He was at Cambridge University from 1928 to 1979. His main interests were historiography, the history of science, eighteenth century constitutional history, Christianity and history, and the theory of international politics. He is mainly remembered for his slim volume entitled *The Whig Interpretation of History* (1931). In *The Whig Interpretation of History*, Butterfield defined "whiggish" history as essentially teleological: "the tendency of many historians to write on the side of Protestants and Whigs, to praise revolutions provided they have been successful, to emphasize certain principles of progress in the past and to produce a story which is the ratification if not the glorification of the present." He had in mind especially the historians of his own country, but his criticism of the retroactive creation of a line of progression toward the glorious present can be, and has subsequently been, applied more generally.

He found Whiggish history objectionable because it warps the past to see it terms of the issues of the present, to squeeze the contending forces of, say, the mid-seventeenth century into those which remind us of ourselves most and least, or to imagine then struggling to produce our wonderful selves. They were, of course, struggling, but not for that. Whiggishness is too handy a 'rule of thumb' by which the historian can select and reject, and can make his points of emphasis.[83] That is astoundingly profound, because even I understand it. Remember all those historians, especially in the Nationalisn chapter, that went to great pains to show how far back their ancestry went, especially to someone noble like the Greeks and Saxons, so they could show how noble they were today. I found seventeen citations on Butterfield.

Lessons Learned:

-Henry Brooks Adams and his *The Education of Henry Adams*, which I do not recommend.

-Brooks Adams, brother of Henry above.

-Dunning was noted for his controversial Reconstruction studies.

-Bury, frequently cited, wrote about the ancient Romans and Greeks.

-Turner was highly influential about America's westward movement.

-Pirenne had ideas about the Middle Ages, Belgian history and wrote while in a WW I prisoner-of-war camp.

-Robinson was a philosopher of history who believed the past should be subordinated to the present.

-Fisher could not find the harmonies and rhythms than other historians found.

-Wells was a plagiarist.

-Vasiliev was a foremost expert on Byzantine history.

-Haskins is considered to be America's first medieval historian.

-Rostovtzeff was recognized as the world's preeminent authority on ancient history of South Russia and Ukraine.

-Huizinga decided the book market on Indian jesters was limited.

-Gooch wrote about other historians, as I am.

-Lefebvre was a leading authority on the French Revolution.

-Beard was the leader of the "Progressive School" of historiography.

-Trevelyan's histories are engaged and partisan.

-Febvre and Bloch founded the *Annales* School.

-Tawney was an economic historian.

-Bloch and Febvre founded the *Annales* School. Bloch was killed by the Nazis.

-Geyl challenged Toynbee.

-Collingwood was a noted philosopher of history.

-Toynbee "discovered" cycles in the rise and fall of civilizations.

-Barnes was a leader of the progressive intelligentsia and his book was an outline for my book.

-Butterfield's *Whiggish* history should be reviewed and understood. It is not too difficult.

This is the story that was mentioned under William of Malmsbury in the chapter, A of B.

...I bought *Bibliomania in the Middle Ages, Being Sketches of Bookworms, Collectors, Bible Students, Scribes and Illuminators, from Anglo-Saxon and Norman periods, to the Introduction of Printing into England; with Anecdotes illustrating the History of the Monastic Libraries of Great Britain in the Olden Time,* by F. Somner Merryweather (288 pages), sometime in 2002. It was a 1933 edition revised and edited by H.B. Copinger from materials compiled by his father, Walter A. Copinger, the first president of the Bibliographical Society in England. Both Copinger's were apparently manuscript experts and collectors. H.B. Copinger was a London barrister. An Introductory Note to the edition stated, in part: "His intention had been evidently to rewrite some of the chapters, and a great part of the work was revised, much of the controversial portion being erased. Mr. Merryweather appears to have been a Protestant of the old school, and many of his denunciations are not, perhaps, in the best taste."

...What exactly is a Protestant of the old school? Could it be someone who denounced some of the practices and activities of the Roman Catholic Church? Is there a new school of Protestants who ignore Roman Catholicism? This has bugged me for four years, and so in 2006 I finally bought a copy of the original 1849 version to discover what was written by Merryweather, but now eliminated from current versions as seen by the holier-than-thou censors, Copinger and son. What follows is an examination of the words missing or added in the 1933 edition, edited by Copinger, from the original of 1849. The page numbers draw from both versions, the deletions are from Merryweather's version and the additions are from Copinger's.

-Preface, page 1, "and believe me when I once for all affirm, that if I admire the monk, I feel no sympathy with the evils of his system; but award praise only when I deem it due to the erudition of the scholar, or to the piety of the Christian."

-Chapter I: Copinger substituted "We" for Merryweather's "I" consistently throughout the book. Why did Copinger do that? Perhaps he thought it was a better style. Maybe he now thought of himself as an equal co-author, and so the "we." When I do my writing and write "I," it is because I really meant that I was alone in that thought. Are there other possible reasons?

-Page 2 (top): "nor let it be deemed ostentation when I say, that the literary anecdotes and bookish memoranda now submitted to the reader, have been taken, and the references to the authorities from whence they are derived have been personally consulted."

-Page 3 (top): "They were fanatics, blind and credulous – I grant it."

-Page 3 (top): "But let not the Protestant reader be too hastily shocked. I am not defending the monastic system, or the corruptions of the cloister – far from it. I would see the usefulness of man made manifest to the world: but I can find in the functions of the monk much that must have been useful in those dark days of feudal tyranny and lordly despotism."

-Page 4: *footnote left out.

-Copinger added from middle of his page 32 to middle of page 34 some value-added information about manuscripts and persons.

-Page 18, 2/3rd down: "but, on the other hand, although the monks possessed many excellent qualities, being the encouragers of literature, the preservers of books, and promulgators of civilization, we must not hide their numerous and palpable faults, or overlook the poison which their system of monarchism *ultimately* infused into the very vitals of society. In the early centuries, before the absurdities of Romanism were introduced, the influence of the monastic orders was highly beneficial to our Saxon ancestors, but, in after ages, the Church of England was degraded by the influence of the fast growing abominations of Popedom. She drank copiously of the deadly potion, and became the blighted and ghostly shadow of herself. Forgetting the humility of her divine Lord, she sought to imitate the worldly splendor and arrogance of her Sovereign Pontiff. These evils too obviously existed to be overlooked; but it is not my place to further expose them; others have done all this, lashing them painfully for their oft-told sins. Frail humanity glories in chastising the frailty of brother man. But we will not denounce them here, for did not the day of retribution come? And was not justice satisfied?"

-Copinger's page 44, added: "About the year 220 Alexander, Bishop of Jerusalem, built a library there for the preservation of the epistles of learned ecclesiastical persons written one to another, and their commentaries on the Holy Scriptures. And in what manner Origen was assisted in literary labors we learn from Eusebius, who tells us that he had more than seven notaries appointed for him, who every one in his turn wrote that which he uttered; and as many more scriveners, together with maidens well exercised and practiced in penning, who were to write copies (Eccles.Hist. Pamphilas lib. 6, cc. 20 and 21)."

-Copinger's page 43 added 18 lines that were not in Merryweather.

-Page 25-6: "But hence arose a circumstance which gave full exercise to their mental powers, and compelled the monk in spite of his timidity to think a little for himself. Unfortunately the fathers, venerable and venerated as they were, after all were but men, with many of the frailties and all the fallibilities of poor human nature; the pope might canonize them, and the priesthood bow submissively to their spiritual guidance, still they remained for all but mortals of dust and clay, and their bulky tomes yet retain the swarthiness of the tomb about them, the withering impress of humanity. Such being the case we, who do not regard them quite so infallible, feel no surprise at a circumstance which sorely perplexed the monks of old, they unchained and unclasped their cumbrous "Works of the Fathers," and pored over those massy expositions with increasing wonder; surrounded by these holy guides, these fathers of infallibility; they were like strangers in a foreign land, did they follow this holy saint they seemed about to forsake the spiritual direction of one having equal claims to their obedience and respect; alas! For poor old weak tradition, those fabrications of man's faulty reason were found, with all their orthodoxy, to clash woefully in scriptural interpretation. Here was a dilemma for the monkish student! Whose vow of obedience to patristical guidance was thus sorely perplexed, he read and reread, analyzed passage after passage, interpreted word after word; and yet, poor man, his laborious study was fruitless and unprofitable! What Bible student can refrain from sympathising with him amidst these torturing doubts and this crowd of contradiction, for we owe to it more than my feeble pen can write, so immeasurable have been the fruits of this little unheeded circumstance. It gave birth to many a bright independent declaration, involving pure lines of scripture interpretation, which appear in the darkness of those times like fixed stars before us; to this, in Saxon days, we are indebted to the labours of Ælfric and his anti-Roman doctrines, whose soul also sympathised with a later age by translating portions of the Bible into the vulgar tongue, thus making it accessible to all classes of the people. To this we are indebted for all the good that resulted from those various heterodoxies and heresies, which sometimes disturbed the church during the dark ages but which wrought much ultimate good, by compelling the thoughts of men to dwell on these important matters. Indeed, to the instability of the fathers, as a sure guide, we may trace the origin of all those efforts of the human mind, which cleared the way for the Reformation, and relieved man from the shackles of these spiritual guides of the monks."

-Copinger's page 44 added: "Fifty years were sometimes employed to produce a single volume, and evidence of which occurred at a sale of Sir Wm. Burrell's books in 1796. Among these was a manuscript Bible, beautifully written on vellum and illuminated, which had taken the writer half a century to execute. The writer, Guido de Jars, began it in his fortieth year, A.D. 1294, in the reign of Philip the Fair, as appeared by the writer's own autograph in the front of the book. Occasionally we meet with ecclesiastics in high offices writing out the Bible. Thus Wiebert, who became Bishop of Hildesheim in the year 880, wrote a Bible with his own hand. The chronicler who records the fact, and who probably wrote in the twelfth century, says, 'Bibliothecam Quæ adhuc in monasterio servatur, propria manu alaboravit.' Olbert, who was Abbot of Gembloux until the year 1048, wrote out a volume containing the whole of the Old and New Testaments."

-Copinger's page 53 added: "In the year 1300 the pay of a common scribe was about one half-penny a-day. (See Stevenson's Suppl. at Bentham's Hist. Of the Church of Ely, p. 51.) At this time there were in Milan about fifty persons who lived by copying. At Bologna it was also a regular occupation at fixed price, and the price for copying a Bible was eighty Bolognese livres, three of which were equal to two gold florins."

-Merryweather's page 36, middle paragraph, was interrupted by Copinger's addition of a page (62) and a half (63) of pricing information.

-Copinger's pages 64-5 about details of manuscripts are new and were inserted at the beginning of Merryweather's page 37.

-Copinger's pages 67-68 main paragraph was added, but it was value-added about the details of manuscripts.

-Copinger's page 69 was new value-added details into the middle of Merryweather's p39.

-Copinger's page 74, lines 7-19, new value-added.

-Copinger's bottom of page 74 and top page 75 added to end of Merryweathers's end of Chapter IV.

-Copinger deleted from Merryweather's bottom page 41 and top page 42: "and I think, from the notes now lying before me, and which I am about to rearrange in something like order, the reader will form a very different idea of monkish libraries than he previously entertained." I object to this segment for two reasons: first, the sense of Merryweather's struggle with organization is lost, and therefore, reader is cheated out of the empathy for the author; and, second, Merryweather's intent to shift the reader's perception of the monkish libraries is lost, which of course, is Copinger's book theme to erase all of Merryweather's opinions of Catholic Church practices and activities.

-Copinger's page 77, 2nd paragraph and page 78, top paragraph are value-added between Merryweather's page 42, 2nd and 3rd paragraphs.

-Copinger's page 83, 6th line from bottom at "transubstantiation," he adds 8 lines ending at top of page 84, but deletes 26 lines from Merryweather's page 47, ending at bottom line ending, "to still better..." I have italicized some of the words that apparently offended the seemingly Catholics, Copinger and son. The deleted words are:

> "...for he there expressly states, in terms so plain that all sophistry of the Roman Catholic writers cannot *pervert its obvious meaning, that the bread and wine is only typical of the body and blood of our Savior.*
>
> To one who has spent much time in reading the lives and writings on the monkish theologians, how refreshing is such a character as that of Ælfrics. Often, indeed, will the student close the volumes of those old monastic writers with a sad, depressed, and almost broken heart; so often will he find *men who seem capable of better things*, who here and there breathe forth all the warm aspirations of a devout and Christian heart, *bowed down and groveling in the dust*, as it were, to *prove their blind submission to the Pope, thinking poor fellows!* – for from my very heart I pity them, - that by doing so they were preaching that humility so acceptable to the Lord.
>
> Cheering then, to the heart it is to find this monotony broken by such an instance, and although we find Ælfric occasionally diverging into the *paths of papistical error*, he spreads a ray of light over the gloom of those Saxon days, and offers pleasing evidence that Christ never forsook his church; that even amidst the peril and darkness of those monkish ages there were some who mourned, though it might have been in a monastery, *submissive to a Roman Pontiff, the depravity and corruption with which the heart of man had marred it.*"

-Copinger's page 94 added lines 4-14.

-Copinger's pages 101-2 added last paragraph, "France was...Departing scholasticism."

-Copinger's page 127 substitutes "six hundred years" for Merryweather's "five hundred years."

-Copinger's page 133 added all but the first six lines and first paragraph on page 134, which is considered value-added.

-Copinger deleted most of Merryweather's pages 92-94 and first paragraph on page 95. The substance was about history, but not directly pertaining to books.

-Copinger added material to bottom of his page 146 and top page 147, which correlated to the middle of Merryweather's p.100, and was value-added information.

-Copinger provided value-added material to the bottom of page 148 and top of page 149.

-Copinger added a few lines at bottom of pages 150, 151 and 154.

-Copinger deleted from Merryweather's page 111, "…and remind us of the more recent wonders wrought by the Jesuit missionaries in India." A footnote about the Jesuits was also deleted from page 111.

-Copinger deleted Merryweather's second paragraph on page 132,

> "Bishop Carpenter built a library for the use of the monastery of Exeter Church, in the year 1461, over the charnal house; and endowed it with £10 per annum as a salary for an amanuensis. But the books deposited there were grievously destroyed during the civil wars; for on the twenty-fourth of September, 1642, when the army under the Earl of Essex came to Worcester, they set about "destroying the organ, breaking in pieces divers beautiful windows, wherein the foundation of the church was lively historified with painted glass;" they also "rifled the library, with the records and evidences of the church, tore in pieces the Bibles and service books pertaining to the quire." Sad desecration of ancient literature! But the reader of history will sigh over many such examples.

It is assumed that Copinger deleted the passage because the damaging action was authorized by King Henry VIII, as part of his major effort to loot the Catholic churches to gain their wealth for himself and his courtiers, as well as destroy the property and will of those who still opposed his Anglican faith.

-Copinger added pages 196-97 (page and a half), "This Ina…on his seventh year," which was value-added information about Ina of Glastonbury Abbey. My wife and I visited the ruins of Glastonbury Abbey in 1998, which is about 110 miles southeast of London.

-Copinger added bottom of page 197 and all of page 198 as value-added about catalog of volumes at Glastonbury Abbey.

-Copinger deleted Merryweather's second paragraph on page 147, (italics added for suspect words that Copinger was apparently unhappy with)

> "But is it not distressing to find that this talented author, no superior in other respects to the crude compilers of monkish history, cannot rise above the superstition of the age? Is it not deplorable that a mind so gifted could rely with *fanatical zeal upon the verity of all those foul lies of Rome called 'Holy" miracles*; or that he could conceive how God would vouchsafe to *make his saints ridiculous in the eyes of man*, by such *gross absurdities* as tradition records, but which Rome

deemed worthy of canonization; but it was then, as now, so difficult to conquer *the prejudices of early teaching*. With all our philosophy and our science, great men cannot do it now; even so in the days of old; they were brought up in the *midst of superstition*; sucked it as it were from their mother's breast, and fondly cradled in its belief; and as soon as the infant mind could think, parental piety dedicated it to God; *not, however, as a light to shine before men, but as a candle under a bushel*; for to *serve God and to serve monarchism were synonymous expressions* in those days."

At the same place Copinger substituted several value-added lines about William of Malmsbury's works.

-Copinger provided value-added material at bottom of page 210 and 2/3rds of page 211.

-Copinger added 26 value-added lines in the middle of page 214.

-Copinger added an 8-line paragraph at the top of page 22.

-Copinger deleted Merryweather's page 160 from the 3rd line, "Yet how cheering....to the 3rd line on page 161, ...me in mind of..."

"Yet how cheering it is to find that the Bible was studied in this little cell; and I trust the monk often drew from it many words of comfort and consolation. Where is the reader who will not regard these instances of Bible reading with pleasure? Where is the Christian who will not rejoice that the Gospel of Christ was read and loved in the turbulent days of the Norman monarchs? Where is the philosopher who will affirm that we owe nothing to this silent but effectual and fervent study? Where is he who will maintain that the influence of the blessed and abundant charity – the cheering promises, and the sweet admonitions of love and mercy with which the Gospels overflow – aided nothing in the progress of civilization? Where is the Bible student who will believe that all this reading of the Scriptures was unprofitable because, forsooth, a monk preached and taught it to the multitude?

Let the historian open his volumes with a new interest, and ponder over their pages with a fresh spirit of inquiry; let him read of days of darkness and barbarity; and as he peruses on, trace the origin of the light whose brightness drove away the darkness and barbarity away. How much will he trace to the Bible's influence; how often will he be compelled to enter a convent wall to find in the gospel student the one who shone as a redeeming light in those old days if iniquity and sin; and will he deny to the Christian priest his gratitude and love, because he wore the cowl and mantle of a monk, or because he loved to read of saints whose lives were mingled with lying legends, or because he chose a life which to us looks dreary, cold, and heartless. Will he deny him a grateful recollection when he reads of how much good he was permitted to achieve in the Church of Christ; of how many a doubting heart he reassured; of how many a soul he fired with a true spark of Christian love; when he reads how the monk preached the faith of Christ, and how often he led some wandering pilgrim into the path of vital truth by the sweet words of the dear religion which he taught; when he reads that the hearts of many a stern Norman chief was softened by the sweetness of the gospel's voice, and his evil passions were lulled by the hymn of praise which the monk devoutly sang to his Master in heaven above. But speaking of the existence of the Bible among monks puts me in the mind of..."

-Copinger deleted the opening 12 lines of Merryweather's Chapter XI. "

"The efficacy of "Good Works" was a principle ever inculcated by the monks of old. It is sad to reflect, that vile deeds and black intentions were too readily forgiven and absolved by the Church on the performance of some *good deed*; or that the monks should dare to shelter or to gloss over those sins which their priestly duty bound them to condemn, because forsooth some wealthy baron could spare a portion of his broad lands or coffered gold to extenuate them. But this forms one of the dark stains of the monastic system; and the monks, I am sorry to say, were more readily inclined to overlook the blemish, because it proved so profitable to their order."

-Copinger deleted 6 lines near the bottom of page 173, "During my search among the old manuscripts quoted in this work, this fact has been so repeatedly forced upon my attention; that I am tempted to regard it as an important hint, and one which speaks favourably for the love of books and learning among the cowled devotees of the monasteries."

-Copinger provided a long value-added paragraph from 1/3rd of page 248 to the middle of page 249.

-Copinger value-added a list of manuscript catalogs at the bottom of page 264 and the top of page 265.

-Copinger value-added to the top of page 272 information about the volumes in Saint Paul's Cathedral, which were probably destroyed during the Great Fire of London in 1666.

-Copinger deleted the 2nd paragraph of page 208,

"I am well aware that many other names might have been added to those mentioned in the foregoing pages, equally deserving remembrance, and offering pleasing anecdotes of a student's life, or illustrating the early history of English learning; many facts and much miscellaneous matter I have collected in reference to them; but I am fearful whether my readers will regard this subject with sufficient relish to enjoy more illustrations of the same kind. Students are apt to get too fond of their particular pursuit, which magnifies in importance with the difficulties of their research, or the duration of their studies. I am uncertain whether this may not be my own position, and await further in the annals of early bibliomania."

-Copinger deleted the last sentence of the first paragraph, page 209, "A merry sound no doubt, was the crackling of those "popish books" for protestant ears to feed upon!"

Copinger deleted the last paragraph of page 209, all of page 210 and 12 half of page 212 to …can live again."

"Some may accuse me of having shown too much fondness – of having dwelt with a too loving tenderness in my retrospection of the middle ages. But in the course of my studies I have found much to admire. In parchment annals coeval with the times of which they speak, my eyes have traversed over many consecutive pages with increasing interest and with enraptured pleasure. I have read of the old deeds worthy of an honored remembrance, where I least expected to find them. I have met with instances of faith as strong as death bringing forth fruit in abundance in those sterile times, and gloring God with its lasting incense. I have met with instances of piety exalted to the heavens – glowing like burning lava, and warming the cold dull cloisters of the monks. I have read of many a student who spent the long night in exploring the mysteries of the Bible truths; and have seen him sketched by a monkish pencil with his ponderous volumes spread around him, and the oil burning brightly by his side. I have watched him in his little cell thus depicted on the ancient parchment, and have sympathized with his painful difficulties in acquiring true knowledge, or enlightened wisdom, within the convent walls; and then I have read the pages of his fellow monk – perhaps, his book-companion; and heard what *he* had to say of that poor lonely Bible student, and have learnt with sadness how often truth had been extinguished from his mind by superstition, or learning cramped by his monkish prejudices; but it has not always been so, and I have enjoyed a more gladdening view on finding in a monk a Bible teacher; and in another, a profound historian, or pleasing annalist.

As a Christian, the recollection of these cheering facts, with which my researches have been blessed, are pleasurable, and lead me to look back upon those old times with a student's fondness. But besides piety and virtue, I have met with wisdom and philanthropy; the former, too profound, and the latter, too generous for the age; but these things are precious, and worth remembering; and how can I speak of them but in words of kindness? It is these traits of worth and goodness that have gained my sympathies, and twined round my heart, and not the dark stains on the monkish page of history; these I have always strove to forget, or to remember them only when I thought experience might profit by them; for they offer a terrible lesson of blood, tyranny and anguish. But this dark and gloomy side is the one which from our infancy has ever been before us; we learnt it when a child from our tutor; or at college, or at school; we learnt it in the pages of our best and purest writers; learnt; that in those days nought existed, but bloodshed, tyranny, and anguish; but we never thought once to gaze at the scene behind, and behold the workings of human charity and love; if we had, we should have found that the same passions, the same affections, and the same hopes and fears existed then, as now, and our sympathies would have been won by learning that we were reading of brother men, fellow Christians, and felloe-companions in the Church of Christ. We have hitherto looked, when casting a backward glance at those long gone ages of inanimation, with the severity of a judge upon a criminal; but to understand them properly we must regard them with the tender compassion of a parent; for if our art, our science, and our philosophy exalts us far above them, is that a proof that there was nothing admirable, nothing that can call forth our love on that infant state, or in the annals of our civilization at its early growth?

But let it not be thought that if I have strove to retrieve from the dust and gloom of antiquity, the remembrance of old things that are worthy; that I feel any love for the superstition with which we find them blended. There is much that is good connected with those times; talent even that is worth imitating, and art that we may be proud to learn, which is beginning after the lapse of centuries to arrest the attention of the ingenious, and the love of these, naturally revive with the discovery; but we need not fear in this superstition and weakness of the middle ages; that the veneration for dry bones and saintly dust, can live again."

Chapter 12

Second-Half, 20th Century

Well, this is the last chapter of personalities. There are many more historians available during this era. But they all seem so commonplace compared to many of the folks in earlier chapters. Modern historians and history books are now just commodities. The earlier historians plowed new ground, developed new theories and wrote under significant handicaps of material accessibility and publisher production processes. The modern historians are just repeating history to make more money for their publisher and themselves. But, we must all remember what the great British lexicographer, Samuel Johnson said, "Sir, no man but a blockhead ever wrote except for money."

Samuel Eliot Morison, July 9, 1887-May 15, 1976, was an American historian born in Boston. He was noted for producing works of maritime history that were both authoritative and readable. A sailor as well as a scholar, he garnered numerous honors, including two Pulitzer Prizes, two Bancroft Prizes, and the Presidential Medal of Freedom. The US military had not prepared for a full-scale history during World War I. It was decided to do so during the Second World War and attached professional historians to all branches of the US military. Morison, a professor of history at Harvard University, was commissioned as a lieutenant commander in the Naval Reserve as a historian. The result was the unmatched *History of United States Naval Operations in World War II*, a work in fifteen volumes that covered every aspect of America's war at sea, from strategic planning and battle tactics to the technology of war and the exploits of individuals in conflict. In recognition of his achievements, the Navy promoted Morison to the rank of Rear Admiral (Reserve).

Samuel Eliot Morison

Morison and Henry Commager Steele wrote *The Growth of the American Republic* in 1930, which became a widely used textbook. Delegations of African-Americans asked that racist language be removed from the 1950 edition. Language such as, "Sambo and pickanninies" were used. Another statement: "Although brought to America by force, the incurably optimistic Negro soon became attached to the country, and devoted to his white folks." The above and other similar judgments were echoes of the thesis of *American Negro Slavery* by Ulrich Bonnell Phillips. This view, popularized by most white historians until the mid-twentieth century, relied on the one-sided personal records of slave-owners and portrayed slavery as a mainly benign institution.[1]

Morison won his Pulitzer Prizes for *Admiral of the Ocean Sea* (1943) and *John Paul Jones* (1960). His Bancroft Prizes were for *The Rising Sun in the Pacific* (1949) and *The European Discovery of America: The Northern Voyages* (1971)

David Hackett Fischer takes Morison to task:

"…who believes deeply in 'history as a literary art.' In an essay published under that title, he urges young historians not to 'bore and confuse the reader with numerous 'buts,' 'excepts,' 'perhapses,' 'howevers,' and 'possibilies.' Instead they are advised to tell beautiful stories for the aesthetic intoxication of their readers. But this, I would think, would be storytelling in more senses than one. A historian who omits all the ugly 'buts,' 'excepts,' 'perhaps,' etc., is falsifying the record. I do not mean to suggest that Morison is a deliberate falsifier—far from it. But his method has a falsifying effect. It is profoundly dysfunctional to serious historical study."[2]

Edward Hallett Carr, June 28, 1892-November 3, 1982, was a British historian, journalist and international theorist born in London. He wrote a fourteen-volume work, *History of Russia* (1950-78). He also wrote *What is History?* (1961), which is one of my frequent references. Vincent describes *What is History?* as combining chattiness, Leftishness, lack of rigor, and thorough skepticism.[3]

Camille-Ernest Labrousse, 1895-1988, was a French historian specializing in social and economic history. He established a historical model centered on three nodes: economic, social and cultural, inventing the quantitative history sometimes now called *Cliometrics*. Not using biographies and the narrative accounts of individuals, he applied statistical methods and influenced a whole generation. Labrousse was not strictly a member of the Annales School of historians, who were influenced by the preconceptions of Marxist historiography to satisfy him, but he collaborated in their efforts to create a new human history centered in historical demography.[4] I found five citations on Labrousse.

"His *Sketch of the Movement of Prices and Revenues in the 18th Century France* (1933) dealt with prices 1701-1817; leading up to *The Crisis of the French Economy* (1944) which emphasized the economic crisis of the late 1780s as a precondition of the [French] Revolution."[5]

Fernand Braudel, August 24, 1902-November 27, 1985, was a French historian born in Luméville-en-Ornois, which is about 120 miles northeast of Paris. He was a student of Lucien Febvre, the co-founder of the Annales School and eventually became his successor. The Annales School of historiography concentrated on meticulous analysis in the social sciences. In 1939 Braudel joined the French army but was captured in 1940 and became a prisoner of war in a camp near Lübeck, Germany near the Baltic Sea. There, working from memory, he put together his first work, *The Mediterranean and the Mediterranean World in the Age of Philip II*, in three volumes which first appeared in 1949. His most famous work is *Capitalism and Material Life, 1400-1800* (1979). It is a broad-scale history of the pre-industrial modern world, presented in minute detail demanded by the school called cliometrics focusing on how people made economics work. Like all his major works, it mixes traditional economic material with much description of the social impact of economic events on everyday life, and gives much attention to food, fashion, social customs and similar areas. He gives importance to the lives of slaves, serfs and peasants, as well as the urban poor, and shows their contributions to the wealth and power of their respective masters and society. Braudel has been considered one of the greatest of those modern historians who have emphasized the role of large socio-economic factors in the making and telling of history.[6] I found nine citations for Braudel.

Henry Steele Commager, October 25, 1902-March 2, 1998, was an American historian born in Pennsylvania. He wrote or edited over forty books and over 700 journalistic essays and reviews. He is well-known for his collaboration with Samuel Eliot Morison, described previously under Morison. He also wrote *Theodore Parker: Yankee Crusader* (1936) and *The Empire of Reason: How Europe Imagined and America Realized the Enlightenment* (1977).[7]

Fischer takes Commager to task in Commager's *The American Mind: An Interpretation of American Thought and Character Since the 1880s* (1950) for listing at least 35 thoughts and characteristics to sixty million Americans (1880) as if they all were exactly the same. Maybe many did, but not all sixty million as one.[8] From what I learned researching my genealogy, as my father's side was around the oil fields of western Pennsylvania and my mother's were farmers in northwestern Ohio, many of Commager's characteristics did not apply.

Alan John Percivale (A.J.P.) Taylor, March 25, 1906-September 7, 1990, was a renowned English historian born in Birkdale, which is on the Irish Sea about 12 miles north of Liverpool. He was perhaps the best-known British historian of the 20th century and probably one of the most controversial. He is deserving of one of the longest of my Wikipedia articles, with good reason. In the 1920s, his mother was a member of the Comintern (Communist International) and one of his uncles a founding father of the British Communist Party. His mother was a suffragette, feminist and advocate of free love who practiced her teachings via a string of extra-marital affairs. Taylor himself was a member of the British Communist Party from 1924 to 1926. He had a great environment for being a *troublemaker*, italics purposeful.

His first book was in 1934, *The Italian Problem in European Diplomacy, 1847-49*. He had been under the influence of Lewis Namier. Taylor's autobiography in 1983 acknowledged his intellectual debt to Namier, he portrayed Namier as a pompous bore. *Troublemaker.* During the 1930s, as the rhetoric heated up between Britain, Germany, and the Soviet Union, he had strong views on everybody and every international happening, and let everybody know about his views. Too complex to be covered here, but he was a *troublemaker*. His books number over thirty, he edited many more and was one of the first television historians. He was opposed to the American revival of West Germany, but said not a word about the Soviet invasion of Hungary in 1957. He condemned the Korean and Vietnam Wars. He was fearless in championing unpopular people and causes. *Troublemaker.*

In 1954, he published his masterpiece, *The Struggle for Mastery in Europe 1848-1918,* and followed it up with *The Trouble Makers* in 1957, a critical study of British foreign policy. In 1961, he published by far his most controversial book, *The Origins of the Second World War*, which earned him a reputation as a revisionist. He argued that Hitler was not just an ordinary German leader, but was also a normal Western leader no better or worse than Stresemann (German), Chamberlain (English) or Dadalier (French). Hitler did not want or plan war, it was just an unfortunate accident caused by mistakes on everyone's part. The reaction was almost unanimously negative and set off a huge storm of controversy and debate that lasted for years. *Troublemaker.*

Taylor had a famous rivalry with the right-wing historian Hugh Trevor-Roper (which you will meet just below), with whom he often debated on television. One of the more famous exchanges took place in 1961. Trevor-Roper said "I'm afraid that your book *The Origins of the Second World War* may damage your reputation as a historian," to which Taylor replied "Your criticism of me would damage your reputation as a historian, if you ever had one."[9] *Hell hath no fury like an historian scorned.*

Before I started this inquiry, I had read a 491-page book about Taylor by Kathleen Burk, titled *Troublemaker.* Never has a title been so understated. I found twelve citations on Taylor.

> "When, exceptionally, a historian like A.J.P. Taylor made what he liked to call 'snap judgment' and issue statements of seemingly dogmatic finality about complex historical issues, it is clear that these were intended to provoke his readers into thinking about the subject rather than to convince then that he was telling the absolute truth about it."[10]

"It is a fairly safe assumption that the brilliance and clarity of Taylor's literary style, the eminent readability of his works, will support any quest for immorality. After all, there are not many men who can write fascinating bibliographies. Some of his wit may fade with time, but the powers of narration should evoke admiration among future generations of students seeking effective ways to organize and present their historical findings."[11]

Fritz Fischer, March 5, 1908-December 1, 1999, was a German historian born in Ludwigsstadt, which is about 115 miles east northeast of Frankfurt. He is best known for his analysis of the causes of World War I. In his book *Germany's Aims in the First World War* (1961, English, 1966), he argued that Germany had deliberately instigated the First World war in an attempt to become a world power. For most Germans at this time, it was acceptable to believe that Germany had caused World War II, but not World War I, which was still widely regarded as a war forced upon Germany. He was criticized and his publisher's offices were firebombed.[12]

C. (Comer) Vann Woodward, November 13, 1908-December 17, 1999, was a pre-eminent American historian focusing primarily on the American South and race relations. He is considered, along with Richard Hofstadter and Arthur Schlesinger, Jr., to be one of the most influential historians of the postwar era, 1940s-1970s, both among scholars and the general public. He was born in Arkansas. In 1974, the House Committee on the Judiciary asked Woodward for a historical study of misconduct in the previous administrations and how the Presidents responded. Woodward led a group of fourteen historians and they produced a thorough 400-page report in less than four months, *Responses of the Presidents to Charges of Misconduct*. This was during Nixon's Watergate scandal and eventual resignation. Woodward won the Pulitzer Prize in 1982 for *Mary Chesnut's Civil War*, an edited version of Mary Chesnut's Civil War diary. He won the Bancroft Prize for *The Origins of the New South*. Martin Luther King Jr. called *The Strange Career of Jim Crow* "the historical bible of the civil rights movement."[13]

Jack H. Hexter, May 25, 1910-December 8, 1996, was an American historian born in Memphis, Tennessee. He was a specialist in Tudor and seventeenth century British history and is well known for his comments on historiography. I am using two of his works, *Reappraisals in History: New Views on History and Society in Early Modern Europe* (1961) and *On Historians* (1979).[14]

Dame Cicely Veronica Wedgwood OM DBE, July 20, 1910-March 9, 1997, was an English historian born in Northumberland, which is about 250 miles north of London and the most northeast shire in Britain and borders with Scotland. She generally goes by C.V. or Veronica on her publications and references. She became a specialist in the English Civil War and the early 17th century. She was highly regarded in academic circles and her books are widely read. *The King's Peace* (1955) was probably her most notable book. Her biography *William the Silent* was awarded the 1944 James Tait Black Memorial Prize. She produced at least fourteen other books.[15]

Hugh Redwald Trevor-Roper, Baron Dacre of Glanton, January 15, 1914-January 26, 2003, was an English historian born in Glanton, Northumberland, which is about 280 miles north of London. He was a notable historian of Early Modern Britain and Nazi Germany. His early career was defined by his political stand-up performances which were deemed offensive and racist. Trevor-Roper's first book was his 1940 biography of Archbishop William Laud, in which Trevor-Roper challenged many of the prevailing perceptions surrounding Laud. Laud was the Archbishop of Canterbury, 1573-1645, and was an outspoken opponent of Puritanism. Laud was executed for treason during the English Civil War for vigorously supporting King Charles I and pushing the Anglican Church as the only church. The Scottish Presbyterians and the Puritans were not happy. He was executed by the Long Parliament despite having a pardon by the King.

In 1945, Trevor-Roper was ordered by the British government to investigate the circumstances of Adolf Hitler's death and to rebut the claims of the Soviet Union that Hitler was alive and living somewhere in the West. The ensuing investigation resulted in Trevor-Roper's most famous book, 1947's *The Last Days of Hitler*, in which he traced the last ten days of the Führer's life.

He was the Regius Professor of Modern History at Oxford University, 1957-1980. He consolidated his reputation as an authority of the Third Reich with books such as *Hitler's Table Talk* (1953) and *The Goebbels Diaries* (1978). He was famous for his disputes with Lawrence Stone and Christopher Hill about whether the gentry (aristocracy or landed class) got better or worse economically in the 17th century. He was involved in other controversies with contemporary historians.

In 1983 Trevor-Roper authenticated the so-called *Hitler Diaries*, which later forensic examination proved to be a fake. He was under pressure from *The Sunday Times* and along with others to authenticate the work. The opinion among experts in the field was by no means unanimous; even David Irving, widely accused of Nazi sympathies, decried them as forgeries. His colleagues at Peterhouse College at Oxford, where he was Master, started to call him "Lord Faker." He had been awarded a life peerage as Lord Dacre in 1979.

Trevor-Roper's endorsement of the alleged Hitler diaries raised questions in the public mind not only about his perspicacity as a historian but also about his integrity, because *The Sunday Times*, a newspaper to which he regularly contributed book reviews and in whose parent company he held a financial interest, had already paid a considerable sum for the right to serialize the diaries. Lord Dacre denied any dishonest motivation, explaining that he had been given certain assurances as to how the diaries had come into possession of their "discoverer" — and that those assurances had been lies. It was after this incident that *Private Eye* nicknamed Trevor-Roper *Hugh Very-Ropey*.[16] You may draw your own conclusions. I found thirteen citations on Trevor-Roper.

Daniel Joseph Boorstin, October 1, 1914-February 28, 2004, was an American historian, professor, attorney and writer born in Atlanta. He served as the U.S. Librarian of Congress from 1975 until 1987. He wrote more than twenty books, including a trilogy on the American experience and one on world intellectual history. The final book of his trilogy, *The Americans: The Democratic Experience* received the 1974 Pulitzer Prize. The other two in the trilogy are *The Americans: The Colonial Experience* and *The Americans: The National Experience*. He also wrote another trilogy, *The Discoverers*, *The Creators* and *The Seekers*, which attempt to survey the scientific, philosophic and artistic histories of humanity respectively.[17]

Daniel Boorstin

Henry Stuart Hughes, May 16, 1916-October 21, 1999, was an American historian, professor and activist born in New York City. His Ph.D. thesis was *The Crisis of the Imperial French Economy, 1810-1812*. His biography is mostly about his peace activism. His major works include: *An Essay of Our Times* (1950); *Oswald Spengler: A Critical Estimate* (1952); *The United States and Italy* (1953); *Contemporary Europe: A History* (1961); and *Prisoners of Hope: The Silver Age of the Italian Jews, 1924-1974* (1983).[18]

"The intellectual historian H. Stuart Hughes has leveled the charge that historians in the United States 'seem to have forgotten—if they ever learned—the simple truth that what one may call progress in their endeavors comes not merely through the discovery of new materials but at least as much through a *new reading* of materials already available.' Hughes of course has a strong vested interest in asserting this 'simple truth,' since he has never discovered any new material himself in any of his publications but devoted his entire career to going over old ground."[19] Take that!

Richard Hofstadter, August 6, 1916-October 24, 1970, was an American historian born in New York. One of the leading public intellectuals of the 1950s, his works include *The Age of Reform* (1955) and *Anti-intellectualism in American Life* (1963) - both of which won the Pulitzer Prize, the former for History and the latter for General Non-Fiction. He also wrote *Social Darwinism in American Thought, 1860-1915* (1944), *The American Political Tradition* (1948) and *The Paranoid Style in American Politics* (1964). He joined the Young Communist League in the early 1930s and the Communist Party in 1938. He wrote at the time:

> "I join without enthusiasm but with a sense of obligation... My fundamental reason for joining is that I don't like capitalism and want to get rid of it. I am tired of talking... The party is making a very profound contribution to the radicalization of the American people... I prefer to go along with it now."

By 1939 he became disillusioned with the Communist Party, but still held his view, "I hate capitalism and everything that goes with it." Hofstadter later moved to the right and became part of the "consensus school." Later he became more conservative.[20] I can only imagine how his writings were influenced by his hatred of capitalism.

> "Indeed, the record of Hofstadter's best-known books shows an almost uninterrupted pattern of interpretative overstatement and of positions that Hofstadter himself would later have to back away from or modify. In a sense, Hofstadter conducted his political and historical education in public. He is remembered for a series of brilliant but inadequate books, all written as a young man."[21]

Eric John Ernest Hobsbawm, June 9, 1917-, is a British Marxist historian and author born in Alexandria, Egypt. He was a long-standing member of the now defunct Communist Party of Great Britain. He is primarily an economic historian. One of his interests is the development of traditions and his work is a study of their construction in the context of the nation state. He argues that many traditions are invented by national elites to justify the existence and importance of their respective nation states. He speaks English, German, French, Spanish and Italian and reads Dutch, Portuguese and Catalan. His works include *The Age of Revolution: 1789-1848* (1962); *Industry and Empire* (1968); *Bandits* (1969); *The Age of Capital, 1848-1875* (1975); *The Invention of Tradition* (1983; editor, with Terence Ranger); and *The Age of Empire* (1987).[22]

Arthur M. Schlesinger, Jr.

Arthur M. Schlesinger, Jr., October 15, 1917-February 28, 2007, was an American historian and social critic whose work explored the liberalism of American political leaders including Franklin D. Roosevelt, John F. Kennedy and Robert F. Kennedy. He was born in Columbus, Ohio. He wrote at least twenty-eight books, including *A Thousand Days* (Kennedy administration) (1965), a trilogy on Franklin Roosevelt's administration, and *The Imperial Presidency* (1973). He won the Pulitzer Prize twice and numerous other awards.[23]

Lawrence Stone, December 4, 1919-June 16, 1999, was an English historian of early modern Britain, born in Epsom, which is about 16 miles southwest of downtown London. He is noted for his work on the English Civil War, and marriage. Stone served as a professor at Oxford University, 1947-1963, and Princeton University, 1963-1990. Those are two prestigious universities, so Stone will be shown as an example of what happens to some historians in this modern era with plenty of data and other resources. No matter what you write, there will be plenty of others who will immediately check it out and attack at the slightest flaw or interpretation.

Stone's best known books were *The Crisis of the Aristocracy, 1558-1641* (1965) and *The Family, Sex and Marriage in England, 1500-1800* (1977). In the former, Stone made a detailed quantitative study of extensive piece of data relating to the economic activities of the English aristocracy to conclude that there was a major economic crisis for the nobility in the 16th and 17th centuries. (This has since been undermined by Christopher Thompson's demonstration that the peerage's real income was higher in 1602 than in 1534 and grew substantially by 1641.) In the latter work, Stone used the same quantitative methods to study family life. Stone's conclusion was there was little love in English marriages before the 18th century. This left him open to devastating counter-attacks from medievalists who pointed out that Stone ignored the medieval period and there is ample evidence that there were many loving marriages before 1700. By the 1980s, Stone had abandoned his thesis.

Stone's work was very controversial. To some, he was a radical trail-blazer, but to more conservative-minded historians, Stone's methods were a disgrace to the historical profession. Stone's thesis that the British political elite was "closed" to new members has undergone important revision. Once widely accepted and popularized in works like Simon Schama's survey of the French Revolution (*Citizens*), this view has recently been challenged. For instance, Ellis Wasson's *Born to Rule: British Political Elites* (2000) shows the ruling class to have been basically open to new members throughout the early period. Stone's claim is shown to have rested on insufficient quantitative evidence.[24]

Geoffrey Rudolf Elton, August 17, 1921-December 3, 1994, was a pre-eminent British historian of the Tudor period. He was born as Gottfried Rudolf Ehrenberg in Tübingen, Germany, which is about 20 miles south of Stuttgart. Elton was most famous for arguing in his 1953 book *The Tudor Revolution in Government* that Thomas Cromwell was the author of modern, bureaucratic government which replaced medieval, household government. His thesis has been widely challenged by Tudor historians and can no longer be regarded as an orthodoxy, but Elton's contribution to the debate has profoundly influenced subsequent discussion of Tudor government, in particular concerning the role of Cromwell.

Elton was also famous for his role in the Carr-Elton debate associated with Leopold von Ranke against Carr's views. Elton wrote his 1967 book *The Practice of History* largely in response to E.H. Carr's book *What is History?* (1961). Both books are among my favorite references. Elton was a strong defender of the traditional methods of history and was appalled by *postmodernism*, which he termed the "intellectual equivalent of crack."[25]

Robert Fogel, July 1, 1926-, is an American economic historian and scientist born in New York City. He won, with Douglas North, the 1993 Nobel Prize in Economics. He is best known as a leading advocate of cliometrics, a name for the use of quantitative methods in history. His first major study involving cliometrics was *Railroads and American Economic Growth: Essays in Econometric History* (1964). This tract sought to quantify railroads' contribution to U.S. economic growth in the 19th century. Its argument and method were each rebuttals to a long line of non-numeric historical arguments that had ascribed much to railroads without rigorous reference to economic data. Examining transportation costs for primary and secondary goods, Fogel compared the actual 1890 economy to a hypothetical 1890 economy in which transportation infrastructure was limited to wagons, canals and rivers. The difference in cost (or "social savings") attributable to railroads was negligible- about 1%. This conclusion made a controversial name for cliometrics. He and Stanley Engerman did a famous and controversial study about slavery, *Time on the Cross* (1974). The study claimed that slaves in the American South lived better than did many industrial workers in the North.[26] The slave study was attacked for flawed statistical procedures, misuse and over interpretation of sources, vague hypotheses, and plain inaccuracy.[27]

Emmanuel Le Roy Ladurie, July 19, 1929-, is a French modernist historian. Undoubtedly one of the most fruitful contemporary historians, he owes much to his mentor, the great historian of the Annales school, Fernand Braudel. He became a specialist in the anthropology history which captures men of the past in the total environment. His doctoral thesis was the *Peasants of Languedoc, 1294-1324* (1966) of 1,035 pages. His most famous work, *Montaillou village Occitan* (1975), was based on the notes of the Inquisitor Jacques Bishop of Parmiers, 1318-1325, translated into French by Jean Duvernoy, to reconstruct the life of a small town in Languedoc at the time of Catharism.[28]

I would like to provide some background on the subject of Ladurie's geographical area of Languedoc, which is the southern-most province of France and borders with Spain. The 600-year Roman Catholic Inquisition started in Languedoc. The Catholic inquisitors were extremely meticulous about recording every bit of minutia about their operations to break the heretics of the Cathar religion. This is a very ugly part of Catholic history. They recorded their actions on the pretense of doing legal activities on behalf of the Church, so the records are a boon to historians. The records also provide the evidence to convict the system of criminal activity.

Hans-Ulrich Wehler, September 11, 1931-, is a German historian with left-wing leanings. He was born in Freudenberg, which is about *who knows how many miles from where* because there are fiour Freudenbergs in Germany. He was educated at the universities of Cologne and Bonn, and at Ohio University in Athens, Ohio. He taught at Bielefeld University (1971-96), which is about 200 miles west of Berlin. As a left-wing historian he sees German history as a result of aggressive foreign policies by the German Empire, and is a leading critic of the efforts of the conservative German historians to whitewash the German past. Needless to say, this position is not always very popular. In 2000, he became the eighth German historian to be inducted as an honorary member of the American Historical Association (AHA). Wehler accepted this honor with some reluctance as previous German historians so honored have included Leopold von Ranke, Gerhard Ritter and Friedrich Meinecke, none of whom Wehler considers to be proper historians. H has a long list of publications to his credit, which I will not mention.[29] That is quite a statement about von Ranke and the others. Do you think he was honored by the AHA for his friendly views on Germany? "...perhaps the most influential (German) historian of the late 1960s and 1970s..."[30]

John Russell Vincent, December 20, 1937-, is a British historian He has been a Professor of modern history at the University of Bristol since 1970. His book, *History* (1995), is one of my references. In 1995 Oxford University Press refused to publish a book on history by Vincent because of the lack of "inclusive" language. This means that he failed to use gender-neutral language, such as he/she, or whatever makes the feminists happy.

In his book on historiography, *An Intelligent Person's Guide to History*, Vincent notes that if we went *solely* by the documentary standards most prized by modern historians nothing would be more historically certain than that there *were* witches in the Middle Ages, given that we have a large volume of solemnly sworn testimony in original documents.[31] Think about that, you budding historians!

Heinrich August Winkler, December 19, 1938-, is a German historian born in Königsberg, which is on the southeast Baltic Sea coast. It is now known as Kaliningrad, which is a Russian enclave surrounded by Lithuania on the north and east, Poland on the south and the Baltic Sea on the west. His major work, *Weimar, A Reading Book of German History, 1918-1933*, is one of the foremost books detailing a comprehensive political history of the Weimar Republic.[32]

The population of the United States increased from 151 million in 1950 to 300 million in 2006. The United States emerged as a super power as a result of World War II, but most importantly was the emergence as an economic giant, which is partially attributable to the Servicemen's Readjustment Act of June 22, 1944 (G.I. Bill). The G.I. Bill was enacted to provide education benefits to the millions of servicemen mobilized for World War II. This was to preclude the shabby treatment and eventual bonus riots that occurred after World War I. The G.I. Bill allowed millions to attend college that was not even a distant dream in America before the end of World War II. This opportunity placed a severe demand on the college and university infrastructure, both in buildings and professors. This resulted in a significant increase of the infrastructure, to include professors of history. The history profession grew, albeit not as much as the engineering profession, but many more were studying history to become professionals. The number of colleges in the United States has been growing dramatically since the 1950s, and the number of people desiring a college degree has been rising faster than the population growth. More history professors are needed.

Professional history professors must write books while they teach, under the "publish or perish" mantra within the profession. This led to more writers producing more books, not just academic books for other historians, but popular history books for the more educated American public since World War II. Publishers soon realized the opportunity to make more money, as did the professors. We are now on our way to the flood of books, although history books are less popular than fiction. The age of computers and printing technologies has changed the dynamics of the publishing business. Books unsold by the retail merchants in 3-4 months are returned and bought by the secondary market at reduced prices, and these prices bring out more buyers. Historians of different genres are able to recycle their material endlessly, whether the Revolutionary period, the Civil War, or World War II. New and old readers are attracted by the marketing slogans mentioned in the preface. Old classics out of print are republished in cheaper versions for school children and adults alike. I use my History Book Club material (every three weeks) to screen for possible purchases, then I go to www.abebooks.com or www.hamiltonbooks.com to make my purchases at better prices.

The so-called Information Age (economy) has been upon us since the last quarter century, but that is not precise because it is constantly and rapidly changing. Computers, the Internet, and the digital world have dramatically revolutionized the information and history business. Old manuscripts and similar materials are now on the Internet in their original form for researchers. Such items were restricted to a very select number of individuals in the past for researching. Books are commodities, and so are history books also commodities. It is all in the marketing by the publisher. By the end of 2000 there had been at least 1,595 books written about Abraham Lincoln. Stand by for a deluge in 2009, Lincoln's 200th birthday. Books about George Washington trail Lincoln, with a paltry 1,094. Books about the best-known former presidents top the never-ending flow of history books.

Joseph Ellis, 1943-, is an American historian who won the 2001 Pulitzer Prize for History for his *Founding Brothers: The Revolutionary Generation*. He also won the National Book Award for *American Sphinx: The Character of Thomas Jefferson*. He also wrote six other books about the Revolutionary period, therefore, he is considered an expert on the Revolutionary period. He is currently a professor of history at Mount Holyoke College, a liberal arts women's college in South Hadley, Massachusetts, which is about 10 miles north of Springfield. Reviewers generally praise Ellis's writing for being both insightful and accessible.

Ellis was involved in a controversy in 1996-98 regarding whether Thomas Jefferson had an affair with his slave, Sally Hemings. Utilized his vast expertise about Jefferson, he concluded "that the likelihood of a liaison with Sally Hemings is remote." In 1998, DNA evidence proved that Thomas Jefferson was the father of Hemings' son, Eston. With this new evidence, Ellis conceded that he had been wrong.

Ellis was involved in another controversy in 2001, the year he won the Pulitzer Prize. Ellis was commissioned as an Army second lieutenant when he graduated from college in 1965, but his active duty was deferred four years while he was in graduate school. He then did his Army service by teaching (no doubt history) at West Point from 1969 until 1972, leaving as a captain. In 2001 he had been teaching at Mount Holyoke for 29 years and was an icon on campus. Probably because he was teaching only girls, he started to embellish his military resume. He started to tell tales about his days as a platoon leader and paratrooper in Vietnam. He said that his unit was nearby when American soldiers massacred hundreds of Vietnamese civilians in the village of My Lai. After that he served on the staff of the U.S. commander in Vietnam, General William Westmoreland. He started to share his classroom stories with journalists and colleagues. The Boston *Globe* pursued the story and discovered his Vietnam experiences were total falsehoods, because he was never there. The story broke and the college president presumed his innocence and defended Ellis as "one of the most respected scholars, writers and teachers in the nation. We at the college do not understand what public interest the *Globe* is trying to serve through a story of this nature."

I immediately wrote a short concise letter of criticism to the college's president. By the time she received it, Ellis had admitted his lies and she wrote back to me, and I'm sure many others, a long one-page letter, expressing her surprise and sadness at the situation and their attempts to investigate the situation. Later Ellis was suspended from the college for one year without pay, but is now back teaching again. His prior scholarship underwent a peer review and it found no errors or misstatements. How could he be so meticulous in his research and writings, yet get trapped in the web of his own lies and aggrandizement?

Paul M Kennedy, June 1945-, is a British historian, political scientist, an expert in military strategy, diplomacy, international relations and author. [That is an impressive set of credentials] He has published fourteen books so far. His most successful, *The Rise and Fall of the Great Powers*, is cited at the beginning of my preface.[33] Evans takes Kennedy to task for exceeding his scope as a historian, by making future predictions based on perceived historical laws. Marx, Engels, Toynbee and Buckle were cited as among those who claimed they discovered the laws of history, only to proven to be false (poor, bad) prophets. "It is always a mistake for a historian to try to predict the future. Life, unlike science, is simply too full of surprises."[34]

Since the early-mid 1990s I have cherished an article [undated despite my efforts to meticulously date each article cut from newspapers and magazines] from the *Wall Street Journal* by Arthur

Schlesinger, Jr., titled *The Future Outwits Us Again*, with the highlighted statement, " Lord Keynes had it right when he said, 'The inevitable never happens. It is the unexpected always.'" The date of the article is dated by the words in the following quotation.

> "Suppose someone a short decade ago had predicted that within ten years the world would see the disappearance of the Soviet Union, the decommunization of Eastern Europe, the unification of Germany, the bloody breakup of Yugoslavia, the end of apartheid in South Africa, the marketization of China, near-revolutionary upheavals in Japan and Italy, and now the handshake on the White House lawn between the prime minister of Israel and the head of the Palestine Liberation Organization."[35]

The handshake by Prime Minister Rabin and Arafat on the White House lawn was on September 13, 1993.

Lessons Learned:

-Morison wrote naval histories and insensitive American history.

-Carr wrote about Russian history and philosophy of history.

-Labrousse was a leader in cliometrics.

-Braudel took over the Annales School from Febvre. He also wrote while in prison.

-Commager was a prolific writer, to include insensitive American history.

-Taylor defended Hitler and was a troublemaker.

-Woodward wrote primarily about the American South and race relations.

-Trevor-Roper wrote about Germany and authenticated the fictitious *Hitler Diaries*.

-Boorstin wrote to glorify America and Americans.

-Hofstadter was an influential historian and leading intellectual in mid-20th century.

-Hobsbawm was a Marxist economic historian.

-Schlesinger was a liberal and promoter of John Kennedy's legacy.

-Stone wrote about the economics of the English aristocracy.

-Elton wrote about Tudor history and a book to counter Carr's.

-Fogel used cliometrics in two studies, which were severely criticized.

-Ladurie was a specialist in the anthropology history.

-Vincent got into trouble about gender language, but I like his books.

-Kennedy was the man who provided the seed for this book.

Is an autobiography history? Is the author a historian? Did he tell facts from the past? Did he introduce facts that no one knew about? Did he interpret those facts? Did he use the present time as the basis for interpreting the past? During the 1990s and early 2000s oral histories were all the rage, primarily because members of Tom Brokaw's *Greatest Generation* (World War II veterans) were rapidly leaving the scene. We needed to have them tell their stories to their own families and others of following generations. Is the speaker a historian? The questions above also apply to the oral historian. Is an amateur historian's story any less than a professional's story? Yes, there are differences in motivation and scope, but many professional stories are made up from eye-witness accounts such as Tom Brokaw's.

Is the memory a reliable source for history? Is it an adequate source for a history? Does an amateur historian stretch the truth more than a professional? We have read numerous chapters filled with historians who were rather loose with the truth, and sometimes outright lied. The professional's motivation is usually money and fame, with maybe a little professional respect, but that respect still does not beat money. Does a veteran or other amateur stretch the truth for fame and respect?

The following story is probably not a typical amateur-historian's effort, but it does demonstrate some of the questions raised above. My current residence town of Huntsville, Alabama has a historical publication published by several entrepreneurs, *Old Huntsville, History and Stories of the Tennessee Valley*. It is published monthly and can be received in the mail by subscription or can be purchased from a box in front of many local establishments. An old issue, number 82, caught my eye because of an article, *They don't make heroes like Roy Rogers anymore*. The author was Chuck Yancurra, Mayor of Madison, a smaller town immediately adjoining Huntsville. He was a retired warrant officer from the U.S. Army, and was quite a vocal and dynamic individual who won his mayoral election. Afterwards it seemed like he was always getting publicity for his actions and his mouth. This article had nothing to do with old Huntsville, but apparently the publishers decided it would be a good story by a local celebrity. Everybody over a certain age knows about Roy Rogers, his wife Dale Evans and his horse, Trigger. I will now quote selective parts of his story.

> "Roy Rogers was a hero to me and my friends when I was a kid growing up in Crafton, Pa., as he was to kids all over the United States....Dale Evans and Rogers' romance turned out to be real, and they were still married the day he died [July 6, 1998]. I actually met Rogers once, although it was under tragic circumstances.
>
> One of his adopted sons was stationed at Bladenheim, Germany, where I was also stationed. If my memory serves me correctly, the year was 1972. At a bar one night, the young soldier imbibed too much hard liquor, later choking on his vomit, and was found dead in his bed the next morning.
>
> It says a great deal about the kind of person Rogers was by how forgiving he was of the battalion commander. However, the group commander was not as forgiving, and the battalion commander was relieved of his command."[36]

Now let me provided an analysis of the above story. To anyone remotely familiar with Germany, a town by the name of Bladenheim has a great element of validity to it. *Heim* means home, so many combinations of prefixes could be attached to the front of *heim*. A random sampling of a German road-atlas index indicated there could logically be at least 500 towns and villages that could end in *heim*. Unfortunately, there are none named Bladenheim.

My wife, Margaret, lived in Gelnhausen, Germany where I was stationed in the early 1960s. I lived there for three years before we came to the States. When it was announced in the newspaper that Rogers' son had died in Gelnhausen, it stuck vividly in our minds. We knew Coleman Kaserne, in Gelnhausen, very well, knew the enlisted men's club and the barracks. When I read the Yancurra's article, we could not remember what year the event took place. Yancurra's memory said 1972, because he was there. Since I was teaching a course about rewriting history to my seniors' learning group, I needed to verify before I spoke. I bought a copy of the Rogers' book, *Happy Trails* (1980) to learn their version of events. The event occurred in October 1965.

Teaching points might be that memories are distorted by many things, to include egos. Memories should be checked by something else more authoritative. I have serious doubts that Yancurra ever met Roy Rogers in Germany. Soldiers do not easily forget the name of the German town they were stationed. You should draw your own conclusions about Yancurra's motivation and credibility as an author, and as a mayor.

As Paul Harvey used to say, "Now for the rest of the story," and it is a sad story taken from Rogers' book. John David (Sandy) Rogers was adopted by the Rogers. His parents were alcoholic, he did not walk until he was two years old, suffered from prolonged malnutrition, and was regularly beaten by his parents. He had troubles in high school. In football, he did not know which way to run. He could not handle a gun. He was a bed-wetter. In January 1965 he wanted to join the Army and did. Apparently the Army pushed him through despite what must have been some obvious personal shortfalls. But this was in the early build-up in Vietnam, so the Army willingly took almost any warm body. In October 1965 he was promoted to private first class and was at his promotion party at the enlisted men's club. "Sandy was at a party Saturday night. Some guys got him to drink a lot of hard liquor, and it killed him."[37]

Do we need more historians because there is more history being made? In 1800 the world's population was just under 1 billion. In 2000 the world's population was 6 billion. That means that there is more history being made, and we need more historians to write about it. And there are more people who want to read about it. Today as I write this sentence, a bridge collapsed in Nepal and people with Internet could know it within a day. One hundred years ago that event would have been unnoticed by the world. But today it is history, today's history for sure, but next year or ten years from now, someone will be including it in their national history, or whatever.

History used to be only written by the winners, and wrote what they wanted to write about their wonderful victory. Today there are more losers writing history because they want to tell their loser's story. They have computers, video cameras, etc. to record for posterity, however long that is. Some of the hottest selling books in today's marketplace are those losers from dysfunctional families, or some other heart-rendering story, who fought their way back to normality and got on Oprah. Did they write history? I think so. All autobiographical material must be history because it tells about something that few people knew. Some day a social historian will collect a hundred sob-stories and write a social history under some theme.

More people. More activity. More information. More history. More historians. Equals more history books.

Chapter 13

Generalizations, Maxims and Quotations

"Advice to persons about to write history—don't." Lord Acton, letter, April 5, 1887,[1] Acton apparently took his own advice. He penned several essays, edited a Catholic monthly journal, wrote many letters and essays, but wrote no history books. He was named the Cambridge Regius Professor of Modern History in 1895, eight years after the previous quotation, but spent his efforts at lecturing and organizing and editing the Cambridge Modern history series.

History has never, in any age, been written without including moral judgments.[2]

The historian is not really interested in the unique, but what is general in the unique.[3]

No matter what or how a historian writes, there will always be plenty of historians to criticize the work.[4]

"...history will always be rewritten," for it was not possible for an historian to take up the pen without "the impulse of the present."[5]

"Every century has the tendency to consider itself the most progressive, and to measure all others according to its own ideas. That is why we study history. An age must always be brought to a realization of its own image and of how it came to be."[6]

"Unreadable history books foster ignorance of history....All this ignorance—at a time when we have more professional historians than ever before.[7]

"As a historian, I am naturally, professionally, interested in truths...In any definition of truth, reality is mentioned or implied. What is said to be true must relate to something experienced and must state that experience accurately....The only thing sure is that mankind is eager for truth, lives by it, will not let it go, and turns desperate in the teeth of contradiction....Truth is a goal and a guide that cannot be dispensed with....Our love of order impels us to make theories, systems, sets of principles. We need them both for comfort and for action. A society, however pluralist, needs some beliefs in common and will not trust them unless they are labeled truths.... man should not be called seeker and finder of truth but fallible and reviser of truths."[8]

"The main work of the historian is not to record, but to evaluate; for if he does not evaluate, how can he know what is worth recording."[9] E.H. Carr (1892-1982), *What is History?* 1962.

"The historian seldom defines....He arbitrarily expands, restricts, distorts the meanings-without warning the reader; without always fully realizing it himself."[10]

"All works of history are in a sense autobiographical, particularly if the author is dealing with a historical personality that he finds sympathetic."[11]

"Academic historians remain committed to their discipline even if they differ about what that discipline exactly is. They revel in the complexity and the opportunity to seek out new areas for study. They persist in stressing that people in the past experienced material realities from day to day, and they valorize rigorous attempts to uncover the past and try to understand it. They use theory to help them understand the possibilities of interpretation rather than a substitute for the necessarily painstaking research required of them. They struggle to write for the general reader. **?????** Historical writing remains dynamic at the start of the third millennium.[12]

"A historian, like any other researcher, has a vested interest in answering his own questions. His job is at stake, and his reputation, and most important, his self-respect."[13] David Hackett Fischer (1935-), *Historians' Fallacies: Toward a Logic of Historical Thought*, 1970.

"Historian. A broad-gauge gossip."[14] Ambrose Bierce (1842-1914, *The Devil's Dictionary*, 1881-1906.

"History and biography and historical fiction are imaginative presentations of points of view, shaped by the author's own frame of mind and by the social and cultural context in which the author wrote."[15]

"The five most influential medievalists of the past half century in the American context have been Bloch, Curtius, Panofsky, Southern, and Strayer, *authoritarian egotists all*."[16] My italics.

"Writers, like teeth, are divided into incisors and grinders."[17] Walter Bagehot (1826-1877), *Estimates of Some Englishmen and Scotchmen*, 1858.

"History repeats itself. Historians repeat each other."[18] Philip Guedalla (1889-1944), *Supers and Supermen*, 1920.

Hell hath no fury like a historian scorned.[19]

"...important maxim: That it is possible for a narrative—however circumstantial—however steadily maintained—however public and however important the events it relates—however grave the authority on which it is published—to be nevertheless an entire fabrication!"[20]

BIBLIOGRAPHY

Archer, Jerome W. & Joseph Schwartz, Editors, *A Reader for Writers*, New York: McGraw-Hill, 1966

Axelrod, Alan, *The Quotable Historian*, New York: McGraw-Hill, 2000

Barnes, Harry Elmer, *A History of Historical Writing*, New York: Dover Publications, 1963

Barraclough, Geoffrey, *History in a Changing World*, Oxford: Basil Blackwell, 1957

Barzun, Jacques and Henry F. Graff, *The Modern Researcher*, New York: Harcourt Brace Jovanovich, 1977

Becker, Carl L., *Detachment and the Writing of History: Essays and Letters of Carl L. Becker*, Ithaca, NY: Cornell University Press, 1958

Beers, Henry Putney, *The French in North America*, Baton Rouge, LA: Louisiana State University Press, 1957

Bierce, Ambrose, *The Devil's Dictionary, New York: Dover Publications, 1958.*

Black, J.B., *The Art of History*, New York: Russell & Russell, 1965

Bloch, Marc, *The Historian's Craft*, New York: Vintage Books, 1953

Burckhardt, Jacob, *Force and Freedom, Reflections on History*, New York: Pantheon Books, 1943

Burckhardt, Jacob, *Judgments on History and Historians*, New York: Garland Publishing, 1984

Burckhardt, Jacob, *The Civilization of the Renaissance in Italy*, New York: The Modern Library, 1954

Burk, Kathleen, *Troublemaker*, New Haven, CT: Yale University Press, 2000

Butterfield, Herbert, *Man on His Past*, Cambridge: Cambridge University Press, 1955

Butterfield, Herbert, *The Origins of History*, New York: Basic Books, 1981

Butterfield, Herbert, *The Whig Interpretation of History*, New York: Charles Scribner's Sons, 1954

Cantor, Norman F., *Inventing the Middle Ages*, New York: William Morrow, 1991

Carr, Edward Hallett, *What is History?*, New York: Alfred A. Knopf, 1964

Certeau, Michel de, *The Writing of History*, New York: Columbia University Press, 1988

Colley, Linda, *Lewis Namier*, New York: St. Martin's Press, 1989

Collingwood, R.G., *The Idea of History*, Oxford: Oxford University Press, 1951

Croce, Benedetto, *History as the Story of Liberty*, London: George Allen and Unwin, 1962

Croce, Benedetto, *History, Its Theory and Practice*, New York: Russell & Russell, 1960

Dahmus, Joseph, *Seven Medieval Historians*, Chicago: Nelson-Hall, 1982

Dalberg-Acton, John Emerich Edward, *Lectures on Modern History*, London: Macmillan, 1960

Davies, W. Watkin, *How to Read History*, New York: George H. Doran, 1924

Dopsch, Alfons, *The Economic and Social Foundations of European Civilization*, London: Routledge & Kegan Paul, 1953

Elton, G.R., *The Practice of History*, New York: Thomas Y. Crowell, 1967

Evans, Richard J., *In Defense of History*, New York: W.W. Norton, 1999

Fernández-Armesto, Felipe, *Amerigo*, New York: Random House, 2007

Fischer, David Hackett, *Historians Fallacies: Toward a Logic of Historical Thought*, New York: Harper Colophon Books, 1970

Foner, Eric, *Who Owns History?*, New York: Hill and Wang, 2002

Fulcher of Chartres, *A History of the Expedition to Jerusalem, 1095-1127*, Knoxville, TN: University of Tennessee Press, 1969

Furber, Elizabeth Chapin, Editor, *Changing Views on British History*, Cambridge, MA: Harvard University Press, 1966

Gay, Peter, *Style in History*, New York: McGraw-Hill, 1974

Gilderhus, Mark T., *History and Historians: A Historiographical Introduction*, Upper Saddle River, NJ, 2003

Given-Wilson, Chris, *Chronicles: The Writing of History in Medieval England*, London: Hambledon & London, 2004

Guilland, Antoine, *Modern Germany & Her Historians*, Westport, CT: Greenwood Press, 1970

Halperin, S. William, Editor, *Essays in Modern European Historiography*, Chicago: University of Chicago Press, 1970

Hobsbawm, Eric, *On History*, New York: The New Press, 1997

Hexter, J.H., *On Historians*, Cambridge, MA: Harvard University Press, 1979

Hexter, J.H., *Reappraisals in History*, Evanston, IL: Northwestern University Press, 1962

Iggers, Georg G., *New Directions in European Historiography*, Middletown, CT: Wesleyan University Press, 1975

Iggers, Georg G., *The German Conception of History*, Middletown, CT: Wesleyan University Press, 1986

Krieger, Leonard, *Ranke, The Meaning of History*, Chicago: University of Chicago Press, 1977

Lucian of Samosata, *How To Write History*.

Macartney, C.A., *The Medieval Hungarian Historians*, Cambridge: Cambridge University Press, 1953

Marsh, Henry, *Dark Age Britain*, New York: Dorset Press, 1970

Merryweather, F. Somner, *Bibliomania of the Middle Ages*, London: Merryweather, 1849

Muller, Herbert J., *The Uses of the Past*, New York: Oxford University Press, 1952

Pares, Richard, *The Historian's Business and Other Essays*, London: Oxford University Press, 1961

Peardon, Thomas, *The Transition in English Historical Writing, 1760-1830*, New York: AMS Press, 1966

Powicke, E.M., *Modern Historians and the Study of History*, London: Odams Press, 1955

Rabb, Theodore K., *The Last Days of the Renaissance*, New York: Basic Books, 2006

Ranke, Ludwig von, *The Secret of World History*, New York: Fordham University Press, 1981

Rogers, Roy, *Happy Trails*, Carmel, NY: Guideposts, 1979.

Sayles, G.O., *The Medieval Foundations of England*, Philadelphia: University of Pennsylvania Press, 1950

Schevill, Ferdinand, *Six Historians*, Chicago: University of Chicago Press, 1956

Schmitt, Hans A., Editor, *Historians of Modern Europe*, Baton Rouge, LA: Louisiana State University Press, 1971

Schorske, Carl E., *Thinking with History*, Princeton, NJ: Princeton University Press, 1998

Shopkow, Leah, *History & Community*, Washington: Catholic University of America Press, 1997

Simkhovitch, Vladimir G., *Approaches to History I*, New York: Academy of Political Science, 1929

Smith, Charlotte Watkins, *Carl Becker: On History & the Climate of Opinion*, Ithaca, NY: Cornell University Press, 1956

Smith, Page, *The Historian and History*, New York: Alfred A. Knopf, 1964

Stephens, Lester D. Editor, *Historiography: A Bibliography,* Metuchen, NJ, The Scarecrow Press, 1975

Thompson, James Westfall, *A History of Historical Writing*, 2 vols., New York: Macmillan, 1942

Thucydides, *The Peloponnesian War*, Indianapolis, IN: Hackett Publishing, 2002

Tillinghast, Pardon E., *The Specious Past: Historians and Others*, New York: Garland Publishing, 1985

Trouillot, Michel-Rolph, *Silencing the Past*, Boston: Beacon Press, 1995

Two Renaissance Book Hunters, The Letters of Poggius Bracciolini to Nicolaus de Niccolis, Columbia University Pres, London, 1974

Vincent, John, *An Intelligent Person's Guide to History*, London: Duckworth Overlook, 2005

Vincent, John, *History*, London: Continuum, 2005

Wedgwood, C.V., *Truth and Opinion*, New York: Macmillan, 1960

White, Hayden, *The Content of the Form*, Baltimore: John Hopkins Press, 1989

William, Archbishop of Tyre, *A History of Deeds Done Beyond the Sea*, New York: Columbia University Press, 1943

Yancurra, Chuck, *They don't make heroes like Roy Rogers anymore.*

Zamoyski, Adam, *Holy Madness*, New York: Viking, 2000

NOTES

Preface
1. Axelrod, Alan, *The Quotable Historian*, p. 75.
2. Evans, Richard J., *In Defense of History*, p. 71.
3. Johnson, Paul, *Art, A New History*, Preface,.
4. Axelrod, Alan, *The Quotable Historian*, p. 76.

Chapter 1 –Points to Ponder
1. Wikipedia.
2. Barnes, Harry Elmer, *A History of Historical Writing*, p. 67-68.
3. Lucian of Samosata.

Chapter 2 – Classical
1. Wikipedia.
2. Gilderhus, Mark T., *History and Historians: A Historiographical Introduction*, p. 15.
3. Collingwood, R. G., *The Idea of History*, p. 18
4. Wikipedia.
5. Croce, Benedetto, *History, Its Theory and Practice*, p. 181.
6. Wikipedia.
7. Barnes, Harry Elmer, *A History of Historical Writing*, p. 27-8.
8. Ibid., p. 15.
9. Wikipedia.
10. www.loyno.edu/history/journal/1998-9/Pipes.htm.
11. Elton, G.R., *The Practice of History*, p. 6.
12. Croce, Benedetto, *History, Its Theory and Practice*, p. 35.
13. Schorske, Carl E., *Thinking with History*, 9. 221.
14. Davies, W. Watkin, *How to Read History*, p. 46-7.
15. Wall Street Journal, June 9, 2007, p. P 8.
16. Wikipedia.
17. Davies, W. Watkin, *How to Read History*, p. 46, 48-9.
18. Ranke, Ludwig von, *The Secret of World History*, p. 164.
19. Foner, Eric, *Who Owns History?*, p. xvii.
20. Evans, Richard J., *In Defense of History*, p. 71-2.
21. Barnes, Harry Elmer, *A History of Historical Writing*, p. 30-1.
22. Gilderhus, Mark T., *History and Historians: A Historiographical Introduction*, p. 18.
23. Thucydides, *The Peloponnesian War*, p. 1.
24. Wikipedia.
25. Davies, W. Watkin, *How to Read History*, p. 52.
26. Wikipedia.
27. Ibid.
28. Ibid.
29. Ibid.
30. Ibid.
31. Ibid.
32. Gilderhus, Mark T., *History and Historians: A Historiographical Introduction*, p. 18.
33. Davies, W. Watkin, *How to Read History*, p. 65.
34. Croce, Benedetto, *History, Its Theory and Practice*, p. 197.
35. Smith, Page, *The Historian and History*, p. 14.
36. Ibid., p. 27.
37. Davies, W. Watkin, *How to Read History*, p. 67-8.
38. Barnes, Harry Elmer, *A History of Historical Writing*, p. 36-7.
39. Wikipedia.

40. www.etext.library.adelaide.edu.au/v/voltaire/disctioany/chapter159.html.
41. Wikipedia.
42. Ibid.
43. www.quotationspage.com.
44. Wikipedia.
45. Ibid.
46. Barnes, Harry Elmer, *A History of Historical Writing*, p. 38.
47. Wikipedia.
48. Ibid.
49. Gay, Peter, *Style in History*, p. 25.
50. Butterfield, Herbert, *Man on His Past*, p. 221.
51. Schevill, Ferdinand, *Six Historians*, p. 194-5.
52. Collingwood, R. G., *The Idea of History*, p. 38-9.
53. Black, J.B., *The Art of History*, p. 174.
54. Carr, Edward Hallett, *What is History?*, p. 130.
55. Barnes, Harry Elmer, *A History of Historical Writing*, p. 38-9.
56. Ibid., p. 102-3.
57. www.holysmoke.org/sdhok/jesus5.htm.
58. Fernández-Armesto, Felipe, *Amerigo*, p. 67.
59. Wikipedia.
60. Barnes, Harry Elmer, *A History of Historical Writing*, p. 39.
61. Wikipedia.
62. Ibid.
63. Ibid.
64. Ibid.

Chapter 3 – Early Christian
1. Wikipedia & Catholic Encyclopedia.
2. Ibid.
3. Wikipedia.
4. www.littleboh.com/darkages.
5. Wikipedia.
6. Barnes, Harry Elmer, *A History of Historical Writing*, p. 134.
7. Croce, Benedetto, *History, Its Theory and Practice*, p. 206.
8. Barnes, Harry Elmer, *A History of Historical Writing*, p. 47.
9. Ibid., 51.
10. Wikipedia & Catholic Encyclopedia.
11. Barnes, Harry Elmer, *A History of Historical Writing*, p. 50.
12. Ibid., 122-3
13. Wikipedia.
14. Ibid.
15. Catholic Encyclopedia.
16. Deeds, Tyre, 58, n.19.
17. Wikipedia & Catholic Encyclopedia.
18. Collingwood, R. G., *The Idea of History*, p. 51.
19. Barnes, Harry Elmer, *A History of Historical Writing*, p. 48.

Chapter 4 – A of B
1. Wikipedia.
2. Wikipedia & Catholic Encyclopedia.
3. Wikipedia.
4. Ibid.
5. Catholic Encyclopedia.
6. Wikipedia.
7. www.monarchieliga.de/moeller.
8. Wikipedia.

9. Vincent, John, *History*, p. 113.
10. Marsh, Henry, *Dark Age Britain*, p. 109-10.
11. Wikipedia.
12. Wikipedia & Catholic Encyclopedia.
13. Wikipedia.
14. www.fordham.edu/halsall/basis/einhard.html.
15. Wikipedia & Catholic Encyclopedia.
16. Ibid.
17. Ibid.
18. Wikipedia.
19. Barnes, Harry Elmer, *A History of Historical Writing*, p. 75.
20. Wikipedia & Catholic Encyclopedia.
21. Wikipedia.
22. www.nipissingu.ca/department/history/MUHLBERGER/chroniqu/texts/GLEBAKE...
23. Wikipedia & Catholic Encyclopedia.
24. Vincent, John, *History*, p. 113-4.
25. Barnes, Harry Elmer, *A History of Historical Writing*, p. 71.
26. Marsh, Henry, *Dark Age Britain*, p. 190.
27. Given-Wilson, Chris, *Chronicles: The Writing of History in Medieval England*, p. 4.
28. Wikipedia.
29. Barnes, Harry Elmer, *A History of Historical Writing*, p. 75.
30. www.fordham.edu/halsall/basis/villehardouin.html
31. Given-Wilson, Chris, *Chronicles: The Writing of History in Medieval England*, p. 130.
32. Wikipedia.
33. Given-Wilson, Chris, *Chronicles: The Writing of History in Medieval England*, p. 4.
34. Wikipedia.
35. Barnes, Harry Elmer, *A History of Historical Writing*, p. 70.
36. Given-Wilson, Chris, *Chronicles: The Writing of History in Medieval England*, p. 1.
37. Ibid., 71.
38. Wikipedia.
39. Ibid.
40. Catholic Encyclopedia.
41. Wikipedia.
42. Catholic Encyclopedia.
43. Given-Wilson, Chris, *Chronicles: The Writing of History in Medieval England*, p. 33-4.
44. Wikipedia.
45. Barnes, Harry Elmer, *A History of Historical Writing*, p. 82.
46. Wikipedia.
47. Catholic Encyclopedia.
48. Wikipedia.
49. www.fordham.edu/halsall/basis/goldenlegend/GL-vol1-prologue.html
50. Tillinghast, Pardon E., *The Specious Past: Historians and Others*, p. 7.
51. Wikipedia.
52. Gilderhus, Mark T., *History and Historians: A Historiographical Introduction*, p. 52-53.
53. Croce, Benedetto, *History, Its Theory and Practice*, p. 214.
54. Smith, Page, *The Historian and History*, p. 23.
55. Tillinghast, Pardon E., *The Specious Past: Historians and Others*, p. 93.
56. Barnes, Harry Elmer, *A History of Historical Writing*, p. 71.
57. www.csudh.edu/oliver/smt310-handouts/jocelin/jocelin.htm.
58. Wikipedia.
59. Barnes, Harry Elmer, *A History of Historical Writing*, p. 90.
60. Wikipedia & Catholic Encyclopedia.
61. Ibid.
62. Barnes, Harry Elmer, *A History of Historical Writing*, p. 82-3.
63. Wikipedia and Catholic Encyclopedia.
64. Barnes, Harry Elmer, *A History of Historical Writing*, p.78.

65. Ibid., 83.
66. Wikipedia and Catholic Encyclopedia.
67. Wikipedia.
68. Ibid.
69. Wikipedia & Catholic Encyclopedia.
70. Wikipedia.
71. Given-Wilson, Chris, *Chronicles: The Writing of History in Medieval England*, p. 74-5.
72. Gilderhus, Mark T., *History and Historians: A Historiographical Introduction*, p. 24.
73. Barnes, Harry Elmer, *A History of Historical Writing*, p. 72.
74. Catholic Encyclopedia.
75. Wikipedia.
76. Ibid.
77. Catholic Encyclopedia.
78. Barnes, Harry Elmer, *A History of Historical Writing*, p. 63.
79. Catholic Encyclopedia & www.spartacus.schoolnet.co.uk.
80. Barnes, Harry Elmer, *A History of Historical Writing*, p.70-1.
81. Ibid., 84-5.
82. Wikipedia & Catholic Encyclopedia.
83. Ibid.
84. Barnes, Harry Elmer, *A History of Historical Writing*, p. 62.
85. Ibid., 62-3.
86. Ibid., 87.
87. Wikipedia.
88. www.newadvent.org.
89. Wikipedia.
90. Barnes, Harry Elmer, *A History of Historical Writing*, p. 74.
91. Wikipedia & Catholic Encyclopedia.
92. Wikipedia.
93. Wikipedia & Catholic Encyclopedia.
94. Wikipedia & Barnes, Harry Elmer, *A History of Historical Writing*, p. 71.
95. Given-Wilson, Chris, *Chronicles: The Writing of History in Medieval England*, p. 31-2 & 48.
96. Ibid., 63-4.
97. www.encyclopedia.jrank.org.
98. Wikipedia.
99. Ibid.
100. Barnes, Harry Elmer, *A History of Historical Writing*, p. 73.
101. Given-Wilson, Chris, *Chronicles: The Writing of History in Medieval England*, p. 189.
102. www.bartleby.com.
103. Given-Wilson, Chris, *Chronicles: The Writing of History in Medieval England*, p. 139.
104. Ibid., 182.
105. www.berkshirehistory.com.
106. Wikipedia.
107. Barnes, Harry Elmer, *A History of Historical Writing*, p. 74.
108. Wikipedia.
109. Wikipedia & Catholic Encyclopedia.
110. Barnes, Harry Elmer, *A History of Historical Writing*, p. 72.
111. Wikipedia.
112. Barnes, Harry Elmer, *A History of Historical Writing*, p. 74.
113. Wikipedia, Catholic Encyclopedia and Barnes, Harry Elmer, *A History of Historical Writing*, p. 86-7.
114. www.fordham.edu/halsall/basis/suger-louisthefat.html.
115. Barnes, Harry Elmer, *A History of Historical Writing*, p. 52.
116. Wikipedia & Barnes, Harry Elmer, *A History of Historical Writing*, p. 69.
117. Barnes, Harry Elmer, *A History of Historical Writing*, p. 90.
118. Wikipedia, Catholic Encyclopedia, & Barnes, Harry Elmer, *A History of Historical Writing*, p. 75.
119. Wikipedia & Catholic Encyclopedia.
120. Ibid.

121. Barnes, Harry Elmer, *A History of Historical Writing*, p. 69.
122. Marsh, Henry, *Dark Age Britain*, p. 155-74.
123. Merryweather, F. Somner, *Bibliomania of the Middle Ages*, p. 206.
124. Wikipedia, Catholic Encyclopedia, and Barnes, Harry Elmer, *A History of Historical Writing*, p. 72.
125. Vincent, John, *History*, p. 112.
126. www.deremilitare.org/resources/sources/puylaurens.
127. Wikipedia & Catholic Encyclopedia.
128. Wikipedia.
129. Barnes, Harry Elmer, *A History of Historical Writing*, p. 75.
130. Smith, Page, *The Historian and History*, p. 22.

Chapter 5 -- Renaissance
1. Croce, Benedetto, *History, Its Theory and Practice*, p. 224.
2. Wikipedia.
3. Barnes, Harry Elmer, *A History of Historical Writing*, p. 81.
4. Wikipedia.
5. Gilderhus, Mark T., *History and Historians: A Historiographical Introduction*, p. 30.
6. Rabb, Theodore K., *The Last Days of the Renaissance*, p. 32-3.
7. Wikipedia.
8. Gilderhus, Mark T., *History and Historians: A Historiographical Introduction*, p. 26.
9. Wikipedia.
10. Ibid.
11. Ibid.
12. Barnes, Harry Elmer, *A History of Historical Writing*, p. 102.
13. Ibid., 102-3.
14. *Two Renaissance Book Hunters, The Letters of Poggius Bracciolini to Nicolaus de Niccolis,* Columbia University Pres, London, 1974, p.46.
15. Ibid, 55.
16. Ibid, 195.
17. Wikipedia.
18. Ibid.
19. Croce, Benedetto, *History as the Story of Liberty*, p. 111-2.
20. Barnes, Harry Elmer, *A History of Historical Writing*, p. 104.
21. Wikipedia.
22. Barnes, Harry Elmer, *A History of Historical Writing*, p. 103.
23. Wikipedia.
24. Ibid.
25. Barnes, Harry Elmer, *A History of Historical Writing*, p. 107.
26. Croce, Benedetto, *History, Its Theory and Practice*, p. 169.
27. Gilderhus, Mark T., *History and Historians: A Historiographical Introduction*, p. 31.
28. Schevill, Ferdinand, *Six Historians*, p. 61-2.
29. Wikipedia.
30. Barnes, Harry Elmer, *A History of Historical Writing*, p. 114.
31. Collingwood,R.G., *The Idea of History*, p. 58.
32. Wikipedia.
33. Wikipedia & Catholic Encyclopedia.
34. Ranke, Ludwig von, *The Secret of World History*, p. 39.
35. Wikipedia.
36. Gilderhus, Mark T., *History and Historians: A Historiographical Introduction*, p. 31.
37. Schevill, Ferdinand, *Six Historians*, p. 139.
38. Guilland, Antoine, *Modern Germany & Her Historians*, p. 27.
39. Wikipedia.
40. Barnes, Harry Elmer, *A History of Historical Writing*, p. 111-2.
41. Ibid., 113.
42. Wikipedia & Barnes, Harry Elmer, *A History of Historical Writing*, p. 116.
43. Wikipedia.
44. Barnes, Harry Elmer, *A History of Historical Writing*, p. 110.

45. Wikipedia.
46. Gilderhus, Mark T., *History and Historians: A Historiographical Introduction*, p. 34.
47. Barnes, Harry Elmer, *A History of Historical Writing*, p. 173.
48. Wikipedia.
49. Ibid.
50. Barnes, Harry Elmer, *A History of Historical Writing*, p. 115.
51. Wikipedia.
52. Barnes, Harry Elmer, *A History of Historical Writing*, p. 113.
53. www.litencyc.com.

Chapter 6 – Reformation and Counter-Reformation
1. Barnes, Harry Elmer, *A History of Historical Writing*, p. 122.
2. Wikipedia & Barnes, Harry Elmer, *A History of Historical Writing*, p. 123.
3. Wikipedia.
4. Barnes, Harry Elmer, *A History of Historical Writing*, p. 126.
5. Ibid. 125-6.
6. Ranke, Ludwig von, *The Secret of World History*, p. 39.
7. Wikipedia.
8. Barnes, Harry Elmer, *A History of Historical Writing*, p. 123-4.
9. Wikipedia.
10. Ibid.
11. Vincent, John, *History*, p. 121.
12. Barnes, Harry Elmer, *A History of Historical Writing*, p. 124.
13. Wikipedia.
14. Barnes, Harry Elmer, *A History of Historical Writing*, p. 127.
15. Wikipedia.
16. Ibid.
17. Barnes, Harry Elmer, *A History of Historical Writing*, p. 129.
18. Catholic Encyclopedia.
19. Wikipedia.
20. Ibid.
21. Ibid.
22. Barnes, Harry Elmer, *A History of Historical Writing*, p. 130.
23. Ibid., 130-1.
24. Catholic Encyclopedia.
25. Barnes, Harry Elmer, *A History of Historical Writing*, p. 129-30.

Chapter 7 – Social and Cultural
1. Wikipedia.
2. Ibid.
3. Ibid.
4. Barnes, Harry Elmer, *A History of Historical Writing*, p. 144.
5. Ibid.
6. Wikipedia.
7. Barnes, Harry Elmer, *A History of Historical Writing*, p. 165.
8. Collingwood,R.G., *The Idea of History*, p. 78-9.
9. Wikipedia.
10. Carr, Edward Hallett, *What is History?*, p. 20.
11. Collingwood,R.G., *The Idea of History*, p. 1.
12. Krieger, Leonard, *Ranke, The Meaning of History*, p. 1.
13. Becker, Carl L., *Detachment and the Writing of History: Essays and Letters of Carl L. Becker*, p. 27.
14. Burckhardt, Jacob, *Force and Freedom, Reflections on History*, p. 56.
15. Davies, W. Watkin, *How to Read History*, p. 185.
16. Hexter, J.H., *On Historians*, Cambridge, p. 48.
17. Barzun, Jacques and Henry F. Graff, *The Modern Researcher*, p. 46.
18. Smith, Page, *The Historian and History*, p. 31.
19. Black, J.B., *The Art of History*, p. 29.
20. Wikipedia.

21. Barnes, Harry Elmer, *A History of Historical Writing*, p. 155.
22. Peardon, Thomas, *The Transition in English Historical Writing*, p. 272-3.
23. Wikipedia & Barnes, Harry Elmer, *A History of Historical Writing*, p. 144.
24. www.newadvent.org/cathen.
25. www.infopt.demon.co.uk'wincklem.htm.
26. www.nndb.com/people/267/0O0049120/.
27. Black, J.B., *The Art of History*, p. 15.
28. Ibid., 117.
29. Ibid., 118-9.
30. Ibid., 128.
31. Wikipedia.
32. Barnes, Harry Elmer, *A History of Historical Writing*, p. 166.
33. Peardon, Thomas, *The Transition in English Historical Writing*, p. 49.
34. Wikipedia.
35. Ibid.
36. Hobsbawm, Eric, *On History*, p. 113.
37. Butterfield, Herbert, *Man on His Past*, p. 49.
38. Wikipedia.
39. Gilderhus, Mark T., *History and Historians: A Historiographical Introduction*, p. 38.
40. Archer, Jerome W. & Joseph Schwartz, Editors, *A Reader for Writers*, p. 296.
41. Hobsbawm, Eric, *On History*, p. 57-8.
42. Dalberg-Acton, John Emerich Edward, *Lectures on Modern History*, p. 14.
43. Schevill, Ferdinand, *Six Historians*, p. 196.
44. Evans, Richard J., *In Defense of History*, p. 92.
45. Powicke, E.M., *Modern Historians and the Study of History*, p. 235.
46. Gilderhus, Mark T., *History and Historians: A Historiographical Introduction*, p. 4.
47. Vincent, John, *History*, p. 78.
48. Davies, W. Watkin, *How to Read History*, p. 46 & 74.
49. Barnes, Harry Elmer, *A History of Historical Writing*, p. 167.
50. Peardon, Thomas, *The Transition in English Historical Writing*, p. 96-98.
51. Barnes, Harry Elmer, *A History of Historical Writing*, p. 164.
52. Butterfield, Herbert, *Man on His Past*, p. 210.
53. Wikipedia.
54. Zamoyski, Adam, *Holy Madness*, p. 46.
55. Gilderhus, Mark T., *History and Historians: A Historiographical Introduction*, p. 43.
56. Wikipedia.
57. Barnes, Harry Elmer, *A History of Historical Writing*, p. 164.
58. Ibid., 169.
59. Krieger, Leonard, *Ranke, The Meaning of History*, p. 81.
60. Butterfield, Herbert, *Man on His Past*, p. 51.
61. Ibid., p. 92.
62. Wikipedia.
63. Butterfield, Herbert, *Man on His Past*, p. 88-9.
64. Barnes, Harry Elmer, *A History of Historical Writing*, p. 162.
65. Peardon, Thomas, *The Transition in English Historical Writing*, p. 255.
66. Wikipedia.
67. Ibid.
68. Butterfield, Herbert, *Man on His Past*, p. 210.
69. Barnes, Harry Elmer, *A History of Historical Writing*, p. 168.
70. Krieger, Leonard, *Ranke, The Meaning of History*, p. 29.
71. Collingwood,R.G., *The Idea of History*, p. 53.
72. Wikipedia.
73. Barnes, Harry Elmer, *A History of Historical Writing*, p. 167.
74. Wikipedia.
75. Black, J.B., *The Art of History*, p. 10.
76. Burckhardt, Jacob, *Judgments on History and Historians*, p. 181.
77. Barnes, Harry Elmer, *A History of Historical Writing*, p. 171.

78. Wikipedia.
79. Halperin, S. William, Editor, *Essays in Modern European Historiography*, p. 223.
80. Barnes, Harry Elmer, *A History of Historical Writing*, p. 170.
81. Ibid., 365.
82. Wikipedia.
83. Barnes, Harry Elmer, *A History of Historical Writing*, p. 162-3.
84. Peardon, Thomas, *The Transition in English Historical Writing*, p. 207.
85. Ibid., 212.
86. Ibid., 171.
87. Wikipedia.
88. Ibid.
89. Barnes, Harry Elmer, *A History of Historical Writing*, p. 233.
90. Black, J.B., *The Art of History*, p. 127.
91. Ibid., 127-28.
92. Wikipedia.
93. www.newadvent.org/cathen.
94. Wikipedia.
95. Ibid.,
96. Ibid.

Chapter 8 – Romanticism and Philosophy of History

1. Wikipedia.
2. Barnes, Harry Elmer, *A History of Historical Writing*, p. 244.
3. Dopsch, Alfons, *The Economic and Social Foundations of European Civilization*, p. 6.
4. Smith, Charlotte Watkins, *Carl Becker: On History & the Climate of Opinion*, p. 53-4.
5. Wikipedia.
6. Ibid.
7. Ibid.
8. Barnes, Harry Elmer, *A History of Historical Writing*, p. 182.
9. Wikipedia.
10. Ibid.
11. Iggers, Georg G., *New Directions in European Historiography*, p. 3.
12. Wikipedia.
13. Barnes, Harry Elmer, *A History of Historical Writing*, p. 195.
14. Wikipedia.
15. Guilland, Antoine, *Modern Germany & Her Historians*, p. 26-7.
16. Wikipedia.
17. Barnes, Harry Elmer, *A History of Historical Writing*, p.180.
18. Wikipedia.
19. Krieger, Leonard, *Ranke, The Meaning of History*, p. 82.
20. Wikipedia.
21. Ibid.
22. Daniel Goldman, Wall Street Journal, November 1, 2005.
23. Davies, W. Watkin, *How to Read History*, p. 209-10.
24. Schmitt, Hans A., Editor, *Historians of Modern Europe*, p. 91.
25. Butterfield, Herbert, *Man on His Past*, p. 217.
26. Barnes, Harry Elmer, *A History of Historical Writing*, p. 189.
27. Wikipedia.
28. Schevill, Ferdinand, *Six Historians*, p. 198.
29. Davies, W. Watkin, *How to Read History*, p. 118-9.
30. Zamoyski, Adam, *Holy Madness*, p. 309, 449.
31. Evans, Richard J., *In Defense of History*, p. 60.
32. Wikipedia.
33. Iggers, Georg G., *The German Conception of History*, p. 68-9.
34. Wikipedia.
35. Barnes, Harry Elmer, *A History of Historical Writing*, p. 200-201.
36. Wikipedia.

37. Davies, W. Watkin, *How to Read History*, p. 166.
38. Barnes, Harry Elmer, *A History of Historical Writing*, p. xi.
39. Wikipedia.
40. Evans, Richard J., *In Defense of History*, p. 46.
41. Peardon, Thomas, *The Transition in English Historical Writing*, p. 162.
42. Barnes, Harry Elmer, *A History of Historical Writing*, p. 190.
43. Davies, W. Watkin, *How to Read History*, p. 73.
44. Ibid., 172.
45. Wikipedia.
46. Barnes, Harry Elmer, *A History of Historical Writing*, p. 202.
47. Burckhardt, Jacob, *Force and Freedom, Reflections on History*, p. 355.
48. Smith, Page, *The Historian and History*, p. 48.
49. Black, J.B., *The Art of History*, p. 1.
50. Wikipedia.
51. Ibid.
52. Hobsbawm, Eric, *On History*, p. 18.
53. Wikipedia.
54. Barnes, Harry Elmer, *A History of Historical Writing*, p. 134.
55. Wikipedia.
56. Barnes, Harry Elmer, *A History of Historical Writing*, p. 311.
57. Wikipedia.
58. Black, J.B., *The Art of History*, p. 10.
59. Dalberg-Acton, John Emerich Edward, *Lectures on Modern History*, p. 340n..
60. Barnes, Harry Elmer, *A History of Historical Writing*, p. 201.
61. Collingwood,R.G., *The Idea of History*, p. 142-43.
62. Croce, Benedetto, *History, Its Theory and Practice*, p. 71.
63. Barnes, Harry Elmer, *A History of Historical Writing*, p. 193.
64. Wikipedia.
65. Halperin, S. William, Editor, *Essays in Modern European Historiography*, Annie Popper, p. 142.
66. Iggers, Georg G., *New Directions in European Historiography*, p. 28.
67. Barnes, Harry Elmer, *A History of Historical Writing*, p. 206.
68. Ibid., 205.
69. Evans, Richard J., *In Defense of History*, p. 26.
70. Wikipedia.
71. Schmitt, Hans A., Editor, *Historians of Modern Europe*, p. 8.
72. Barnes, Harry Elmer, *A History of Historical Writing*, p. 205.
73. Iggers, Georg G., *The German Conception of History*, p. 141.

Chapter 9 – Nationalism and Historical Writing
1. Wikipedia.
2. Barnes, Harry Elmer, *A History of Historical Writing*, p. 210.
3. Wikipedia.
4. Ibid.
5. Ibid.
6. Ibid.
7. Iggers, Georg G., *The German Conception of History*, p. 104.
8. *Huntsville Times*, August 12, 2007.
9. Iggers, Georg G., *New Directions in European Historiography*, p. 24.
10. Guilland, Antoine, *Modern Germany & Her Historians*, p. 215-6.
11. Croce, Benedetto, *History as the Story of Liberty*, p. 133.
12. White, Hayden, *The Content of the Form*, p. 99.
13. Wikipedia.
14. Ibid.
15. Ibid.
16. Ibid.
17. Guilland, Antoine, *Modern Germany & Her Historians*, p. 171.

18. Ibid., 172.
19. Ibid., 177.
20. LoveToKnow 1911.com.
21. Wikipedia.
22. Zamoyski, Adam, *Holy Madness*, p. 425.
23. Davies, W. Watkin, *How to Read History*, p. 215-16.
24. Wikipedia.
25. Barzun, Jacques and Henry F. Graff, *The Modern Researcher*, p. 169.
26. Barnes, Harry Elmer, *A History of Historical Writing*, p. 311.
27. Wikipedia.
28. Barnes, Harry Elmer, *A History of Historical Writing*, p. 215.
29. Wikipedia.
30. Ibid.
31. Barnes, Harry Elmer, *A History of Historical Writing*, p. 216.
32. Wikipedia.
33. Ibid.
34. Dalberg-Acton, John Emerich Edward, *Lectures on Modern History*, p. 12.
35. Hobsbawm, Eric, *On History*, p. 75.
36. Wikipedia.
37. Barnes, Harry Elmer, *A History of Historical Writing*, p. 216.
38. Ibid., 289.
39. www.answers.com.
40. Wikipedia.
41. Ibid.
42. Burckhardt, Jacob, *Judgments on History and Historians*, p. xix.
43. Carr, Edward Hallett, *What is History?*, p. 25.
44. Krieger, Leonard, *Ranke, The Meaning of History*, p. 220-1.
45. Becker, Carl L., *Detachment and the Writing of History: Essays and Letters of Carl L. Becker*, p. 66.
46. Tillinghast, Pardon E., *The Specious Past: Historians and Others*, p. 70.
47. Davies, W. Watkin, *How to Read History*, p. 190.
48. Guilland, Antoine, *Modern Germany & Her Historians*, p. 42.
49. Powicke, E.M., *Modern Historians and the Study of History*, p. 166.
50. Davies, W. Watkin, *How to Read History*, p. 196.
51. Gay, Peter, *Style in History*, p. 97.
52. Butterfield, Herbert, *Man on His Past*, p. 222.
53. Barnes, Harry Elmer, *A History of Historical Writing*, p. 218.
54. Ibid., 219.
55. Wikipedia.
56. Black, J.B., *The Art of History*, p. 10.
57. Furber, Elizabeth Chapin, Editor, *Changing Views on British History*, p. 3.
58. Barzun, Jacques and Henry F. Graff, *The Modern Researcher*, p. 187.
59. Wikipedia.
60. Peardon, Thomas, *The Transition in English Historical Writing, 1760-1830*, p. 210.
61. Black, J.B., *The Art of History*, p. 11.
62. Barnes, Harry Elmer, *A History of Historical Writing*, p. 218.
63. Vincent, John, *History*, p. 127.
64. Barnes, Harry Elmer, *A History of Historical Writing*, p. 220.
65. Dalberg-Acton, John Emerich Edward, *Lectures on Modern History*, p. 1-2.
66. Black, J.B., *The Art of History*, p. 19.
67. Barnes, Harry Elmer, *A History of Historical Writing*, p. 220.
68. Wikipedia.
69. www.amazon.com.
70. Wikipedia.
71. Davies, W. Watkin, *How to Read History*, p. 101.
72. Wikipedia.
73. Croce, Benedetto, *History, Its Theory and Practice*, p. 256.
74. Wikipedia.

75. Barnes, Harry Elmer, *A History of Historical Writing*, p. 221.
76. Ibid.
77. Ibid.
78. Wikipedia.
79. Barnes, Harry Elmer, *A History of Historical Writing*, p. 221.
80. Davies, W. Watkin, *How to Read History*, p. 144.
81. Barnes, Harry Elmer, *A History of Historical Writing*, p. 321.
82. Wikipedia.
83. Barnes, Harry Elmer, *A History of Historical Writing*, p. 223.
84. Wikipedia.
85. Ibid.
86. Barnes, Harry Elmer, *A History of Historical Writing*, p. 223.
87. Wikipedia.
88. Barnes, Harry Elmer, *A History of Historical Writing*, p. 223.
89. Wikipedia.
90. Barnes, Harry Elmer, *A History of Historical Writing*, p. 224.
91. Ibid.
92. Ibid.
93. Ibid., p. 224-5.
94. Wikipedia.
95. Ibid.
96. Ibid.
97. Ibid.
98. Ibid.
99. Barzun, Jacques and Henry F. Graff, *The Modern Researcher*, p. 177.
100. Beers, Henry Putney, *The French in North America*, p. 40-41.
101. Wikipedia.
102. Davies, W. Watkin, *How to Read History*, p. 243.
103. Wikipedia.
104. Ibid.
105. Smith, Charlotte Watkins, *Carl Becker: On History & the Climate of Opinion*, p. 192.

Chapter 10 – Critical Historical Scholarship
1. Wikipedia.
2. Gay, Peter, *Style in History*, p. 73.
3. Wikipedia.
4. Ibid.
5. Barzun, Jacques and Henry F. Graff, *The Modern Researcher*, p. 46.
6. Barnes, Harry Elmer, *A History of Historical Writing*, p. 143.
7. Wikipedia.
8. Ibid.
9. Iggers, Georg G., *New Directions in European Historiography*, p. 18.
10. Guilland, Antoine, *Modern Germany & Her Historians*, p. 49.
11. Wikipedia.
12. Ibid.
13. Croce, Benedetto, *History as the Story of Liberty*, p. 156.
14. Gay, Peter, *Style in History*, p. 75.
15. Guilland, Antoine, *Modern Germany & Her Historians*, p. 52.
16. Ibid., 63.
17. Ibid., 67-8.
18. Ibid., 68.
19. Wikipedia.
20. Collingwood, R.G., *The Idea of History*, p. 132.
21. Croce, Benedetto, *History, Its Theory and Practice*, p. 191.
22. Ibid., 192.
23. Gilderhus, Mark T., *History and Historians: A Historiographical Introduction*, p. 46.
24. Guilland, Antoine, *Modern Germany & Her Historians*, p. 117.

25. Smith, Page, *The Historian and History*, p. 49.
26. Ranke, Ludwig von, *The Secret of World History*, p. 2.
27. Wikipedia.
28. Dopsch, Alfons, *The Economic and Social Foundations of European Civilization*, p. 15.
29. Wikipedia.
30. Gay, Peter, *Style in History*, p. 201.
31. Hobsbawm, Eric, *On History*, p. 228.
32. Evans, Richard J., *In Defense of History*, (Defense, p. 54-55.
33. Wikipedia.
34. Ranke, Ludwig von, *The Secret of World History*, p. 24.
35. Smith, Page, *The Historian and History*, p. 61.
36. Butterfield, Herbert, *Man on His Past*, p. 21-22.
37. Schorske, Carl E., *Thinking with History*, p. 8.
38. Wikipedia.
39. Ibid.
40. Davies, W. Watkin, *How to Read History*, p. 84.
41. Wikipedia.
42. Powicke, E.M., *Modern Historians and the Study of History*, p. 142.
43. Wikipedia.
44. Butterfield, Herbert, *Man on His Past*, p. 77.
45. Barnes, Harry Elmer, *A History of Historical Writing*, p. 212.
46. Fischer, David Hackett, *Historians Fallacies: Toward a Logic of Historical Thought*, p. 293.
47. Ibid., 304.
48. Croce, Benedetto, *History as the Story of Liberty*, p. 191-92.
49. Wikipedia.
50. Black, J.B., *The Art of History*, p. 10.
51. Peardon, Thomas, *The Transition in English Historical Writing, 1760-1830*, p. 207.
52. Dalberg-Acton, John Emerich Edward, *Lectures on Modern History*, p. ix.
53. Ibid., xv.
54. Collingwood, R.G., *The Idea of History*, p. 281.
55. Elton, G.R., *The Practice of History*, p. 17.
56. Ranke, Ludwig von, *The Secret of World History*, p. 20.
57. Tillinghast, Pardon E., *The Specious Past: Historians and Others*, p. 35.
58. Butterfield, Herbert, *Man on His Past*, p. 62.
59. Wikipedia.
60. Halperin, S. William, Editor, *Essays in Modern European Historiography*, p. xvi-xvii.
61. Ibid., 298.
62. Wikipedia.
63. Vincent, John, *History*, p. 131.
64. Wikipedia.
65. Ibid.
66. Hexter, J.H., *Reappraisals in History*, p. 195.
67. Powicke, E.M., *Modern Historians and the Study of History*, p. 129.
68. Ibid., 220.
69. Vincent, John, *History*, p. 128.
70. Elton, G.R., *The Practice of History*, p. 107.
71. Wikipedia.
72. Gay, Peter, *Style in History*, p. 61.
73. Gilderhus, Mark T., *History and Historians: A Historiographical Introduction*, p. 111-12.
74. Wikipedia.
75. Ibid.
76. Barnes, Harry Elmer, *A History of Historical Writing*, p. 249.
77. Simkhovitch, Vladimir G., *Approaches to History I*, p. 492.
78. Wikipedia.
79. Ibid.
80. Ibid.
81. Colley, Linda, *Lewis Namier*, p. 1.
82. Vincent, John, *History*, p. 95.

83. Ibid., 96-97.

Chapter 11 – First- -Half, 20th Century
1. Wikipedia.
2. Schevill, Ferdinand, *Six Historians*, p. 177.
3. Ibid., 181.
4. Wikipedia.
5. Stephens, Lester D. Editor, *Historiography: A Bibliography,* p. 71.
6. Wikipedia.
7. *The Columbia Encyclopedia*, www.bartleby.com.
8. Smith, Charlotte Watkins, *Carl Becker: On History & the Climate of Opinion*, p. 103.
9. Wikipedia.
10. Elton, G.R., *The Practice of History*, p. 107-8.
11. www.dreamofpassamaquoddy.com.
12. Barnes, Harry Elmer, *A History of Historical Writing*, p. 12.
13. Wikipedia.
14. Carr, Edward Hallett, *What is History?*, p. 71.
15. Wikipedia.
16. Barzun, Jacques and Henry F. Graff, *The Modern Researcher*, p. 181.
17. Gilderhus, Mark T., *History and Historians: A Historiographical Introduction*, p. 112.
18. Smith, Page, *The Historian and History*, p. 150.
19. Ibid., 216.
20. www.abaa.org.
21. Wikipedia.
22. Ibid.
23. Ibid.
24. Tillinghast, Pardon E., *The Specious Past: Historians and Others*, p. 31.
25. Wikipedia.
26. Evans, Richard J., *In Defense of History*, p. 26.
27. Fischer, David Hackett, *Historians Fallacies: Toward a Logic of Historical Thought*, p. 124-25.
28. Wikipedia.
29. Ibid.
30. Ibid.
31. Ibid.
32. Hexter, J.H., *Reappraisals in History*, p. 26-27.
33. Elton, G.R., *The Practice of History*, p. 107.
34. Wikipedia.
35. Barnes, Harry Elmer, *A History of Historical Writing*, p. 64-65.
36. Wikipedia.
37. Ibid.
38. Ibid.
39. Ibid.
40. Carr, Edward Hallett, *What is History?*, p. 22-23.
41. findarticles.com.
42. Barnes, Harry Elmer, *A History of Historical Writing*, p. 403.
43. Wikipedia.
44. Barnes, Harry Elmer, *A History of Historical Writing*, p. 280.
45. Ibid., 21-22.
46. Wikipedia.
47. Halperin, S. William, Editor, *Essays in Modern European Historiography*, p. 243.
48. Wikipedia.
49. Evans, Richard J., *In Defense of History*, p. 75.
50. Ibid., 23.
51. Gilderhus, Mark T., *History and Historians: A Historiographical Introduction*, p. 86.
52. Schorske, Carl E., *Thinking with History* p. 21.
53. Wikipedia.
54. Ibid.
55. Vincent, John, *History*, p. 56-7.

56. Davies, W. Watkin, *How to Read History*, p. 116.
57. Ibid., 231.
58. Evans, Richard J., *In Defense of History*, p. 22.
59. Wikipedia.
60. Stephens, Lester D. Editor, *Historiography: A Bibliography,* #1185.
61. www.northamptonshirerecordsociety.ord.uk.
62. Wikipedia.
63. Gilderhus, Mark T., *History and Historians: A Historiographical Introduction*, p. 116-17.
64. Wikipedia.
65. Ibid.
66. Furber, Elizabeth Chapin, Editor, *Changing Views on British History*, p. 59.
67. Wikipedia.
68. Ibid.
69. Ibid.
70. Ibid.
71. Ibid.
72. Ibid.
73. Ibid.
74. Evans, Richard J., *In Defense of History*, p. 26.
75. Fischer, David Hackett, *Historians Fallacies: Toward a Logic of Historical Thought*, p. 3.
76. Wikipedia.
77. Fischer, David Hackett, *Historians Fallacies: Toward a Logic of Historical Thought*, p. 288-89.
78. Evans, Richard J., *In Defense of History*, p. 47.
79. Barnes, Harry Elmer, *A History of Historical Writing*, p. 378.
80. Smith, Page, *The Historian and History*, p. 105.
81. Schmitt, Hans A., Editor, *Historians of Modern Europe*, p. 65.
82. Wikipedia.
83. Ibid.

Chapter 12 – Second--Half, 20th Century
1. Wikipedia.
2. Fischer, David Hackett, *Historians Fallacies: Toward a Logic of Historical Thought*, p. 89-90.
3. Vincent, John, *History*, p. 168.
4. Wikipedia.
5. Vincent, John, *History*, p. 165-66.
6. Wikipedia.
7. Ibid.
8. Fischer, David Hackett, *Historians Fallacies: Toward a Logic of Historical Thought*, p. 191.
9. Wikipedia.
10. Evans, Richard J., *In Defense of History*, p. 93.
11. Schmitt, Hans A., Editor, *Historians of Modern Europe*, p. 93.
12. Wikipedia.
13. Ibid.
14. Ibid.
15. Ibid.
16. Ibid.
17. Ibid.
18. Ibid.
19. Evans, Richard J., *In Defense of History*, p. 73.
20. Wikipedia.
21. McClay, Wilfred M., reviewing *Richard Hofstadter: An Intellectual Biography*, by David S. Brown, Wall Street Journal, May 13, 2006.
22. Wikipedia.
23. Ibid.
24. Ibid.
25. Ibid.
26. Ibid.
27. Evans, Richard J., *In Defense of History*, p. 35.

28. Wikipedia.
29. Ibid.
30. Iggers, Georg G., *New Directions in European Historiography*, p. 94.
31. Wikipedia.
32. Ibid.
33. Ibid.
34. Evans, Richard J., *In Defense of History*, p. 52-53.
35. Arthur Schlesinger, Jr., *Wall Street Journal*, circa early 1990s.
36. Yancurra, Chuck, *Old Huntsville*, No. 82.
37. Rogers, Roy, *Happy Trails*, p. 201.

Chapter 13 – Generalizations, Maxims and Quotations
1. Axelrod, Alan, *The Quotable Historian*, p. 74.
2. Tillinghast, Pardon E., *The Specious Past: Historians and Others*, p. 154.
3. Carr, Edward Hallett, *What is History?*, p. 80.
4. Hays, Paul A., *An Inquiry.........*, p. 182.
5. Ranke, Ludwig von, *The Secret of World History*, p. 21.
6. Ibid,, 257.
7. Boot, Max, Wall Street Journal, October 17, 2002.
8. Barzun, Jacques, author of more than 30 books, to include *From Dawn to Decadence. Forbes ASAP*, October 2, 2000.
9. Axelrod, Alan, *The Quotable Historian*, p. 76.
10. Bloch, Marc, *The Historian's Craft*, p. 175.
11. Cantor, Norman F., *Inventing the Middle Ages*, p. 352.
12. Axelrod, Alan, *The Quotable Historian*, p. 78.
13. Ibid., 75.
14. Ibid., 74.
15. Cantor, Norman F., *Inventing the Middle Ages*, p. 15.
16. Ibid., p. 412.
17. Axelrod, Alan, *The Quotable Historian*, p. 75.
18. Ibid., p. 77.
19. Hays, Paul A., *An Inquiry.........*, p. 183.
20. Whately, Archbishop Richard, *Historic Doubts Relative to Napoleon Buonaparte*.

INDEX

The page number is only for the major description of the cited author.